JESUS 2000

CONSULTING EDITORS

DR RICHARD BAUCKHAM
Lecturer in Christian Thought, University of Manchester, England.

THE REV. DR R.T.FRANCE
Principal, Wycliffe Hall, Oxford, England.

MELBA MAGGAY
Director, Institute for Study of Asian Church and Culture, Philippines.

DR JAMES STAMOOLIS
formerly Secretary for Theological Education, International Fellowship for Evangelical Students, United States.

DR CARSTEN PETER THIEDE
Editor, Brockhaus Verlag, Wuppertal; Member of Board, German Institute for Education and Knowledge, Paderborn, West Germany.

ORGANIZING EDITOR
Robin Keeley

DESIGN AND CHARTS
Tony Cantale Graphics
Gerald Rogers

PICTURE EDITOR
Jo Egerton

EDITORS
Vernon Blackmore
Jenny Hyatt
Jeanette Robson

ADDITIONAL RESEARCH
Kathy Keay

Copyright © 1989 Lion Publishing

Published by
Lion Publishing plc
Sandy Lane West, Littlemore, Oxford, England
ISBN 0 7459 1416 0

Lion Publishing Corporation
1705 Hubbard Avenue, Batavia, Illinois 60510, USA
ISBN 0 7459 1416 0

Albatross Books Pty Ltd
PO Box 320, Sutherland, NSW 2232, Australia
ISBN 0 7324 0154 2

Printed and bound in Spain

JESUS 2000

A LION BOOK

Oxford · Batavia · Sydney

CONTENTS

SPECIAL FEATURES

CONTRIBUTORS

Helen Alexander, Producer 'This is the Day', British Broadcasting Corporation, London, England, *Jesus and the modern media.*

Dr Richard Bauckham, Lecturer in Christian Thought, University of Manchester, England. *God in a human life; The finality of Jesus; The human Jesus; Francis of Assisi; Ignatius and the Exercises; The Imitation of Christ; The martyrs.*

The Rev. Kwame Bediako, Director, Akrofi-Christoller Memorial Research Centre, Ghana. *Into all the world.*

The Rev. John L.Bell, Co-ordinator of Worship for Iona Community, Scotland. *Worshipping Jesus today.*

Dr Craig Blomberg, Assistant Professor of New Testament, Denver Theological Seminary, United States. *The four evangelists; Jesus the miracle-worker.*

The Right Rev. Dr George Carey, Bishop of Bath and Wells, England. *The authority of his teaching.*

The Rev. Colin Chapman, Lecturer in Mission and Religion, Trinity Theological College, Bristol, England. *Repent and believe; Conversion and new birth.*

Dr William Craig, Associate Professor of Religious Studies, Westmont College, Santa Barbara, United States. *Raised from death.*

Dr Theo Dankwa, Regional Secretary for Africa, International Fellowship of Evangelical Students, Ghana. *Growing opposition; Powers of evil.*

The Rev. Brian Donne, Minister, Emmanuel Baptist Church, Trowbridge, England. *The ascension.*

Dr John Drane, Lecturer in Religious Studies, University of Stirling, Scotland. *'When you pray'; The people of God; Pharisees and Sadducees; The Trinity.*

The Rev. Dr R.T.France, Principal, Wycliffe Hall, Oxford, England. *How do we know about Jesus? The witness of the Gospels; The kingdom of God; 'Are you the coming one?' Jesus and God; Galilee and Jerusalem; Jesus, God's servant; The Son of Man.*

Bruce L. Guenther, Youth Worker studying at Regent College, Vancouver, Canada. *Advocate of the young.*

Professor Donald Hagner, Professor of New Testament, Fuller Theological Seminary, Pasadena, United States. *Were the Jews to blame?*

Dr James Houston, Lecturer in Spirituality and Pastoral Studies, Regent College, Vancouver, Canada. *The Christian tradition of prayer.*

Tony Jasper, Musical journalist and author, London, England. *Jesus the musical.*

Dr Donald Lewis, Assistant Professor of Church History, Regent College, Vancouver, Canada. *Jesus and the revivalists.*

The Rev. Dr Alister McGrath, Lecturer in Christian Doctrine, Wycliffe Hall, Oxford, England. *The death of Jesus.*

Melba Maggay, Director, Institute for Study of Asian Church and Culture, Philippines. *Jesus the liberator; Being made whole.*

Professor I. Howard Marshall, Professor of New Testament Exegesis, University of Aberdeen, Scotland. *God the Father; Jesus worshipped as Lord; Jesus the living presence; Jesus and Paul.*

Dr Rainer Riesner, Research Fellow, University of Tubingen, West Germany. *Jesus the teacher; The twelve.*

Professor Klaas Runia, Professor of Practical Theology, University of the Reformed Churches, Kampen, Netherlands. *Understanding who Jesus is.*

The Rev. Graeme Rutherford, Vicar, St John's Camberwell, Victoria, Australia. *The beginning; Born of a virgin? The Messiah; The temptations.*

The Rev. Dr David Seccombe, Vicar, St Matthew's Shenton Park, West Australia. *The call to follow.*

Dr Manfred Siebald, Reader in American Language and Literature, University of Mainz, West Germany. *Jesus in modern literature.*

The Rev. Vera Sinton, Lecturer in Pastoral Theology and Ethics, Wycliffe Hall, Oxford, England. *The way of love; The neighbour; Law and love.*

Elaine Storkey, Lecturer in Sociology, Open University, England. *Jesus and women.*

Dr Carsten Peter Thiede, Editor, Brockhaus Verlag, Wuppertal, West Germany. *The Gospel manuscripts; First-century archaeology; Jesus in his setting; The Dead Sea Scrolls; John the Baptist; What languages did Jesus speak? Communicating Jesus.*

The Rev. Dr Stephen H. Travis, Director of Academic Studies, St John's College, Nottingham, England. *A vision for the future; The second coming.*

Dr Max Turner, Lecturer in New Testament, University of Aberdeen, Scotland. *The promise of the Holy Spirit; The church begins.*

PREFACE

For nearly 2,000 years people have been fascinated by Jesus – and never more so than in our own day, in a mass of books, films and television programmes. He has been portrayed in numerous guises, from hippy to revolutionary, from new-age cult leader to clown.

This book investigates who Jesus really was. It mounts a full-scale enquiry into him, centring on the evidence of the first century AD, but also considering the influence of Jesus over two millennia since then.

It is a step-by-step investigation. The first part looks at the evidence about Jesus from his own times. What can definitely be known about him? Part two takes up well-known stories about Jesus' birth, and the beginning of his brief public appearance. The third part is the longest, since it surveys eleven key themes of Jesus' teaching. Part four focuses down on the last week of Jesus' life – the events that led to his death, and what happened after it. The fifth part draws some conclusions and builds up to a statement of who Jesus was. Then a brief final section brings the story up to date, looking at three aspects of the impact of Jesus today.

The enormous influence of Jesus over the centuries cannot be ignored in any such investigation. Throughout the book, special features illustrate this influence, and show how people have been affected by him in different historical periods and in different parts of the world. A few of these are major features, but others are simply brief snapshots of the impact of Jesus on people and situations, many of them taken from our own day.

Thirty writers have co-operated in this venture, drawn from eight countries. They write from expert knowledge, but have presented their material for the benefit of non-specialists, so that all can now gain access to the most recent discoveries and interpretations of the facts about Jesus. What is the truth about some of the sensational 'discoveries' claimed in popular books and on television?

Any serious investigation of Jesus takes us beyond idle fascination to see the importance of Jesus for world history and for our lives today. It is hoped that many people worldwide will find that this book brings their picture of him into sharper focus, and helps them to a clearer appreciation of Jesus as he really was – or should it be, as he really is?

PART

1

THE EVIDENCE

This investigation into Jesus begins with the evidence.
How do we know about Jesus at all? How solid is the evidence?

The core of the evidence is in the four contemporary
documents, the Gospels. We look closely at them. What is a Gospel?
How reliable are Matthew, Mark, Luke and John? What picture
do they give of Jesus?

CONTENTS

SPECIAL FEATURES

The lunatic fringe
What languages did Jesus speak?
Galilee and Jerusalem
Other Gospels
Jesus the musical
Jesus in literature today
Jesus on the screen

1.1

HOW DO WE KNOW ABOUT JESUS?

In these days you can easily know quite a lot about a public figure, even if you never meet them. You watch the television and read books and newspapers. But Jesus belongs to another world. It was long ago and, for most of us, far away in a foreign culture. In his world there was no television and no newspapers. Even if you could read, hand-copied books were an expensive luxury. And of the books which were written, many have not survived: at least half the known writings even of the great Roman historian Tacitus are lost.

We know comparatively little about even the great political leaders and military commanders of those days. Julius Caesar wrote records of his own campaigns, and Tacitus left us a graphic (if very biased) account of life in the imperial court. But Jesus was not a great political figure, and wrote no books.

Indeed, from the point of view of the literary world of his time he might as well not have existed. He was a countryman with only a basic education who had a few years of popularity as an itinerant preacher. He taught not in Rome or Athens but among a generally despised tribe in a little-known sub-prefecture of the most easterly province of the Roman empire. The only time he came to official notice was when his own fellow-countrymen persuaded the Roman governor to have him executed. Why should such a man leave any trace in the pages of history?

How can we know anything about Jesus?

Jesus in non-Christian writing

The earliest mention of Jesus by a Roman writer is when Tacitus (about AD115) describes Nero's attacks on Christians in Rome. He explains who these 'Christians' are by mentioning that in Judea 'the originator of that name, Christus, had been

▲ Until 1961 there was no record outside the Gospels that Pontius Pilate existed. Then in 1961 this stone slab was discovered at the port of Caesarea. It carries the name 'Pontius Pilate', and the title of a building in honour of Emperor Tiberius.

executed when Tiberius was emperor by order of the procurator Pontius Pilatus'. That is all, and Tacitus is probably only repeating what Christians in his day were saying about their origins.

At about the same time Suetonius also mentions that there were 'Christians' in Rome, but he says nothing about their origins. Pliny, the governor of Bithynia (now part of Turkey), writes about the problems Christians were causing for him, but the only mention of Jesus in his long letter is that they sang 'a hymn to Christ as to a god'. There is not much basis here for a knowledge of Jesus as a historical figure!

The only other non-Christian writer within a century of Jesus' lifetime who offers us information about him is the Jewish historian, Josephus. But it is very little, and hard to assess. In all his twenty-eight volumes of Jewish history, written towards the end of the first century AD, there are just two passages which mention Jesus.

▲ The earliest known pictorial representation of Jesus is part of a giant floor mosaic in a Roman villa at Hinton St Mary, Dorset, England. It is from the mid-fourth century AD. In early Christian art, Jesus was always beardless.

He tells of the execution in AD62 of James 'the brother of Jesus the so-called Messiah', but gives no further information at that point about Jesus himself.

In an earlier passage, however, he had written a brief paragraph about this Messiah. The trouble is that Josephus' works were preserved for posterity by Christians, and it is generally agreed that the passage about Jesus has been adapted from what Josephus originally wrote. It speaks of Jesus in a way only a Christian would—and Josephus was certainly no Christian. Jesus, the passage says, was 'a wise man, if indeed one should call him a man. For he was a performer of astonishing deeds, a teacher of men who are happy to accept the truth. He won over many Jews, and indeed also many Greeks. He was the Messiah.' The passage goes on to tell of his crucifixion by Pilate at the instigation of Jewish leaders, and of how 'he appeared to his followers on the third day alive again' as the prophets had foretold.

Scholars argue over what Josephus himself may have written. A few think the whole thing is a Christian addition. Others have proposed less 'believing' words: they think that Josephus did in fact describe Jesus as a miracle-worker and teacher who won an enthusiastic following and was crucified at Jewish instigation, even if not as 'the Messiah'. It is very likely that Josephus wrote *something* about Jesus of Nazareth, since otherwise his later reference to 'Jesus the so-called Messiah' would be left hanging in the air. But we cannot be sure just how he described him.

Other Jewish writings offer us little help. There are a few probable references to Jesus in the Rabbinic texts, but they are hard to interpret and contain little factual information. Jesus appears as a magician who 'led Israel astray'. The clearest reference (and probably the earliest—it may derive from the second century) mentions that for these offences 'Yeshu' was 'hanged' on Passover Eve after due trial.

So there is, apart from Josephus, very little evidence about Jesus from contemporary or near-contemporary non-Christian writers, and what there is comes from some generations after his time. But why should we expect more? Until the Christian movement began to spread and to attract attention (usually unfavourable!) from the authorities, why should the historians and writers of the day have had any idea of his existence? Jesus did not move in that sort of company.

Can archaeology help?

Our knowledge of the world Jesus lived in is becoming clearer all the time as a result of archaeological discovery (see *First Century Archaeology*). We can picture the places where Jesus went and the people he met. Well-known stories and sayings of Jesus take on new meaning.

But this can only be background information. Archaeological discovery has not added anything to our specific knowledge about Jesus himself, only to our awareness of his environment. A few people are specifically mentioned on inscriptions (such as Pontius Pilate's name on a stone at Caesarea). But Jesus was not that sort of person; he held no public office and no buildings were dedicated in his honour. A few individuals are mentioned by name

on the boxes in which their bones were preserved ('ossuaries'). One box belonged to a Cyrenian Jew, Alexander son of Simon—could this be the man mentioned in Mark 15:21? But no such relic of Jesus has ever been found—indeed it would be very disconcerting for Christians if it were!

Archaeology has given us immense help in understanding the Gospel accounts of Jesus. It has in various ways confirmed that the Gospel-writers can be trusted. But it cannot be expected in itself to offer us any new information about Jesus himself.

Jesus in Christian tradition

Most of what people today know (or think they know) about Jesus comes from the four Gospels of the New Testament, and we shall have more to say about these special writings. But people did not stop writing and thinking about Jesus when those four books had been written. This book is itself an example of the way Christians have always wanted to talk and write about Jesus.

As time has gone on a great deal has been added to what was in the four Gospels. People are sometimes surprised to find how much they have come to accept something which is not in fact in the Bible. The original Gospels do not tell us, for example, that Jesus was born in a stable. They only say he was laid in a manger, which is not the same thing, whatever our cultural patterns may lead us to assume. Nor do they claim he was visited by three kings; still less do they name the wise men, or make one of them black, or have a fourth who got lost on the way! But the stories of Jesus have been expanded and interpreted over the years, sometimes by pious imagination, sometimes by sheer misunderstanding.

We have many Christian writings from the second century AD onwards which tell additional stories of Jesus or which offer further accounts of his teaching. Generally classed together as the 'apocryphal gospels', they are in fact a very varied range of writings. There are lively stories about the miracle-working child Jesus, and imaginative accounts of the pious home from which his mother came and of her unique experiences in becoming the 'mother of God'. There are familiar New Testament stories with new twists to them, and familiar sayings expanded to offer teaching very different from what the four Gospel-writers recorded. There are long discourses about the secrets of the universe presented as sayings of the risen Jesus.

Is it possible that among this rich growth of

Christian tradition there are some genuine facts and sayings? Might they have preserved something from the historical ministry of Jesus which the New Testament Gospels did not record? Yes, of course it is possible, even likely. John, in his Gospel, tells us that to record all that Jesus did would take more books than the world could contain! Even though the 'apocryphal' books were written a century or more after Jesus' lifetime, some of his unrecorded acts and sayings could have been remembered and faithfully incorporated into the new books about him. But the problem is to know how any such genuine historical material can be recognized. So much that is in these books is clearly legendary, or seems designed to support new forms of teaching (particularly 'Gnosticism', a teaching which has

some points of contact with twentieth-century 'new age' ideas).

But some of this traditional material has been confidently claimed as historical, especially some of the sayings preserved in the 'Gospel of Thomas'. This is an early second-century anthology of 'sayings of Jesus' which was discovered in Egypt in 1946 as part of a collection of ancient Gnostic writings. But while some of the sayings in the Gospel of Thomas are very similar to those found in the New Testament Gospels, others are already clearly Gnostic. And the fact that scholars disagree about which sayings or stories may be historical means that any attempt to learn about the historical Jesus from such sources will inevitably be subjective.

The Christian tradition of the second century

The Lunatic Fringe

In 1970 John Allegro published *The Sacred Mushroom and the Cross*. Allegro was an eminent scholar at Manchester University, England, specializing in philology, the study of language. He had been one of several scholars to link Jesus with a figure mentioned in the Dead Sea Scrolls—the Teacher of Righteousness, expected by the Essene community at Qmran.

Now, in what was to become a bestselling book, he claimed that Jesus did not exist at all. Allegro noted that certain New Testament names do not mean what they are supposed to mean. The brother apostles, James and John, were called 'Boanerges', said to mean in Aramaic 'sons of thunder', but according to Allegro it does not mean this. Allegro saw such words as clues to the coded message he believed the New Testament to be: not a historical story about a real person, but the coded book of a cult centred on the use of a halucinogenic mushroom.

This seems an extraordinary explanation for the Gospels, which tell the story of a man

who has had such a deep influence ever since. A group of fifteen scholars 'of several faiths and none' wrote to the London *Times* because they felt it was 'their duty to let it be known that the book is not based on any philological or other evidence which they can regard as scholarly'.

It is far-fetched to deny that Jesus ever existed, because his existence is so fully attested. As Hans Kung has written: 'The Christ of the Christians is a quite concrete, human, historical person. . . no other than Jesus of Nazareth.' But other recent books, while accepting that Jesus lived, have given accounts of him which are at variance with the man we meet in the pages of the Gospels.

The Holy Blood and the Holy Grail was published in 1982. Written by three writers—Biagent, Leigh and Lincoln—the book consists of a vast number of interlocking hypotheses spanning many centuries. It has the fascination of a complex mystery, and was another bestseller. Two aspects of the writers' account of Jesus are particularly striking—that

he was married and that he did not die on the cross. The marriage was apparently to Mary Magdalene and the wedding John describes at Cana in Galilee was Jesus' own wedding. This is pure supposition; there is no good evidence for it. But the other idea contradicts the New Testament even more starkly. We are introduced to a conspiracy between Pontius Pilate, Joseph of Arimathea and Jesus himself, which led to Jesus hanging from the cross but being rescued by his friends before his death. He then set the events in train which are hypothesized in the rest of the book.

So, on this theory, there was no resurrection, and the message which swept the world was based on a hoax, for which many good people died.

Soon after came *Jesus: the Evidence*, both a book and a television series broadcast on Britain's Channel 4. This put forward an account of Jesus which required that the Gnostic Gospel fragments be given more credence than Matthew, Mark, Luke and John. The result was a strange, new-age kind of figure who would never have made the deep impact on the world that Jesus actually did.

These ideas sold hundreds of thousands of books, even

though their theories were forgotten quite quickly. They are testimony to the continuing fascination Jesus exercises on people's minds. Each fails to answer the two crucial questions. If Jesus did not exist, or was quite different from how the first Christians understood him, how did those Christians convince so many people so quickly? And if the Jesus of the Gospels is an invention, how did the Gospel-writers create a figure of such power that he has changed the world?

and beyond gives us a lot of information about the development of Christian devotion. But it offers us little more reliable evidence for the Jesus of history than do the writings of non-Christians of the same period.

The New Testament Gospels

If our knowledge of Jesus came only from the sources we have so far considered, we could conclude that he was a popular leader who was executed in Judea under Pontius Pilate. But that would be about all. It would not be much of a foundation for the world's greatest religion!

But what we have so far left out of account is what any responsible historian must recognize as the primary evidence for Jesus: the four books about him which were written by his followers. These accounts were written down within two generations of his death—indeed some would date some or all of the four Gospels no later than the sixties of the

▲ Twentieth-century New Testament scholars have approached the reliability of the Gospel accounts of Jesus in different ways. They have also interpreted their meaning differently. Rudolf Bultmann (left, 1884–1976) took scepticism about the historical Jesus to its limits; in his view faith in Christ should need no support from history. Karl Barth (right, 1886–1968) saw in Jesus 'the humanity of God', the way God had revealed himself and reconciled us to him. Wolfhart Pannenberg (born 1928) begins his theology with the man Jesus, known to us by historical research. Jurgen Moltmann (born 1926) focuses on Jesus' death and resurrection, showing how God suffers alongside people, and how Jesus is the basis of Christian hope for the world's future. Edward Schillebeeckx (born 1919) holds that historical study of Jesus should be done from within faith, not outside and against it. All these have important things to teach, but each of us can read the Gospels for ourselves and let them make their own impact on us.

first century, only one generation away from the events they record.

In the ancient world it was not uncommon for the lives of great philosophers, politicians or religious leaders to be written by their followers. In a few cases we have more than one such record. For example, there are very different accounts of

Socrates by Plato and by Xenophon. But there is no parallel to the *four* 'lives' of Jesus which now form the first books of our New Testament.

The Gospels of Matthew, Mark and Luke are in fact quite closely related to each other, and we will explore this in a later section. But while a great deal of the material is shared between them, each writer sets out his own independent portrait of Jesus. Each Gospel is similar to the others in much of the basic content, but is filled out with a lot of new material. And even where the authors tell the same story, there is sometimes a degree of independence which can be quite embarrassing for readers today who want to iron out all the differences. As for John's Gospel, it is so different in tone and content that in places you could be forgiven for wondering if it is the same Jesus he is writing about!

So we have four witnesses to the life and teaching of Jesus. Or, to be more accurate, we have four collections of traditions about him, traditions which must have been treasured and passed on by many of his earliest followers before they were incorporated into the books as we know them. In some cases the authors will be passing on their own direct memories of Jesus; in others they are repeating what they have heard from others. We shall have more to say of the process by which the Gospel traditions were preserved. But compared with the majority of ancient figures we have a remarkably full collection of early evidence for Jesus.

Can we trust the Gospels?

Why should we assume that these earlier accounts of Jesus are any more historically reliable than the imaginative contributions of the later 'apocryphal gospels'? If later Christians could embellish the traditions, why should the first generations of disciples not have done the same? Indeed some scholars believe that they did. And so they are doubtful about the historical value of much of the material in the New Testament Gospels. Some, like Rudolf Bultmann, have gone so far as to declare that we can know little more about Jesus than the bare fact that he existed.

Most modern scholarship is not so sceptical. While there are disputes about many individual incidents and sayings, there is now general agreement that the broad outlines of Jesus' ministry and teaching given by the Gospels can be trusted. They represent the historical figure of Jesus and not just the piety of his followers.

We must remember that the period of time between Jesus' activity and the writing of the first accounts of him is likely to have been quite short. Luke records at the beginning of his own Gospel that he already knew of 'many' such accounts. And even where the memories were passed on by word of mouth, we must not assume from modern Western experience that oral tradition is always unreliable. In the ancient East they valued oral tradition more highly than written, and spoken stories and words were retold virtually unaltered for many generations, particularly among the Jews. But in any case, at the time the New Testament Gospels were compiled, there were still plenty of people around who had been present during Jesus' lifetime. They could (and surely would) have prevented any serious misrepresentation of Jesus as they had known him.

Does it matter that all the substantial evidence for Jesus comes to us from Christian sources? We can expect no more since Jesus' place in society was not such as to cause anyone else to preserve a record of him. But does this mean that the evidence is too biased to be trusted? Certainly, we are not reading objective, unbiased reports. The Gospel-writers tell about Jesus because they think he is worth telling about, and they want others to follow him as well. But what worthwhile history or biography has ever been written by people who have no personal interest in what they write? Why should a 'bias' in favour of the subject render the history unreliable? Surely those who had been captivated by Jesus might be expected to take pains to pass on *truth* about him.

1.2

THE GOSPEL MANUSCRIPTS

There are more than five thousand New Testament manuscripts known to us today. An almost incredible number, by far exceeding the textual evidence for any other collection of texts from antiquity. And yet no original of any of the Gospels, or of any New Testament writing, has survived. This may sound disappointing, but there are good historical reasons.

▲ The text of the Gospels survived through being repeatedly copied, usually in monasteries. In time, the copyists began to illuminate their texts most beautifully. This title page of Mark's Gospel is from the Coptic (Egyptian) tradition.

The material most commonly used for writing on in the first century, papyrus, was not meant to last for centuries. Nor was the more precious vellum or parchment. Only if the scrolls were used sparingly and kept carefully could they survive the wear and tear of more than a generation or two. However, people at that time did not acquire the Gospels to line their library shelves with impressive volumes. These scrolls would pass from hand to hand, from study group to study group. After a while copies would be made, and copies of copies, for easier reading and for distribution.

In the early second century, the roll-like scroll gave way to the codex—a smaller, handier format, text on both sides of the sheets, more like a book as we know it today. This innovation was to relegate the traditional scroll to second rank and, eventually, to oblivion. The few manuscripts which outlived their normal life expectancy were prone to be destroyed by the pagan authorities, as one persecution after another hit the Christians. The only manuscripts with a chance of survival were well hidden (like the Dead Sea Scrolls at Qumran) or had been discarded, after re-copying, to rubbish dumps in protective climates (as at Oxyrynchus and other places in Egypt).

When finally, early in the fourth century, Christianity became the state religion of the Roman Empire, Constantine commanded his court librarian Eusebius to arrange for fifty 'codices', collections of

▼ **Letters are the form of writing to have survived most plentifully from classical times. This papyrus letter, from the first century AD, begins: 'Prokleios to his good friend Pekysis, greetings...' Letters form a significant part of the New Testament.**

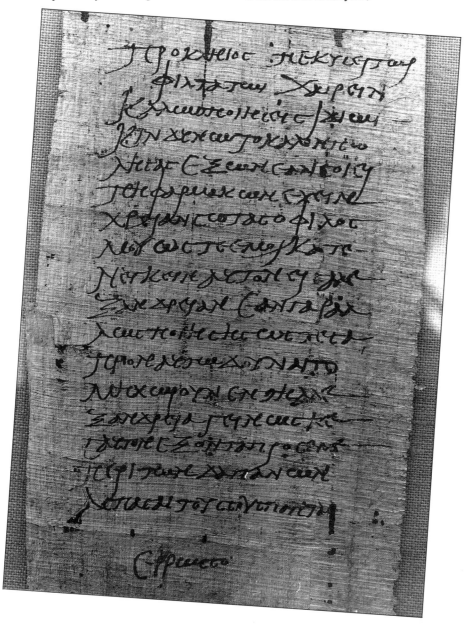

▲ Codex Sinaiticus can be seen today in the British Museum. Dating from the fourth century, it contains parts of the Greek Bible. It is written on vellum.

the Old and New Testaments in one volume, to be written. Yet not a single one of these copies has survived! The only two fourth-century codices of the Bible in Greek to have come down to us are the Codex Sinaiticus, in London's British Museum, and the Codex Vaticanus, in Rome's Vatican Library. And they originate from other, unknown, sources.

So instead of being disappointed at the lack of original Gospel manuscripts, we should be grateful for the impressive number which do exist, and indeed for the very early date of some of them:

■ **The earliest surviving manuscript collection of the four Gospels** is the so-called papyrus *p 45*. This has been separated into two parts, one in the Chester Beatty collection in Dublin, the other in the Austrian National Library in Vienna. Its approximate date is the early third century, that is, soon after AD200. This is more than a century after the last of the Gospels was written, but more than a century before the copying of Christian texts was to enjoy state sanction.

■ **The oldest manuscript fragment of any part of a Gospel** may well belong to Mark. A papyrus

▲ At St Catherine's
Monastery, near the foot of
Mount Sinai, Konstantin von
Tischendorf located a
manuscript containing

considerable parts of the
Greek Bible. Now known as
Codex Sinaiticus, this text is
vital to the whole manuscript
tradition.

fragment from Cave 7 at Qumran, the *7Q5*, has been dated to around AD50. This tiny fragment of Mark chapter 6 verses 52 to 53 is still hotly disputed by some scholars of repute, but it may eventually be commonly accepted as evidence of a New Testament manuscript, if not the first then at least of the second generation of Christian scribes. (It would also be the only known New Testament fragment from a scroll rather than from a codex.)

▪ **The earliest known fragmentary manuscripts of Matthew** known as *p 64* and *p 77*, are late second century.

Where does this leave Luke and John? For Luke, *p 69* and *p 75*, both late second or early third century, are important fragments. And John's Gospel, for a long time regarded as the latest and historically least reliable of the four, is impressively documented in the fragment *p 52* which dates from the early second century and, apart perhaps from Mark's *7Q5*, is the oldest New Testament manuscript known today: and in the *p 66* we have a near-complete codex, probably from about AD130.

These datings mean that some Gospel manuscripts which have survived to today were written very early on: not many years from when people who had seen Jesus and the apostles were still alive. The copyist of the *p 52* (let alone the scribe of *7Q5*) could theoretically have known the author of the fourth Gospel. No other literary text of any importance from antiquity—except for some private letters and legal documents which have survived in the original—comes as close, in its textual tradition, to its authors. Up to eight centuries separate the great classical authors, such as Homer and Tacitus, from the oldest known manuscript collections of their works.

And yet the very wealth of earlier and later Gospel manuscripts presents a challenge to the editors of the Greek New Testament. If no originals have survived, what was the original text? Should we accept the so-called Byzantine group, the Majority Text, which is made up of more than 90 per cent of all known New Testament manuscripts and on which the English King James Bible or Authorized Version was based? Or should we say, as most scholars convincingly do today, that the Majority Text is a purified group of manuscripts, dating from a later stage when a concerted effort was first made to remove real or imagined scribal errors?

If the latter is true, then we must take every single early manuscript very seriously indeed. And even some of the later ones: for a late copy may well have preserved an extremely reliable text otherwise lost.

The number of actual errors in New Testament manuscripts is absolutely minimal if compared to non-biblical manuscripts of antiquity. It would be easy to imagine an organized effort to 'harmonize' the Gospels, once Christianity had become the established religion of the empire. A second-century heretic called Marcion tried unsuccessfully to do this: he discarded all the Gospels apart from Luke, and even Luke he 'edited' to fit his own theological purposes. The early Christians could have done something similar—but they did not. The contents of the Gospels were handed down as they had been compiled by their authors, and the human errors or well-meant 'corrections' affecting certain passages in certain manuscripts cannot detract from the faithfulness which prevailed.

There remain a few disputed areas. Were verses 9 to 20 of Mark chapter 16 added on later? Or where should the story of the woman caught in adultery be placed? Is it original to its present position in John or was an independent story placed there at a later stage?

With the exception of the last verses of John, the Gospels give no indication of authorship. Later writers, from the early second century onwards, have supplied this information, and we have retained the names they mention. However, men such as Papias, Irenaeus and others did not invent the names of Matthew, Mark, Luke and John: independent early evidence is contained in some of the manuscripts (*p 66* for John, *p 75* for Luke and John, and *p 64/77* for Matthew, followed by other early codices). A document such as Luke's Gospel, dedicated to a high-ranking Roman official, Theophilus, would most certainly have included a reference to the author, the 'dedicator' and sender.

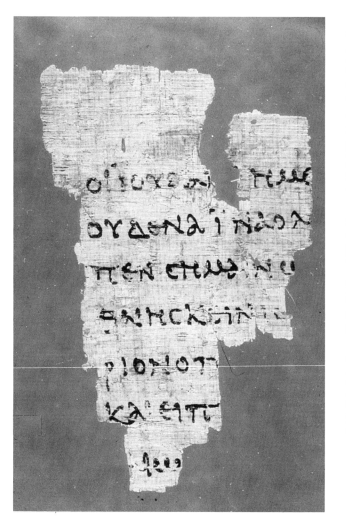

The place for this, in ancient scrolls, was a parchment strip called *sittybos*, attached to the outside cover or handle. This would contain the title of the work inside, and, if there was more than one work of the same title—such as 'Gospel'—the name of the author. Thus, during the lifetime of the first Christians, before the end of the first century, the names of the authors of the four Gospels would have been known, if not from a reference within the text, definitely from the parchment strip attached to the outside.

When the Gospels, after a brief period of oral tradition, were written down, the language the writers chose was *koine*, common, Greek—not the highly cultivated literary idiom of classical literature. The first copyists were untrained laypeople, as we can see from any of the surviving first, second and third century manuscripts. God used average men and women to transmit his word in the texts of the Gospels. And in a sense, he still does today.

◀ **This tiny fragment from John's Gospel – parts of chapter 18 – may be the earliest surviving Gospel text. Written on papyrus, and found in Egypt, it dates from AD125–50.**

1.3

FIRST-CENTURY ARCHAEOLOGY

The New Testament writers did not intend to provide us with a guidebook to places which would later become sites of Christian pilgrimage. For them, *what* actually happened was decisive, not exactly *where* it happened.

John, it is true, gives a useful description of the Pool of Bethesda, near the Sheep Gate, and there are thirty-two other examples in his Gospel. On the other hand, what is venerated today as the *Via Dolorosa*, Christ's route to his death at Golgotha, is most certainly unhistorical: the Gospel-writers simply did not describe the streets he walked. Only recently have archaeologists begun to put together the evidence for the most plausible route, which includes the so-called *Gennath*, or Garden Gate, mentioned by Josephus and rediscovered last year.

Even the Empty Tomb is described in such general terms that only the locals would have found it. As a result, it was some time before the dispute about the actual site, 'Garden Tomb' or 'Church of the Holy Sepulchre', was finally settled in favour of the latter by archaeologists and historians.

In other words, while the existence of these places as real sites in real life was briefly recounted, they were never highlighted as holy places of worship. So what is the point and importance of the archaeology of the time of the first Christians, and what can we draw from it?

This kind of archaeology has passed through three stages:

▪ **There was a genuine interest among Christians to see the places where Jesus and the apostles had been, to tread the same stones.** We We have impressive accounts written by travellers to the Holy Land in the fourth century who visited Jerusalem, Galilee, Judea and Samaria and who wrote descriptions of such locally-venerated places as Peter's house in Capernaum where Jesus used to stay. The mother of Emperor Constantine, Helena, carried Christian archaeology to its first extremes when she visited Jerusalem in AD330. According to fourth-century reports, she found and acquired there such items as the cross, the nails and the robe of Jesus. Even the 'Holy Staircase', the *Scala Santa*, according to legend the staircase which Jesus climbed in Pilate's palace, she brought to Rome, as tradition has it, where it can still be seen today. Thus, at this stage, three centuries after the events, fact and legend, belief and make-belief were sometimes barely distinguishable.

And yet without those early travellers and discoverers, many traces of historical sites, later destroyed by wars or hidden under new structures, might well have been lost for ever. Their journals and accounts have remained invaluable guides to modern archaeologists, and churches built at that time helped to preserve first-century traces underneath. Thus, the Church of the Holy Sepulchre, built between AD326 and 335, guards the historical sites of both Golgotha and the Empty Tomb.

▪ **Curiosity, veneration, preservation and the rise of Christianity as a state religion with all its political undertones shaped the first stage.** The second stage is, to a certain extent, still with us today: it is the stage of the *archaeology of apologetics.* This was an attempt to defend the authenticity of the Gospel accounts. If so-called enlightened sceptics doubted the historicity of such-and-such New Testament event, should one not rebut them by discovering and analyzing the actual places, the

inscriptions, the documents? Let the facts speak! This was and is an entirely legitimate approach, as long as the scientific tools of the trade are being applied without bias.

Spurred on by their convictions, the great Franciscan archaeologists Corbo and Loffreda discovered, a few years ago, the first-century synagogue of Capernaum, where Jesus and the disciples worshipped. Since only a fourth-century structure had been in evidence—and can still be seen by any tourist going there—the 'missing' synagogue of Jesus' time puzzled everyone. Now its existence underneath the later building is safely substantiated.

Or take the Benedictine archaeologist Bargil Pixner. He persevered until he had established the sites of the Essene Gate in Jerusalem and, quite recently, the probable place of Matthew's 'tax office'. In fact, since the work of William Albright in the middle years of this century, we have used the discoveries of archaeologists to validate the reliability of the New Testament writers and to explain the

▲ This octagonal building at Capernaum dates from the fifth century. But beneath it is a first-century house, whose site and characteristics so precisely fit the description given in Mark chapter 1 verses 29 to 33 that many believe it is Peter's house.

historical context of New Testament events. The Pool of Bethesda is one example; another is the Gallio-inscription found at Delphi, which corroborates the presence of a consul of that name mentioned in the book of Acts, and gives us the dates when he was in Corinth.

▪ **A third form of archaeology makes the attempt to be disinterested.** For this approach, it does not matter whether one believes in the New Testament accounts or not; there is a job to be done, and the results will be published with no 'ulterior motives'. Most of the Pauline sites in modern Turkey may belong to this category.

Sometimes this 'neutral', 'unbiased' approach may seem ideal, but it is not realistic. There are too many vested interests—and the furtherance of

▲ A first-century fishing boat was recently unearthed on the shores of Lake Galilee. Much larger than expected, its basic design suggests a raised platform in the stern, exactly as described in Mark chapter 4 verse 38, when Jesus calmed a storm.

tourism is only one of them.

When, thanks to the receding water level, an ancient fishing boat was accidentally discovered on the shores of the Lake of Galilee a couple of years ago, neutral evaluation was hardly possible. The label 'The boat of Peter and Jesus' was attached to it almost immediately. Careful analysis was delayed by triumphant reporting and tourists flocking to the site. In the meantime, analytical carbon-14 dating has shown that the boat may well be of Jesus' time, and that its stern has a characteristic form which may explain Mark's reference, 'Jesus was in the stern, sleeping on a cushion'. A kind of covered area in the stern, where a person could sleep, is suggested by the boat now found, and a New Testament passage long regarded as a literary device could in fact go back to an eyewitness account.

In 1972, the tentative identification of New Testament manuscripts from a cave at Qumran (which had been sealed in AD68) was greeted with such exuberant triumph by certain scholars, who saw in them the final downfall of modern schools of Gospel criticism, that others rejected them equally firmly out of hand, sometimes without looking at the real evidence. The slow process of correct and unbiased evaluation is still being hampered by preconceived ideas of what could or could not be found.

First-century archaeology is an ongoing business. Hard evidence, hypotheses and speculations will continue to accompany it. But fascinating as it may be, our faith in the trustworthiness of the New Testament should not be made to rely on its results.

1.4

JESUS IN HIS SETTING

Look at a map of the Roman Empire in the time of Jesus and you will, after a while, discover that tiny region in the east, the province of Judea, the 'Kingdom' of Herod Antipas, the Tetrarchy of Philip: that is where Jesus and the disciples lived the lives of a wandering preacher with his followers.

This was a remote area of the empire; no governor had ever asked to be sent there from Rome. And yet Judea was not totally a place apart. It belonged to the whole: its culture, its way of life were influenced by Greek and Roman literature, philosophy, and arts, as well as by pagan religions, and by international trade linking the south and east with the west and north.

Imagine Nazareth, an unimportant hamlet in Galilee, not even mentioned in any Jewish writings before the time of Jesus. And nearby, within walking distance, as it were, was Sepphoris, a major cultural centre with a beautiful theatre (now fully excavated). Practically everyone, even a mere carpenter's son, could have gone to Sepphoris to see the tragedies and comedies of the great Greek and Roman playwrights (see also the article *What language did Jesus speak?*). Some scholars have suggested that Mark's Gospel is constructed like a Greek tragedy. Absurd? Well, even someone like Mark could have been influenced by the formal stringency of a drama he had watched in a place like Sepphoris. Or again Paul: the book of Acts tells us that he was a pupil of Gamaliel; and Gamaliel belonged to school of teachers using Greek literature and philosophy to exemplify certain points of Jewish thinking. Thus, to hardly anyone's surprise, Greek classical quotations pop up in Paul's teaching and in his letters. In his first letter to the Corinthians, Paul quotes from the

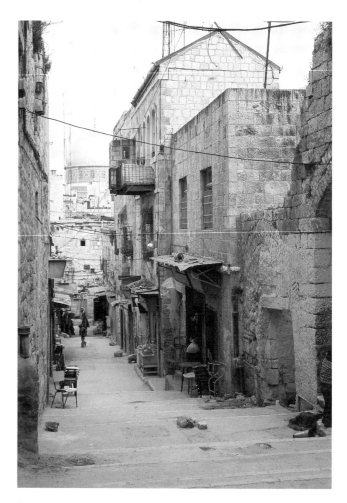

▲ Old Jerusalem today contains many narrow, crowded streets, with much of life lived outdoors. In this way it is not very different from the Jerusalem of Bible times.

What Languages Did Jesus Speak?

People (especially English-speakers) are generally happy to speak and write one language fluently and correctly. But at the time of Jesus, one language was not sufficient—not even for the rulers of the empire, the Romans. Their own language, Latin, had a rival in Greek, used by educated people in their writings, letters and conversations.

And Greek was not simply Greek. There were different forms of dialects, used for different literary genres; there was the lower, 'hellenistic' everyday literary style; and there was the common language accessible to practically everyone, even the uneducated. This internationally-current type of Greek (much more correct than, say, Pidgin English today) is known as *koine*, the common one. It was in this Greek that the New Testament was later to be written.

And then, of course, every country, every province of the Roman Empire would have its own native language. In Palestine, there were two: Hebrew, the ancient, traditional language of Bible and synagogue, and Aramaic, the everyday language, almost as old as Hebrew and closely related to it (and used occasionally in the Old Testament).

To begin with, every male Jew who attended elementary school would have been fluent in Hebrew and Aramaic. Those working in commerce would have acquired at least a good working knowledge of Greek. Remarkably, not a single coin minted in Palestine between 37BC and AD67 has been found with even one Hebrew letter, let alone a complete Hebrew (or Aramaic) inscription. People using coins (nearly everyone, that is) were thus almost forced to learn at least basic elements of Greek.

Jesus is likely to have spoken Aramaic as his normal, everyday language. But he was brought up in Galilee, a region thoroughly permeated by Greek influence. As a carpenter, he would have encountered Greek-speaking people quite frequently as he travelled around, long before the beginning of his public ministry. And inscriptions found in Galilee and elsewhere in Palestine demonstrate that Greek was acceptable even to orthodox, believing Jews who used it in the synagogues or on tombstones, in the theatres, and even in the Temple of Jerusalem.

To this indirect evidence, which makes it quite plausible that Jesus was able to use Greek in everyday dealings, we can add the evidence of the New Testament. There are at least two instances which hint at a conversation in Greek:

■ **Jesus once met a Syrian Phoenician woman**. The woman was Greek, born in Syrian Phoenicia, Mark tells us. She would, in all probability, not have been able to speak Aramaic or Hebrew. No interpreter was present at this meeting in a house in the vicinity of Tyre. Thus we must assume that they spoke Greek.

■ **And of course he also talked with Pontius Pilate**, whose languages were Greek and Latin. Here too, no interpreter was present. So again we must assume that Jesus spoke Greek (if not Latin).

Recently it has been suggested by Benedict Schwank that Jesus' saying, 'Give to Caesar what is Caesar's, and to God what is God's', was originally spoken in Greek, as it plays on the inscription of a coin of the emperor Tiberius, minted with the Greek for 'Caesar', for which there was no everyday Aramaic equivalent. And as every Jew in Palestine would have used those coins and known their inscriptions, it would not have been unusual for Jesus to use Greek immediately. Also, when Jesus talked with Peter at the lakeside to test his continuing love for him, the structure of the sentences shows a play on shades of meaning in the Greek words for 'to love', 'to know' and 'flock' which cannot be repeated in Aramaic or Hebrew. And we should bear in mind that the brothers Peter and Andrew came from hellenized background; even Andrew's name is entirely Greek, and Peter's original name, Simon, is documented in Greek texts much earlier than in Hebrew and Aramaic ones. Philip, too, is an entirely Greek name. Apparently, even Mary of Magdala used to speak Greek: John explicitly notes that she switched to Aramaic near the empty tomb. She turned towards him and cried out in Aramaic, "Rabboni!" (which means Teacher), after a previous passage obviously spoken in Greek.

And Latin? A working knowledge of the language cannot be ruled out, and, theoretically at least, the conversations with the Roman centurion and with Pilate could as well have taken place in Latin as in Greek. Enough everyday Latin would have been spoken in regions with Roman army contingents for it to be thinkable. However, the circumstantial evidence in favour of Greek even on these occasions is much stronger.

So although the Gospels were written down in common Greek and not Hebrew or Aramaic, this does not necessarily distance us from Jesus' other words. This Greek was a part of the everyday experience of Jesus and his disciples. And in some instances it was the language actually used by Jesus himself.

playwright Menander; in the letter to Titus, from Epimenides and Callimachus; in his speech in Athens he alluded to Aratus and Cleanthes.

Jesus himself grew up as a law-abiding, orthodox Jew. And none of his later teachings were meant to overthrow the Mosaic framework of the Torah, the Law, or the message of the prophets, but rather to fulfil them. He was called Master and Rabbi by his

▶▼ The Gospels focus on
Galilee – rural and provincial,
and Jerusalem – the focal city
of the region.

Galilee and Jerusalem

Today we think of Palestine in Roman times as all one region. A man of Nazareth would be quite at home in Jerusalem. But that is not so.

For one thing, Jerusalem was a large and impressive city, once the proud capital of an independent kingdom. But Nazareth was only a little-known village in the hills seventy miles to the north. And Nazareth was in Galilee. As far as the people of Jerusalem were concerned, it was foreign territory, even though its people were also Jews.

For most of its history since the death of King Solomon, nearly a thousand years earlier, Galilee had been under different government from Judea. Sometimes the region had even belonged to a different empire. It was known as 'Galilee of the Gentiles' and its population was so mixed that in the period of the Maccabean wars a century and a half before Jesus was born the minority Jewish population had had to be evacuated to the south. It was only after military conquest that Galilee was forcibly 'rejudaized'. The village in which Jesus grew up, protected by its ring of hills, was Jewish enough. But four miles away in the valley was the Greek city of Sepphoris, the administrative capital of Galilee. And down by the lake stood the Greek city of Tiberias, founded during Jesus' boyhood by Galilee's ruler, Herod Antipas, as his new capital.

To reach Judea from Galilee, you either had to travel through the hostile territory of the Samaritans or cross the Jordan and make your way through the Gentile territory of Decapolis. On all sides Galilee was surrounded by non-Jewish territory.

Galilee is more fertile than Judea, and its people tended to be more prosperous. But in the eyes of Jerusalem Jews they were not to be trusted. Galileans faithfully made their way to the temple in Jerusalem for the prescribed festivals, but they were never as enthusiastic as Judeans in their observance of scribal rules. They had a reputation for being less concerned about proper observance of the Law. A religious teacher from Galilee could expect a rough ride among the Pharisees of Jerusalem.

Judean Jews made fun of the accent of the Galileans. They regarded them as uncultured. So Jesus and his followers, with their northern accent, would have seemed as 'foreign' in Jerusalem as an Irishman in London or a Texan in New York. After Jesus' arrest Peter was easily identified as one of the disciples because of his accent.

When Jesus, the prophet from Nazareth with his band of Galilean disciples, presented himself to the people of Jerusalem as the Messiah of Israel, the reaction was predictable: 'How can the Messiah come from Galilee?' they said.

▲ This silver tetradrachm is from the city of Tyre. Each city had its own standard of weight for its coins, which explains the balances used by the temple merchants as they weighed out coinage. Jesus was enraged by this trade.

▶ The Forum at Rome was the centre of a great and well-ordered empire, of which Judea was a remote, insignificant part.

followers, and there were, at first sight, others like him, wandering teachers preaching and performing miracles, men such as Hanina Ben-Dosa still known to us from later sources. Jesus was working in a setting in which he did not appear superficially very unusual—the first to perceive his chosen role after his infancy were John the Baptist and Simon Peter.

Climate of expectation

Jesus, although brought up like any ordinary Jew of his time, should be set against a wider backcloth than just an Old Testament one. Yes, there were Jewish expectations that someone great would be born. Had not Isaiah predicted that he would be born of a virgin? (And do not let the force of this be diminished by some critics who dismiss this as a misinterpretation: *parthenos*, the word in the Greek version, and *alma*, the word in Hebrew, both mean 'virgin'—with a very few exceptions where it means 'young, unmarried woman', a synonym in those days for 'virgin' anyway.) But the wider Roman Empire showed instances of a similar expectation.

A unique birth, the coming of the ruler of the world, the bringer of peace—these were looked for by many peoples at the time: the Babylonians, the Persians, and the Romans themselves had predicted it for the very period when Jesus was born. We know from ancient and contemporary clay tablets and manuscripts that the 'Great Conjunction', the 'Star of Bethlehem', is not a cosy Christmas myth but a historical fact well documented outside the New Testament, and there is nothing more probable than the historical existence of those wise men, those astrologers from the east who came to see Jesus in Bethlehem.

Even the influential Roman poet Virgil, from the last century BC, wrote a pastoral poem, an 'eclogue' —his fourth—on the expected birth of such a man. Although he very probably was not referring prophetically to Christ, but to the son of a certain Pollio, his poem was taken up by later Christian authors and interpreted as a pre-Christian prophecy pointing to Jesus as the Messiah. In Dante's *Divine Comedy* (1313), the Roman author Statius claims to have become a Christian through Virgil; in the Spanish cathedral of Zamora, a statue of Virgil stands next to one of Isaiah as a prophet.

To understand Jesus and his role in his own time, we have to understand this historical setting which seems so remote to us. Today we are growing used to the idea of a Europe of '1992', with fewer borders, easier trade, and hopefully a growing exchange of cultural and, not least, spiritual experiences. But still the *Pax Augusta*, the peace of the Roman emperor Augustus which had shaped the world of the time of Jesus, seems strangely advanced: no frontiers, a magnificent international road system, working postal services (it took a letter,

▲ These houses at Ostia Antica, Rome's ancient seaport, are built over first-century remains. A number of such sites have yielded evidence of Christian worship and occupation.

say one of Paul's, about a week to reach Italy from Israel; try that today!)—all this contributed to the spreading of the Christian message. On the other hand, Jesus the Jew was crucified under Roman law in Jerusalem; Paul the Jew was beheaded as a Roman citizen outside the walls of Rome. They lived in a world, efficient even in its cruelty, where most Romans did not try to understand the stubborn monotheism of the Jews, so alien to them, and where most Jews did not try to stifle their thirst for revolt against the foreign oppressors. It is a world from which we cannot disentangle the historical Jesus if we are to understand him and his work in the setting where God had made him the Son of man.

A Jesus Acrostic

In the ruins of Pompeii, the city ruined by the eruption of Vesuvius in AD79, there are two instances of a strange acrostic.

```
R O T A S
O P E R A
T E N E T
A R E P O
S A T O R
```

What does it mean? Four levels have been suggested:
- 'Sator', the sower, is an early name for Jesus, so the acrostic is identified as referring to him.
- The letters add up to a double Paternoster, 'our Father', with an extra A and O, alpha and omega, first and last letters of the Greek alphabet, which the writer of Revelation used as a symbol for the eternal Jesus.
- When A and O come near each other, T is between them, standing for the cross at the heart of the eternal Jesus.
- Right in the middle, forming the pattern of the cross, comes the repeated word 'tenet', 'he holds'. This would be a powerful support for Christians then undergoing fierce persecution. In the midst of it all Jesus is with them and he who has been through it himself will sustain them. *Tenet*; he holds.

1.5

THE DEAD SEA SCROLLS

When the moon slowly rises over the waters of the Dead Sea, a mere sixteen miles east of Jerusalem, this arid, unwelcoming region suddenly looks far from 'dead', and one can easily imagine a religious community, the Essenes, settling there. The Essenes, with the Pharisees and the Sadducees, were one of the great rival groups within ancient Judaism. They lived a closely guarded, strictly regulated life, and wrote their own theological works as well as copying and interpreting the writings of the Bible, or the Old Testament as it was then.

As far as we know today, the ruins of Qumran, where the Essenes had established themselves, had been settled for some time, with only brief interruptions. Community life there came to an end when the Romans occupied the site in AD68, on their march towards Jerusalem, which they besieged and destroyed in AD70. Some settlers returned later, but no traces of community life after AD68 have been found.

This isolated spot, so suddenly cut off from history, became a focus of world attention in 1947, when the chance discovery of a cave with jars containing manuscript rolls was made known. They were found, not by an archaeologist, but by a Palestinian goat-herd looking for a lost animal. Soon afterwards, they were put on sale in Jerusalem. As so often with important art treasures and literary finds, the exact spot where they had been discovered remained obscure, until two years later when a group of researchers identified the cave. This led to further archaeological campaigns, and between 1952 and 1956 a further ten caves were discovered. During those years, the settlement of Qumran was excavated, and the visitor today can walk through the ruins of the buildings, among them the *scriptorium*, or 'writing rooms', where most of the manuscripts were written, and can see the sites of caves nearby where they were hidden when the Roman Tenth Legion approached in AD68.

But what makes these 'Dead Sea Scrolls' so exciting? When the first scrolls from Cave 1 finally reached the hands of the experts, their importance soon became clear.

■ **They were the first authentic documents from this Jewish community**, previously only known about by virtue of second-hand information: the 'Manual of Discipline', the 'War Scroll', the 'Thanks-giving Hymns'. Also, in Cave 3, the fascinating 'Copper Scroll', enabled the archaeologist Bargil Pixner to identify where the Essenes' treasures were hidden in the Jerusalem area.

■ **There were also unique commentaries on particular Old Testament books** (such as the 'Habakkuk Commentary').

■ **Above all, the scrolls included the oldest known manuscripts of Old Testament writings**, such as the world-famous 'Isaiah Scroll', dating to the second century BC, which represents a giant step towards the development of a reliable history of the textual tradition of the Old Testament.

Since the library was closed, as it were, in AD68, its final period coincided with the beginnings of Christianity. And indeed, some of the Qumran teachings have been compared with the teachings of Jesus and of John the Baptist. Certain similarities do exist. There is, for example, a common emphasis on baptism. But Essene baptism was very different from John's baptism. And most of the similarities,

◀ In this desert monastery, a group of the Jewish sect of Essenes lived out their lives and copied their manuscripts until the day when the Romans broke up their community.

▲ These caves at Qumran by the Dead Sea were the scene of a manuscript discovery which has transformed scholarly confidence in the accuracy of the Old Testament text.

close or distant, real or imagined, between Essenes, and John the Baptist and the first Christians, can be explained from their joint Old Testament background.

There is, however, a notable link going back to the days of Jesus' ministry in Jerusalem. As recent archaeology has shown, the Essene quarter in Jerusalem was next to the centre of the first Christian community on Mount Zion. Essene Jews may have been interested in the uncompromising lifestyle of their neighbours, and the followers of Jesus may have wanted to find out more about the unique attitude towards law and tradition held by the Essenes, which was so different from that of the Pharisees and Sadducees. Some scholars think that the room where the Last Supper took place was in a house belonging to the Essenes 'around the corner'. Others think that the unusual sharing of property within the Christian community in Jerusalem was reinforced, if not inspired, by the neighbouring Essene way of life. The Essenes may have been among the first practising Jews to convert to Christianity.

All this takes us directly back to the Dead Sea Scrolls. Without the geographical and social connections between Christians and Essenes in

▲ The task of repairing and piecing together the many manuscripts of the Dead Sea Scrolls has continued ever since their discovery in 1948. Much work remains to be done.

Jerusalem, an almost sensational discovery in Cave 7 at Qumran would be difficult to understand. A Spanish papyrologist, Jose O'Callaghan, suggested in a series of articles in 1972 that of the nineteen tiny fragments found in that cave, all of them in Greek and on papyrus (whereas the other caves held almost exclusively Hebrew and Aramaic texts on parchment), up to nine could be from New Testament writings. Leaving the question of the individual identifications aside (and recent debate is pointing towards the acceptance of at least one of them, 7Q5, being part of Mark chapter 6, verses 52–53), historians have suggested that there are two main reasons for the existence of Christian texts in this peculiar cave with the Greek papyri: Essenes converted to Christianity or Jewish Christians interested in visiting the headquarters of the Essenes could have taken the scrolls with them to Qumran, perhaps even as evangelistic tools. Cave 7 would then have contained their reference library. Or, the Jerusalem Christians entrusted their most valuable manuscripts to their Essene neighbours for safekeeping when they left the city in AD66 to withdraw to Pella, and the Essenes hid them in a separate cave at Qumran.

Thus, the Qumran caves contain not only the oldest known Hebrew Old Testament manuscripts but also, in all probability, the oldest Greek New Testament manuscript or manuscripts known today.

Quite a few of these identifications (not only of the Greek Cave 7!) are the object of controversy among international scholars. Literally hundreds of Dead Sea Scrolls fragments are still waiting to be edited, more than thirty years after their discovery. And some of them may well contain further important information for us on the environment of Jesus and the first Christians.

1.6

THE WITNESS OF THE GOSPELS

The Greek word *euangelion*, which we translate as 'gospel', means simply 'good news'. When Mark began his book with the words 'The beginning of the *euangelion* of Jesus Christ, the Son of God. . .', he used the word to refer not to his book but to its subject-matter. The 'good news' was what was being preached, and Mark was putting it down on paper. But the fact that he used the word, right at the beginning, soon led to the use of *euangelion* as a convenient label for this new type of book. As far as we know it was never used as the title of a book before the New Testament.

What is a Gospel?

There was nothing new about writing a record of the deeds and sayings of a great man. Biographies were common in the Greek and Roman world, and we even know of a few Jewish examples. Their subjects might be kings, military leaders, philosophers or poets—anyone who had made a mark in the world of their time. Such 'lives' were usually not so much detailed accounts of all that their hero did and experienced, but rather collections of reminiscences and memorable sayings designed to provide a model for others to follow.

In many ways the New Testament Gospels fit this pattern. But what is different is the nature of their subject and the authors' attitude to him. Jesus was not a prominent public figure, nor is he presented as primarily a great teacher. He is not even first and foremost an example for his disciples to copy. His 'biographers' are not very interested in the majority of his life. Nor are they concerned with background and psychological development. They

▲ This ancient relief shows Peter dictating his recollections to Mark the Gospel-writer.

Other Gospels

Are the four New Testament Gospels the only source of information about what Jesus said and did? Not quite. Stories and sayings crop up in fragments of manuscript and in quotations from other writers. And at least two other documents have been called 'Gospels'.

■ **The Gospel of Thomas** was found among many ancient papyrus books discovered in 1946 at Naq Hammadi in Egypt. It consists mainly of a collection of sayings attributed to Jesus—114 in all. Some are virtually identical to sayings in the four Gospels. Others are closely related to known sayings, but develop them to make different points. But a great deal is unfamiliar, and serves a philosophy plainly in line with the Gnostics (as is true of all the Naq Hammadi material). The Gnostics held a wide range of ideas, some linked to Christianity; they believed in the importance of a secret

knowledge (or *gnosis*) about the spiritual world. One saying shows the difference in atmosphere: 'Split the wood; I am there. Lift up the stone, and you will find me there.'

■ **The Gospel of Peter** has come down to us in a fragment found in 1886–87, also in Egypt. It is a free retelling of the Gospel account of what happened from the end of Jesus' trial to his resurrection appearances. The writer identifies himself with Simon Peter, the chief apostle. It is plainly part of a longer work, and seems to date to at least as early as the second century. The story we know is embellished to give fuller 'evidence' for the resurrection.

■ **Fragments of manuscripts** with material about Jesus are quite common. One instance is *Egerton Papyrus 2*, preserved in the British Museum. This tiny document, on three pieces of papyrus, contains parts of stories and sayings similar to some in the four Gospels, but also some otherwise unknown material.

■ **Some later writers quote sayings and deeds of Jesus extra to those we know.** But, if collected together, these do not add substantially to the material in Matthew, Mark, Luke and John.

These additional sources about Jesus make a fascinating study. But there is no reason, where their accounts differ from the four Gospels, to prefer them or to revise our understanding of what Jesus said and did.

▼ **Egerton Papyrus 2 contains sayings similar to some in the Gospels, but also some quite different material.**

▲ **A fragment from the Gospel of Thomas.**

▲ The Arch of Titus in Rome shows soldiers in procession celebrating victories in Palestine. They are carrying the great candlestick and other treasures from the Jerusalem Temple, sacked in AD70. Much internal evidence suggests the Gospels may have been composed before this happened.

focus on only a few years of intensive public activity, and then devote as much as a quarter of their books to describing the events leading up to and surrounding his death. The Gospels have even been described as 'passion narratives with extended introductions'!

What makes all this 'good news'? As they wrote, Jesus' biographers were convinced that he was still alive, and that he still called people to follow him. Their books were offered not for information so much as for action. As John put it, 'These are written that you may believe that Jesus is the Messiah, the Son of God, and that by believing you may have life in his name.'

How were Gospels written?

People today perhaps imagine Matthew and the others sitting alone at their study desks working on the printer's drafts sent to them by their publishers. But of course it was not like that.

Matthew, Mark, Luke and John were members of Christian communities, writing in and for the churches to which they belonged. The material they wrote was based on the stories and sayings of Jesus as taught and preached in their churches. The tradition is that Mark acted as a secretary to the apostle Peter, and his Gospel is a compilation of what Peter had been teaching in Rome. Mark set it down in writing so that Peter's message could continue to be available after his death. It is a tradition which may well be true, and which adds that Mark wrote his book because the church leaders asked him to do so.

The evangelists were men with their own individual ideas and emphases, and they wrote their books in their own distinctive ways. But they did not do it in isolation. These are church books intended primarily for reading aloud in the church, many of whose members would not be able to read for themselves. Probably the evangelists themselves were engaged in preaching and teaching, and their books grew out of and continued that work.

Two of the Gospels (Matthew and John) are attributed to two of Jesus' inner circle of disciples, and Mark's is based on Peter's teaching. Luke was not himself a member of the original Jesus-circle,

Jesus the Musical

Jesus the Musical, Jesus the pop star, came together in a major way during the early 1970s, with *Jesus Christ Superstar* and *Godspell*, and endless efforts since to repeat the impact of this showbiz duo have failed.

Superstar was the most successful. Its writers, Tim Rice and Andrew Lloyd Webber, had previously achieved moderate acclaim for a young person's participatory musical *Joseph And The Amazing Technicolour Dreamcoat*. Initially *Superstar* was a double-record album that fetched average reviews. It was the American record and showbiz industry that made it into a sensation, so much so that in theatre terms it became a 'must'. *Godspell* was in all ways a much quieter affair. It was written as a drama thesis by John-Michael Tebelak. The score was by Stephen Schwartz. Its British opening was helped by the casting of an up-coming teen sensation called David Essex. Neither musical was penned by a Christian, although of course both centred on a particular aspect and style of Jesus' life. Christians and churches reacted in varied ways.

▼ **In this scene from 'Jesus Christ Superstar' Jesus is greeted by the people of Jerusalem with palm branches, as a king. It is an ecstatic and dramatic scene – a natural for a musical.**

Godspell continues in theatrical popularity, partly because it is simpler whether in stage set or dialogue. *Superstar* was a forerunner of theatrical stage-set epics; it was noisy and vulgar. *Godspell* seems to possess more of the inner gospel, *Superstar* a showbiz version.

But pop music with an interest in Jesus spreads further than full-blown musicals. A discography of religious and predominantly Christian-flavoured songs in pop history from the mid-1950s onwards lists well over one thousand titles. Musically there is considerable breadth, as shown by the names: Lena Martell, The Rolling Stones, Boney M, Elton John, Paul McCartney, Marvin Gaye, Gram Parsons, David Essex and Queen. Many of them could not claim a particular religious commitment but some would, as for instance Dylan, Cliff Richard, Pete Townshend, Van Morrison, Donna Summer and the duo Seals & Croft.

Since its beginning days the pop phenomenon has had numerous variations and has attracted conflicting loyalties and attachments. The religious, albeit mostly Christian, strain is an important element.

Early rock'n'roll heroes such as Elvis Presley, Jerry Lee Lewis and Little Richard had a grounding in American gospel music. The

church was central to the lives of people and communities where they were reared. Almost all the early British music stars of the early-to-mid 1960s derived their musical love and style from listening to American popular music, and amid the jazz, folk, R&B, country and blues they also heard gospel. The Beatles, Manfred Mann and The Animals are three groups whose early music was influenced by hearing things American.

To hear and see many pop-rock groups is to sense a gospel and black-church presence. This is not confined to expected black quarters, as for instance with James Brown, Earth Wind & Fire and Kool and the Gang, and the so-popular Michael Jackson and Prince. It can be sensed in white acts with The Eurythmics, Dexy's Midnight Runners (and the now-solo Kevin Rowland), Robert Palmer and Talking Heads among those surely qualifying. Few known black acts have escaped an actual church upbringing with the 1980s represented as any

▲ **Michael Jackson is just one popstar whose roots are in church music. The rhythms of black gospel singing underlie the beat of rock music. Many American singers grew up in church communities.**

other with the likes of Whitney Houston, Deniece Williams, Prince, Mica Paris, Will Downing, The Pasadenas, Paul Johnson and Terence Trent D'Arby.

And there are rock writers and chroniclers who would trace in rock music a basic search for redemption. They see much music as expressive of a search for self, for overall meaning in a seemingly cold and alien world. Musicians such as Sting and Peter Gabriel, influenced by Jungian thought, have delved into the whys and wherefores of existence; others, as with the Punk movement, have sent out painful cries for help, shouting the odds of a world without meaning.

Religious, even predominantly Christian, song lyrics have not always been composed or sung by card-carrying Christians and indeed the greater mass

have come from apparent non-believers. Cat Stevens recorded the massive hit *Morning Has Broken* during his flirtation period between Christianity and Buddhism, and later he chose Islam. Oddly enough the pianist on *Morning Has Broken* was Rick Wakeman, and by the end of the 1980s he had made a Christian stand. Occasionally a religious song of one community has been adopted elsewhere, as with George Harrison's Krishna-based *My Sweet Lord* being also sung on record by Cliff Richard.

From time to time the record companies see gospel as the next 'in thing', but they rarely stay with it in the absence of immediate hit singles and albums. However, it has meant a wide outreach for performers such as The London Community Gospel Choir, The Inspirational Choir and Lavine Hudson.

During the 1980s the number of pop people with Christian conviction has grown, although they represent a smallish number on the total scene. But, as a group like U2 has shown, it only needs one big name to achieve considerable media profile. The most pronounced pop-star Christian has been Britain's Cliff Richard, whose career has spanned three decades.

It might be expected that artists who have recorded for religious labels run by Christian-based companies would make chart inroads. But until fairly late into the 1980s much product from such sources was inferior to that of the general record world. However, standards have risen considerably and

▲ 'Godspell' gained its impact by portraying Jesus and his disciples in clown costume. The joy, the sadness and the drama are keenly felt in such a presentation.

in America at least two acts, Amy Grant and the metal band Stryper, have crossed over from religious terrain to general-chart ground. There are other religious label artists who could well achieve something similar, but unfortunately the economics of religious record companies, especially outside the United States, dictate that these artists should lack well-funded and sustained promotion.

Rock stars seem to have general respect for Jesus. Some say their Christian understanding was ruined by bad religious education teaching or memories of church Sunday school. Certainly it is the church that receives a thumbs down. Jesus is alive and well in many pop areas, although there are some Christians who vehemently see the pop world as an arena for the devil to conquer young lives and hearts.

It would be a strange state of affairs if Jesus should be left to non-Christians in one of the most powerful communicative areas of modern times. Fortunately, he is not.

but he tells us that he has been at pains to discover all he could from 'those who from the first were eye-witnesses and servants of the word'. He has thus 'carefully investigated everything from the beginning'. So the material in the Gospels is closely linked with the original apostolic group, whether at first or second hand. Luke also mentions that there were already other accounts of Jesus in existence. Certainly there must have been plenty of oral tradition in circulation among the churches for the evangelists to draw on.

Who copied whom?

The Gospels of Matthew, Mark and Luke are known as the 'Synoptic Gospels'. This is because they have quite similar outlines, and much of their material overlaps, so we can read them 'synoptically'. Christians have been so aware of the similarities, and so keen to read them as if they were a single work, that they have often not done justice to the distinctive ways in which each of the three writers presents his material. In recent studies their individual contributions have rightly been more emphasized. But the degree of similarity remains an intriguing fact, and many explanations have been offered.

The facts are complex. In places all three Synoptic Gospels, or sometimes just two of them, are word-for-word the same for several verses at a time. At other places, while the subject-matter is clearly the same, the wording is very different, as each puts his own slant on the story or teaching. Sometimes we cannot decide whether we are dealing with real parallels (where we have differing accounts of the same original incident) or with quite separate occasions (but where Jesus said or did similar things). In the course of a few years' public activity there must have been times when a similar event occurred or Jesus repeated his teaching on an important matter.

Matthew and Luke are longer than Mark, and for almost all of Mark's Gospel there is a parallel of some sort in one or both of the others. In much of the other material Matthew and Luke are so similar that they must have had some common source or sources. Unless, that is, one of them took his material from the other.

For most of the church's history it was assumed that Matthew wrote first, then Mark 'abbreviated' his work. Matthew and Mark appear as the first two Gospels in our New Testament. Then Luke, so it was thought, used both of the others as the basis of his own Gospel. But the facts do not fit. Where

Jesus in Literature Today

Hundreds of titles could easily be cited to prove that Jesus plays a significant role in the poetry, fiction and drama of the twentieth century. Even in an age of secularization, in which many of the Christian roots of Western culture have been cut off, his figure is manifest, though often in shapes or guises we do not expect. How does Jesus appear in literature today? What are the purposes to which his appearance is put? And how do writers tell us that one of their characters is meant to be a Christ figure?

Some works present Jesus as a historical person in the historical setting of the Roman Empire. In others, such as Upton Sinclair's *They Call me Carpenter* (1922), he steps down from his place in a stained-glass window and enters modern life in person. His face is tattooed onto the main character's skin in Flannery O'Connor's short story *Parker's Back* (1964), which is set in the American South. Günter Herburger's *Jesus in Osaka* (German,

1970) places him in a futuristic society of around the year 2000. Sometimes writers have made a link by giving a character the initials J C. The names of Faulkner's Joe Christmas (*Light in August*, 1932) or Steinbeck's Jim Casey (*The Grapes of Wrath*, 1939) in themselves suggest certain parallels to Jesus. It may also be traits of Jesus' character or sayings of his that mark a fictional person as a Christ figure. Simon in William Golding's *Lord of the Flies* (1954), for example, not only dies an innocent death but has a visionary perception of the truth about good and evil that connects him with Jesus.

Interesting as such parallels are, one should be careful not to mistake every reference to Jesus as an author's personal statement of faith in Jesus as the Son of God. Apart from works with the clear purpose to present this biblical Jesus to a modern age, there are many attempts to reinterpret his person in terms of one ideology or

another, and many others which use him as a frame of reference for interpreting modern dilemmas, or simply endow a modern hero with Christ-like traits in order to lend more depth to a work of art.

The attempts to retell the story of the biblical Jesus include both historical accounts and tales of modern times. In the wake of Giovanni Papini's *Storia di Cristo* (Italian, 1921), which tries to present Christ to a secular audience, we find many literary accounts of Jesus' life in its historical setting. One such attempt is Dorothy L Sayers' cycle of radio plays, *The Man Born to Be King* (1943). Though the place of the action is ancient Palestine, the characters speak colloquial modern English, thereby demonstrating that 'God was executed by people painfully like us, in a society very similar to our own'. Nikos Kazantzakis' *The Last Temptation of Christ* (Greek, 1953) shows how Jesus might have been tempted to exchange the cross for a life of 'simple human pleasures'. Jan Dobraczynski's *Listy Nikodema* (Polish, 1952), Paär Lagerkvist's *Barrabas* (Swedish, 1946), Max Brod's

Der Meister (German, 1952), and Gertrud von le Fort's *Die Frau des Pilatus* (German, 1955) focus on the biblical Jesus from the perspective of a minor figure from the Gospel—Nicodemus, Barrabas, Meleagros (a clerk under Pilate) and Pilate's wife. Such works differ in the degree to which they employ modern language and modern notions, but they all share a serious intention to do justice to the Christ of the Bible.

There are many other works which try to make Jesus into someone else than the Son of God and redeemer that the Gospels show us. Such reinterpretations are as old as David Friedrich Strauss's *Das Leben Jesu* (German, 1835) and Ernest Renan's *Vie de Jesus* (French, 1863), the one distinguishing between a historical Jesus and a Jesus of faith, and the other producing a psychological portrait of a sweet and gentle young Palestinian carpenter. Neither accepted the Gospels as the factual accounts which they had been for previous centuries. Once the factual bottom of the Gospels had been knocked out, the person of Jesus could then be shaped

◄ On the walls of the catacombs at Rome, where Christians gathered in the centuries after Jesus, are painted many scenes from the Gospels. This 'Good Shepherd' painting, at the Callisto cemetery, dates from the third century.

Matthew and Mark tell the same story, Mark does not 'abbreviate'—he usually tells it at much greater length. It is just that he covers far less ground than Matthew.

Since the nineteenth century most scholars have turned to the theory that Mark came first. Matthew and Luke independently drew both on Mark and on another common source or sources, which was subsequently lost. The letter 'Q' has become the accepted name for this common material, sometimes envisaged as a single collection of the sayings of Jesus, sometimes as a variety of traditions, both written and oral, to which Matthew and Luke had access. This remains the favourite theory today.

Another theory, first proposed in the eighteenth

and coloured in whatever way it pleased a writer. For example, Robert Graves' *King Jesus* (1954) claims that Jesus was not born to the virgin Mary but was the rightful heir to the Jewish throne and executed as such deliberately by Pilate for political reasons. William Faulkner re-interprets Jesus as compassionate sufferer in his allegory *A Fable* (1954).

In most works of modern literature, however, the attention is not focused on Jesus himself, but on humankind in a modern age. Jesus is merely used as a parallel to drive home the point a writer wants to make. Three examples demonstrate this:

- *The Rebel*. The Jesus of the Gospels opposed the religious establishment of his time, and some modern writers use this as a means to attack today's religious or political establishment. Thus one of beat poet Lawrence Ferlinghetti's poems makes Christ climb down 'from his bare tree' and run away from the phoniness of modern Christmas celebrations (*Christ Climbed Down*, 1958). Frank Andermann's novel *Das grosse Gesicht* (German, 1970) makes him a rebel against political oppression. In that respect, today's writers follow the model of novelists such as Ignazio Silone (*Pane e Vino*, Italian, 1936) or Arthur Koestler (*Darkness at Noon*, 1941), whose image of Christ is that of a Marxist revolutionary.

- *The Sufferer*. Jesus' suffering is echoed by the suffering of modern humanity—especially during or after the Second World War. Such novels as Anna Seghers' *Das siebte Kreuz* (German, 1942) establish parallels between the unspeakable conditions of Nazi concentration camps and Christ's cross. Heinrich Böll's *Und sagte kein einziges Wort* (German, 1953) presents the suffering of the post-war generation as similar to Jesus' passion.

- *The Irrational*. Much modern literature may be humanistic and without any supernatural dimension, but there is also an irrationalist current that makes references to Jesus as a somewhat vague symbol of mystery and religion. Peter Shaffer's drama *Equus* (1973) invests its horse god with an aura of uncanniness that is, in part, produced by allusions to Christ. German playwright Franz Xaver Kroetz's *Bauern sterben* (1985) makes the Christ on the main characters' crucifix into a complex symbol of home, of non-technological life and of lost faith. Most of the modern literary interest in Jesus does not aim to present him as the biblical Son of God to an unbelieving generation. Yet there is much interest in him. The diversity of responses to Jesus reflect some of the seeming paradoxes of the gospel. In him the infinite God becomes a frail human being; in him God's justice and his love and mercy are united; and his suffering is finally turned into the greatest victory. Modern writers may not subscribe to Christian traditions any more, but they still testify to the uniqueness of Jesus Christ.

century and now taken up again by some scholars, is that Matthew indeed wrote first. Luke based his work on Matthew, and finally Mark used both the others in compiling a shorter Gospel. His Gospel was a sort of compromise between the other two, written for a church which could not agree which of the others was the better!

We should not expect a definite conclusion. Clearly no simple X-copied-Y scheme is ever likely to explain all the data, and the situation was probably less tidy than that. It is likely that during the decades after Jesus' ministry various people in different churches were engaged in compiling traditions about him. As people travelled from one church to another there was ample opportunity for cross-fertilization. The similarities between the Synoptic Gospels are perhaps better explained by such a living and fluid compiling of accounts of Jesus than by any neat scheme of straight literary dependence. And in this sort of scenario John's Gospel finds a natural place, as a more individual account and yet one which is not completely out of touch with the traditions which the others knew.

So in the four Gospels of the New Testament we are not just listening to the personal thoughts of four isolated individuals. We are 'plugging in' to the living traditions of the followers of Jesus as they preached and taught about their master in those crucial decades which followed his brief life on earth. They were firmly convinced that the death they described with such care had been merely the prelude to his resurrection, and that he himself was still with them as their risen Lord.

Jesus on the Screen

▲ In the prewar film 'King of Kings', H.B. Warner as Jesus sets a child in the midst to settle an argument.

▼ Pasolini's 'Gospel according to St Matthew' portrays Jesus as a revolutionary.

▼ Ted Neeley played Jesus in the film version of 'Jesus Christ Superstar'. Unlike the show, it flopped.

▶ Charlton Heston, playing Ben Hur, encounters Jesus on his way to the cross.

1.7

THE FOUR EVANGELISTS

People familiar with the Gospels often take it for granted that the New Testament contains four accounts of the ministry of Jesus. But people coming fresh to them may find this fact more curious. No other part of Bible history is repeated four times.

So why did Christians early in the church's history accept Matthew, Mark, Luke *and* John as part of their Holy Scripture? Primarily because they believed that the story of Jesus' life, death and resurrection formed the very centre of their faith. The details recounted by the four evangelists or Gospel-writers overlap with each other in various ways, yet each Gospel contains its own peculiar themes. The church early on recognized that its understanding of Jesus would be impoverished if any one of the four were jettisoned. The previous chapter (*The Witness of the Gospels*) points out that many stories of Jesus' life and teaching are common to all four Gospels; here we will dwell more on what makes each of them distinctive.

Mark, the story-teller

Mark was a young Jewish travelling companion of the apostle Paul and a friend of Peter. His Gospel was probably the first written. It is the shortest, focusing more on the actions of Jesus than on his teachings. It is written in vivid and sometimes rugged language. Mark often uses the word 'immediately' to connect various incidents, creating a rapidly paced narrative. Almost half of his Gospel describes the events leading up to and including Jesus' death, because Christians believed that the most important thing Jesus did was to die—to pay God's penalty for the sins of humanity. But Mark

▲ Jesus Christ the 'alpha and omega' is the subject of this mid-fourth-century catacomb painting from the Commodille cemetery. First and last letters of the Greek alphabet, alpha and omega represent the beginning and the end of everything there is.

says nothing about Christ's birth and he greatly abbreviates his account of the resurrection.

Mark introduces his book by actually calling it a Gospel ('good news'). In that introduction he also refers to Jesus as Messiah ('Christ' in Greek) and Son of God. But neither of these titles occurs very often in the rest of the book. When people do speak of Jesus in these terms, he often tells them to be silent. Probably this was because most Jews were looking for a political and military leader who would liberate them from Roman rule. Jesus, on the other hand, understood the Messiah to be one who first had to accept the role of a 'suffering servant' (as prophesied in Isaiah) and be crucified. Only much later, on a future date which Christians still await, would he return from heaven as king of all the earth. So probably he avoided using terms which would lead to misunderstanding.

Mark also describes the shortcomings and failures of Jesus' disciples more graphically than do any of the other evangelists. Notice, for example, how he plays down Peter's dramatic realization that Jesus was the Son of God and the 'rock' on which Christ would build his church (Matthew makes much more of this), while highlighting the same disciple's subsequent misunderstanding of Jesus' mission (Mark 8:27–33). Perhaps this reflects the candour of Mark's primary source of information—widely thought to be the apostle Peter himself. And probably Mark was writing to Christians in Rome in the 50s or 60s AD who were beginning to experience persecution for their faith. Mark seems to be saying that if the apostles could so often fail their Lord and yet 'bounce back' to do great things for God, then Christians in difficult circumstances everywhere should be encouraged to persevere in their faith.

Matthew, the teacher

Matthew was one of the twelve apostles, a former tax-collector, and a strong tradition associates him with this Gospel. Almost all of Mark's information about Jesus' life reappears in Matthew. But Matthew begins with two chapters about Christ's birth and early years and ends with a greatly expanded account of the resurrection. He also presents a much larger proportion of Jesus' teaching. Much of this teaching appears in five major sermons of Jesus (chapters 5–7, 10, 13, 18 and 24–25), of which the most famous is the first—the Sermon on the Mount. Some interpreters think that Matthew was portraying Jesus as a new 'lawgiver' like Moses. Is it coincidence that Moses' commandments also came from a mountain and were written in five parts (the books from Genesis to Deuteronomy)?

Matthew seems to be the Gospel most directed to a Jewish audience. Probably he was writing for a Christian church comprised largely of converts from Judaism. This would explain why he can combine harsh denunciations of the Jews who rejected Jesus with regular references to prophecies from the Old Testament which were fulfilled in Jesus' life. He is showing Jewish Christians that they have made the right decision to follow Jesus, even though many of their friends and relatives have rejected them because of it. So it is not surprising that Matthew emphasizes the title 'Son of David' for Jesus and begins his Gospel with a genealogy proving that Jesus was descended both from Israel's greatest king, and from their forefather, Abraham. He is stressing that Jesus has the proper Jewish ancestry which the Old Testament had laid down for the one who would be the Messiah.

Similarly, only Matthew includes such seemingly narrow-minded sayings of Jesus as 'Do not go among the Gentiles or enter any town of the Samaritans', and 'I was sent only to the lost sheep of Israel'. Yet the conclusion to Matthew's Gospel makes it clear that these restrictions were temporary. The Jews were God's chosen people, they needed to hear the gospel first. But after Jesus rose from death, he commissioned his followers to go and make disciples of all nations. And only Matthew's Gospel describes the coming Day of Judgment in which all the peoples of the earth will have to give account for the kind of lives they have led.

In addition, Matthew portrays the disciples in a somewhat better light than Mark does. He emphasizes their faith more than their failures. He is the only Gospel-writer to record Jesus' teaching about establishing the church. And much of Jesus' teaching in Matthew seems especially relevant for church leaders in any age. Matthew probably wrote somewhere between five and twenty years later than Mark, in a Syrian church troubled more with relating its faith and structure to its Jewish roots than with Roman persecution.

Luke, the historian

Luke was the doctor who accompanied Paul on several of his travels. He was probably Greek, and so the only writer of any book in the Bible who was not a Jew. Not surprisingly in the light of this, Luke writes in the most literate Greek of all the four evangelists. He alone begins his Gospel with a preface, dedicating his book to a patron named Theophilus, after the style of ancient Greek and Roman biographers. Luke describes the birth, death and resurrection of Jesus in even more detail than Matthew. He alone has a sequel for his Gospel, the Acts of the Apostles, in which Luke narrates what the risen Jesus continued to do and teach through his disciples. So Luke writes more self-consciously as a historian, as is shown also by his unique references to the various political and religious leaders who held power during the events of Jesus' life.

It is in Luke that Jesus' humanity most clearly shines through. Over and over again, Christ identifies with and shows compassion to the outcasts of his society. These included Gentiles (non-Jews), Samaritans (half-Jew, half-Gentile), tax-collectors (seen as traitors who supported Rome), women, the poor, and those who had a reputation for being particularly wicked or sinful. Luke's most distinctive title for Jesus is Saviour. Christ came 'to seek and to save what was lost', rather than to hobnob with the self-styled righteous. Luke is probably writing to a largely Greek church, perhaps in the early 60s, to assure them that they as Gentiles are as accepted by God as anyone else.

Luke is also concerned to write his Gospel in an 'orderly way' so that his readers may be convinced of the truth of his message (Luke 1:3–4). Many people have assumed that Luke's order was chronological, but this seems unlikely. While basically he follows Mark's sequence of events for the beginning and end of Jesus' ministry, there is a long section—from chapter 9 verse 51 to chapter 18 verse 14—where Luke has almost nothing in common with Mark. These chapters contain almost exclusively collections of Jesus' teaching, some of which is paralleled in Matthew but much of which is unique to Luke. Over twenty parables of Jesus appear here which are found in no other Gospel, including the well-known 'Good Samaritan' and 'Prodigal Son'. Luke seems to be organizing his material geographically, so as to present Jesus' ministry in Galilee, his teaching en route to Jerusalem, and his death in that same city. The other Gospels, especially John, make it clear that Jesus often journeyed to Jerusalem and occasionally travelled beyond Israel's borders. But Luke includes only what fits into his outline. In so doing, he prepares the reader for his second volume in which the disciples will retrace their master's steps—in reverse sequence. In Acts they begin by preaching in Jerusalem but move out from there with the goal of eventually reaching 'to the ends of the earth'. Much like Matthew, but in his own distinctive way, Luke is telling us that the key events of Jesus' ministry and the birth of the church are firmly rooted in Judaism, but the Christian message is one for the whole world.

Luke also stresses the role of prayer and of the Holy Spirit in the lives of Jesus and his followers. The church grows in influence and expands geographically not because of its own power or strategies but because of men and women who have submitted themselves to God's perfect guidance.

John, a call to faith

The fourth Gospel is by far the most distinctive. Early church tradition claimed that the apostle John wrote it, although the evangelist deliberately keeps

What comes in Matthew?

1:1–4:16 THE PERSON OF JESUS CHRIST
1:1–25 Jesus' parentage and birth
2:1–23 From Bethlehem via Egypt to Nazareth
3:1–17 John the Baptist and the baptism of Jesus
4:1–16 Jesus is tempted in the desert; he moves to Capernaum

4:17–16:20 JESUS CHRIST IS PUBLICLY PROCLAIMED
4:17–25 Jesus preaches, calls his disciples and heals
5:1–7:29 The Sermon on the Mount: the first great speech
8:1–9:34 Ten miracles and other scenes from Jesus' work in Galilee
9:35–38 A summary of Jesus' work
10:1–11:1 Jesus sends out the Twelve: the second great speech
11:2–19 Jesus and John the Baptist
11:20–30 Cries of judgment and salvation
12:1–45 Conflict and argument between Jesus and the Pharisees
13:1–53 Parables of the kingdom: the third great speech
13:54–58 Jesus is rejected in Nazareth
14:1–12 John the Baptist is executed
14:13–36 Feeding the five thousand; walking on water
15:1–20 Purity: the inward and the outward kinds
15:21–39 A healing and a feeding
16:1–12 The Pharisees, the Sadducees and Jesus
16:13–20 Jesus is the Christ, Son of the living God

What comes in Mark?

1:1–13 THE BEGINNING OF THE GOOD NEWS OF JESUS

1:14–8:21 JESUS' WORK IN GALILEE
1:14–45 The power and authority of Jesus
2:1–3:12 Jesus' freedom and authority
3:13–19 Jesus commissions the Twelve
3:20–35 Misunderstanding who Jesus is and who may belong to his family
4:1–34 The disciples learn through parables
4:35–5:43 The disciples learn through Jesus' miracles
6:1–6 Jesus misunderstood again and rejected by his own people
6:7–13 Jesus sends the Twelve on mission
6:14–29 Interlude: the death of John the Baptist
6:30–8:21 The disciples misunderstand Jesus' teaching and miracles, even though a non-Jewish woman trusts Jesus to heal her daughter

8:22–10:52 THE GRADUAL UNDERSTANDING OF JESUS' TEACHING ABOUT HIMSELF AND DISCIPLESHIP
8:22–26 Blind eyes, at first, only partially opened
8:27–30 Peter states that Jesus is the Messiah
8:31–9:1 Jesus' first prediction of his death misunderstood
9:2–13 Jesus is transfigured; the disciples misunderstand
9:14–29 The disciples fail in their mission
9:30–41 Jesus' second prediction of his death misunderstood
9:42–10:31 Wise sayings and teachings on discipleship

16:21–28:20 JESUS CHRIST'S SUFFERING, DEATH AND RESURRECTION
16:21–28 First prediction of suffering: what it means to follow Jesus
17:1–21 Jesus is transfigured, and the immediate sequel
17:22–27 Second prediction of suffering; the temple tax
18:1–35 Jesus teaches his disciples: the fourth great speech
19:1–15 Marriage, divorce and the little children
19:16–20:16 The rich man, and the reward of true discipleship
20:17–28 Third prediction of suffering; true greatness
20:29–21:11 From Jericho up to Jerusalem
21:12–22 The cleansing of the temple and the cursing of the fig tree
21:23–22:46 Searching questions, and more parables
23:1–39 Judgment on the scribes and the Pharisees
24:1–25:46 The destruction of Jerusalem, and parables about the end of the age; the fifth great speech
26:1–16 The prelude to Jesus' suffering
26:17–56 The last supper; Jesus' agony in Gethsemane; his arrest
26:57–75 Jesus' trial before the high priest; Peter's denial
27:1–31 Jesus' trial before Pilate; the soldiers torture him
27:32–56 The crucifixion
27:57–66 Jesus' burial; the guarding of the grave
28:1–15 The resurrection of Jesus
28:16–20 Jesus' great command

▶ Matthew had the form of a man.

10:32–45 Jesus' third prediction of his death misunderstood
10:46–52 Jesus completely opens the eyes of a blind man who becomes a disciple

11:1–13:37 THE LAST DAYS IN JERUSALEM BEFORE THE CROSS
11:1–11 Jesus' triumphant entry into Jerusalem
11:12–33 Jesus' teaching and action about the temple
12:1–44 Parable and questions
13:1–37 Teaching on times before the end

14:1–16:8 THE DEATH AND RESURRECTION OF JESUS
14:1–72 The last acts of Jesus
15:1–21 The trial of Jesus and the death sentence
15:22–47 Jesus is crucified, dies and is buried
16:1–8 The resurrection

▶ Mark was represented by a lion.

What comes in Luke?

1:1–4 PREFACE

1:5–2:52 THE BIRTH AND CHILDHOOD OF JESUS
1:5–25 John's birth foretold 1:26–38 Jesus' birth foretold
1:39–56 Mary's visit to Elizabeth
1:57–80 The birth of John
2:1–20 The birth of Jesus
2:21–40 The presentation of Jesus at the temple
2:41–52 The Passover visit of Jesus to the temple

3:1–4:13 THE CREDENTIALS OF JOHN AND JESUS
3:1–20 John's ministry
3:21,22 Jesus' baptism
3:23–38 The ancestors of Jesus
4:1–13 Jesus' temptation

4:14–9:50 JESUS IN GALILEE
4:14–30 Jesus declares who he is
4:31–6:11 The miracles begin to arouse controversy
6:12–49 The choosing of the Twelve and the Sermon on the Plain
7:1–50 The compassion of Jesus
8:1–21 The parables of Jesus
8:22–56 The power of Jesus
9:1–50 The inner-circle and Jesus

9:51–19:44 THE JOURNEY TO JERUSALEM
9:51–10:24 Lessons in discipleship
10:25–11:13 The characteristics of disciples
11:14–54 Opposition mounts
12:1–13:9 Ready and alert for the coming crisis
13:10–35 The kingdom's victory
14:1–24 Dinner with a Pharisee
14:25–35 Disciples
15:1–32 Three parables of the lost
16:1–31 Warnings to the rich
17:1–10 Teaching about service and gratitude
17:11–19 Jesus heals
17:20–18:8 The coming of the king
18:9–19:10 The scope of the kingdom
19:11–27 Towards Jerusalem: a parable about a rejected king
19:28–44 Towards Jerusalem: Jesus enters on a colt

19:45–21:38 JESUS IN JERUSALEM
19:45–48 The cleansing of the temple
20:1–21:4 The growth of opposition
21:5–38 The signs of the last days

22:1–24:53 CRUCIFIXION AND RESURRECTION
22:1–38 The Last Supper
22:39–53 The agony and arrest of Jesus
22:54–71 The Jewish trial
23:1–25 The Roman trial
23:26–49 Jesus crucified
23:50–56 The burial of Jesus
24:1–53 The resurrection of Jesus

▶ **Luke was given the symbol of a bull.**

What comes in John?

1:1–12:50 THE MINISTRY OF JESUS
1:1–18 The Prologue, introduction to the Gospel
1:19–40 John the Baptist, who he was and the scope of his ministry
1:41–51 The call of the first disciples
2:1–12 The marriage at Cana, Jesus' first miracle or 'sign'
2:13–25 Jesus cleanses the temple
3:1–21 Jesus meets Nicodemus and explains what it means to be 'born again'
3:22–36 John the Baptist and Jesus are compared
4:1–42 Jesus meets a Samaritan woman
4:43–54 Jesus heals the son of the ruler of the synagogue
5:1–18 Jesus heals a paralytic
5:19–47 Jesus proclaims himself the agent of God
6:1–25 The feeding of the 5,000
6:26–71 Jesus the Bread of Life
7:1–13 The Feast of the Tabernacles
7:14–52 A division arises among the Jews over Jesus
8:1–11 A woman caught in adultery is brought to Jesus (This passage is not in all Greek manuscripts and is omitted in some translations)
8:12–20 Jesus defends his claims
8:21–59 Jesus confronts his hearers with his claims
9:1–41 The healing of the man born blind; Jesus' followers and enemies are clearly shown

10:1–42 Jesus, the Good Shepherd, interprets his coming death
11:1–44 The raising of Lazarus
11:45–57 The plot to arrest Jesus is hatched
12:1–8 Mary anoints Jesus
12:9–19 Jesus enters Jerusalem in triumph
12:20–50 Jesus anticipates his coming rejection and death

13:1–17:26 JESUS TEACHES HIS DISCIPLES ON HIS LAST NIGHT WITH THEM
13:1–20 Jesus washes the disciples' feet
13:21–38 Judas betrays Jesus
14:1–31 The promises of Jesus for the believers
15:1–16:4 The call for believers to abide in Jesus' word
16:5–15 The promise of the Holy Spirit
16:16–33 The promise of help after sorrow
17:1–26 Jesus makes a final prayer for his disciples

18:1–21:25 ARREST, CRUCIFIXION AND RESURRECTION
18:1–40 Betrayal, arrest and trial
19:1–42 Crucifixion, death and burial
20:1–31 Resurrection appearances to Mary, the disciples and Thomas
21:1–25 Epilogue: an appearance to Peter and the beloved disciple

▶ **John was an eagle.**

his identity secret. It has also long been held that John wrote much later than Matthew, Mark and Luke. Probably, it is thought, his work dates from the 90s, and he deliberately avoids repeating most of the contents of his three predecessors. As the last living apostle, he realized that there was much more about the story of Jesus which had not been written down. So he chose to retell further details of Christ's life which would encourage people to believe in him or strengthen what faith they already had (John 20:31). Today many scholars think that, although John wrote independently of the other three evangelists, he may not have written later, and a few think his Gospel may date as early as the 60s. But they still largely accept John's stated purpose for writing—to provoke faith.

John is the only evangelist to describe three visits of Jesus to Jerusalem for the annual Jewish Passover feast. Without this information, we might easily assume that Jesus' ministry lasted for less than a year; as it is we know it lasted more than two. In the first half of his narrative, John describes seven major miracles of Jesus which he calls 'signs'—pointers to Christ's divine nature. He alone also records seven remarkable claims which Jesus made, and the discourses in which they were embedded. Each begins, 'I am. . .': the Bread of Life, the Light of the World, the Good Shepherd, the Door of the Sheepfold, the Resurrection and the Life, the Way, Truth and Life, and the True Vine. In the second half of his Gospel, John includes five unique chapters containing the teaching Jesus gave to his disciples privately during the last night of his life. Here again Jesus stresses the oneness he has with God his Father, as well as the unity which should characterize his followers.

In fact, John regularly portrays Jesus' divinity more plainly than do Matthew, Mark or Luke. Only John calls Jesus the 'Word of God' who 'was God' (John 1:1). Instead of telling about Jesus' birth, John begins by explaining how he was with God from before the creation of the universe and in fact was the agent by whom God created the heavens and the earth. Only John tells of Jesus claiming to be 'one' with his heavenly Father in a way which the Jews interpreted as blasphemous. Only John has 'doubting Thomas' exclaim, as he saw and touched the risen Christ, 'My Lord and *my God*!' (John 20:29).

Yet, even though the modern reader might assume that John's primary purpose in all this was to convince sceptics that Jesus was more than a man, his aim was probably precisely the opposite. Church tradition from early on taught that John was writing to Christians in the Asian city of Ephesus (in modern-day Turkey) and that his purpose was to refute the false teaching current there which held that while Jesus was fully God he only *seemed* to be human. So John writes his Gospel to make clear that although he also strongly believes in Jesus' divinity, it is crucial to believe in his humanity as well, as God in the life of a man. In John's words, 'The Word became flesh and made his dwelling among us'. God truly became fully human in the person of Jesus of Nazareth.

A long list could be compiled of other distinctive themes in the fourth Gospel. Foremost among these are an emphasis on 'eternal life' as beginning already in this world the moment a person puts his or her trust in Jesus, the fact that Jesus will never abandon those who put their faith in him, and the promise that the Holy Spirit will come to help Jesus' followers remember everything he taught them. John loved striking contrasts—light over against darkness, 'life' opposed to 'death', love versus judgment. He wrote too of 'witness', 'truth' and 'abiding' (having a close personal relationship) with Jesus.

What are we to make of these four diverse portraits of Jesus? Surely we should learn from their very diversity. Two approaches can be held in balance:

■ **Expect historical reliability**. Many contemporary critics find the evangelists at odds with one another and speak of numerous irreconcilable discrepancies. And yet historically Christians have almost always believed that the Gospels complement rather than contradict one another. A fair assessment of this debate requires a careful analysis of almost every passage in Matthew, Mark, Luke and John. But plausible solutions to every alleged contradiction have been proposed, so the burden of proof rests with the sceptic to demonstrate that the Gospels are not historically reliable. Certainly the first three evangelists seem to try to put themselves back into the days before the fuller understanding that followed Jesus' resurrection.

■ **Do justice to the differences**. If all we are concerned with is a harmonization of the four accounts of Jesus' life, then we become insensitive to the very way in which God originally inspired the evangelists—guiding each to emphasize certain themes rather than others.

If we want to understand the Gospels as their original audiences did, then we must hear each evangelist speak on his own terms, without trying to interpret every passage in one Gospel by means of related verses in another. The richness of the Gospels owes much to their very variety.

▶ **This brilliantly illuminated frontispiece to the Gospel section of the Celtic Book of Kells makes use of the four traditional emblems of the Gospel-writers.**

PART 2

HOW IT ALL BEGAN

This enquiry into the story of Jesus starts with his
birth and childhood. Bethlehem and Nazareth set the scene for his early life.
Then years later he was baptized by John the Baptist, tempted in the wilderness, and reached a new
beginning, as he started to teach and to heal.

CONTENTS

SPECIAL FEATURES

Birth, life, death... and beyond
The Messiah
The Herodian family
The temptations
The Virgin Mary
Jesus' birth and childhood
The twelve
Jesus' ministry begins
Communicating Jesus
Jesus and the modern media
The miracles of Jesus

BIRTH, LIFE, DEATH – AND BEYOND

1. JESUS' BIRTH AND CHILDHOOD

NAZARETH

JESUS' BIRTH IS FORETOLD
(THE 'ANNUNCIATION')
THE VIRGIN MARY IS PROMISED
THAT SHE WILL CONCEIVE A SON
'BY THE HOLY SPIRIT'.

▶ MATTHEW 1:18-24

BETHLEHEM

JESUS IS BORN (THE 'NATIVITY')
JOSEPH AND MARY TRAVEL TO
BETHLEHEM FOR A TAX CENSUS.
THERE JESUS IS BORN.
SHEPHERDS ARE FIRST TO HEAR
OF HIS BIRTH.

▶ LUKE 2:1-20
▶ MATTHEW 1:25

NAZARETH

CHILDHOOD IN NAZARETH
JESUS IS BROUGHT UP AT
NAZARETH IN GALILEE.

▶ MATTHEW 2:19-23
▶ LUKE 2:39-40,51-52

2. JESUS' MINISTRY BEGINS

RIVER JORDAN

JESUS IS BAPTIZED
JESUS ASKS JOHN FOR BAPTISM.
THE HOLY SPIRIT COMES ON HIM.

▶ MATTHEW 3:13-17
▶ MARK 1:9-13
▶ LUKE 3:21-22

JUDEAN WILDERNESS

JESUS IS TEMPTED
FORTY DAYS FASTING IN THE
WILDERNESS; JESUS IS TEMPTED
BY THE DEVIL.

▶ MATTHEW 4:1-11
▶ MARK 1:12-13
▶ LUKE 4:1-10

3. THREE CENTRAL EVENTS

GALILEE

**JESUS APPOINTS THE
APOSTLES**
HE CHOOSES TWELVE TO LIVE
CLOSE TO HIM AND SHARE HIS
MINISTRY.

▶ MATTHEW 10:1-42
▶ MARK 3:13-19
▶ LUKE 6:12-16

CAESAREA PHILLIPPI

THE GREAT CONFESSION
PETER DECLARES THAT JESUS
IS MESSIAH.

▶ MATTHEW 16:13-28
▶ MARK 8:27-38
▶ LUKE 9:18-27

MT. HERMON

JESUS' GLORY IS REVEALED
(THE 'TRANSFIGURATION')
THREE APOSTLES SEE JESUS FOR
WHO HE REALLY IS.

▶ MATTHEW 17:1-13
▶ MARK 9:2-13
▶ LUKE 9:28-36

4. THE LAST WEEK

JERUSALEM

THE LAST SUPPER
JESUS AND THE APOSTLES SHARE
A FINAL PASSOVER MEAL.

▶ MATTHEW 26:17-30
▶ MARK 14:12-26
▶ LUKE 22:7-38

THE AGONY IN GETHSEMANE
JESUS STRUGGLES TO ACCEPT
THE ORDEAL OF DEATH.

▶ MATTHEW 26:36-46
▶ MARK 14:32-42
▶ LUKE 22:39-46

JESUS IS ARRESTED
BETRAYED BY JUDAS, JESUS IS
TAKEN BY THE JEWISH
AUTHORITIES.

▶ MATTHEW 26:47-56
▶ MARK 14:43-52
▶ LUKE 22:47-53
▶ JOHN 18:1-14

CRUCIFIED!
JESUS IS TORTURED, THEN TAKEN
TO A HILL CALLED GOLGOTHA,
OR CALVARY, AND CRUCIFIED. HE
DIES FORGIVING HIS
EXECUTIONERS.

▶ MATTHEW 27:27-56
▶ MARK 15:16-41
▶ LUKE 23:26-49
▶ JOHN 19:16-37

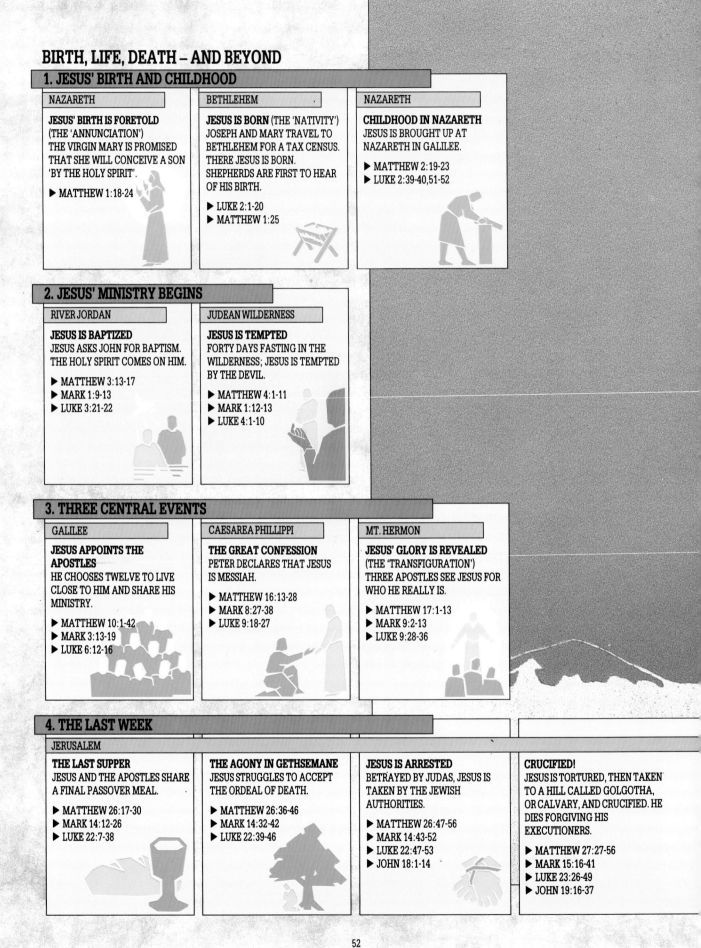

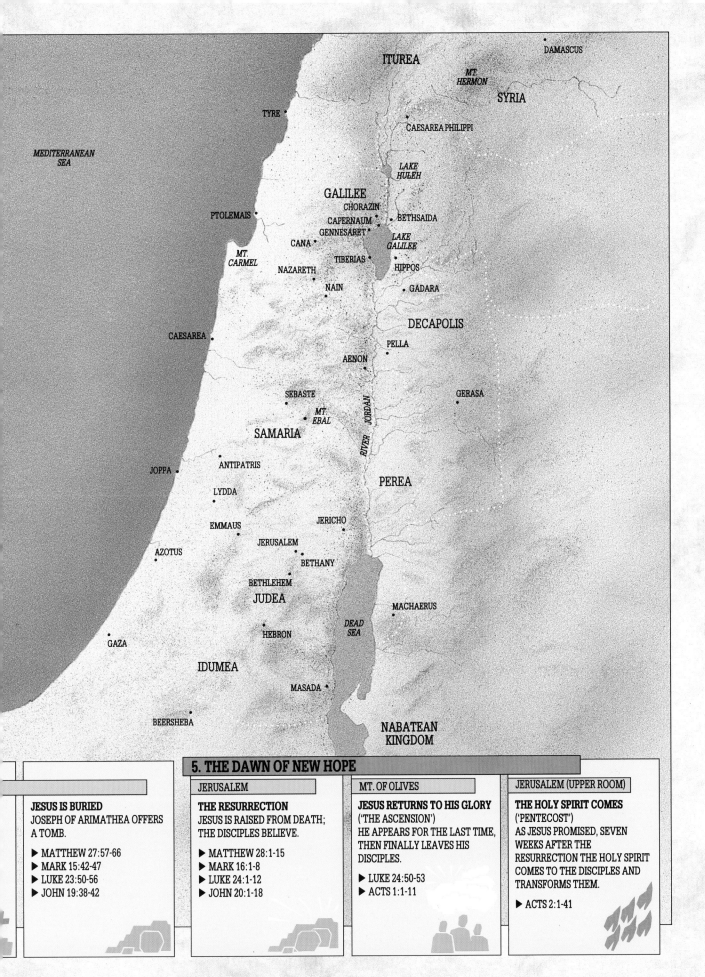

DAMASCUS

ITUREA

MT.
HERMON

SYRIA

TYRE

CAESAREA PHILIPPI

MEDITERRANEAN
SEA

LAKE
HULEH

GALILEE

CHORAZIN

PTOLEMAIS

CAPERNAUM   BETHSAIDA

GENNESARET

LAKE
GALILEE

CANA

MT.
CARMEL

TIBERIAS

HIPPOS

NAZARETH

NAIN

GADARA

DECAPOLIS

CAESAREA

PELLA

AENON

SEBASTE

MT.
EBAL

GERASA

SAMARIA

JOPPA   ANTIPATRIS

PEREA

LYDDA

EMMAUS   JERICHO

JERUSALEM

AZOTUS   BETHANY

BETHLEHEM

JUDEA

MACHAERUS

GAZA   HEBRON

DEAD
SEA

IDUMEA

MASADA

BEERSHEBA

NABATEAN
KINGDOM

5. THE DAWN OF NEW HOPE

JESUS IS BURIED
JOSEPH OF ARIMATHEA OFFERS
A TOMB.

▶ MATTHEW 27:57-66
▶ MARK 15:42-47
▶ LUKE 23:50-56
▶ JOHN 19:38-42

THE RESURRECTION
JESUS IS RAISED FROM DEATH;
THE DISCIPLES BELIEVE.

▶ MATTHEW 28:1-15
▶ MARK 16:1-8
▶ LUKE 24:1-12
▶ JOHN 20:1-18

JESUS RETURNS TO HIS GLORY
('THE ASCENSION')
HE APPEARS FOR THE LAST TIME,
THEN FINALLY LEAVES HIS
DISCIPLES.

▶ LUKE 24:50-53
▶ ACTS 1:1-11

THE HOLY SPIRIT COMES
('PENTECOST')
AS JESUS PROMISED, SEVEN
WEEKS AFTER THE
RESURRECTION THE HOLY SPIRIT
COMES TO THE DISCIPLES AND
TRANSFORMS THEM.

▶ ACTS 2:1-41

2.1

THE BEGINNING

Each Gospel-writer begins his story at a different place. Mark omits all reference to Jesus' birth and boyhood. He plunges almost immediately into Jesus' public ministry. John goes to the other extreme and sets the scene beyond the realm of history. He reflects on the Son of God's existence before he became man. As 'the Word', God's creative power, he was also with God. John stresses not only his existence before his human birth, and his role in creation, but also his divine nature. He was himself God. John goes on to tell us in a short, sharp sentence that 'the Word became flesh'.

This staggering claim at once raises the question in what circumstances such a thing happened. Matthew and Luke supply the answer. The two writers narrate the birth of Jesus with remarkable restraint. Their accounts are complementary to each other.

The first Christmas

The Christmas story which they tell is so familiar that it is difficult for us to recapture its original significance. There were devout people among the Jews who eagerly awaited the coming of the Messiah. Their expectations were shaped by Old Testament prophecy and centred on the town of Bethlehem. No one, however, expected his coming to happen as it did.

That there was no room in the inn is not surprising. A census was taking place, and travellers were returning to their birthplaces. So all available accommodation would soon be occupied. Whether the manger that Joseph finally found was attached to a humble resting-place for travellers or was part of a

▲ Jesus was born in the days of the Emperor Augustus. This bronze statue of Augustus was found in the Sudan.

cave-dwelling, as some traditions suggest, is impossible to say. Traditionally, it has been held to be a stable, but a stable is never in fact mentioned. It is a deduction from the word 'manger', and in ancient Palestine animals were generally not kept in separate stables away from where people lived. There are many caves in the vicinity of Bethlehem and it is possible that the family found shelter in one such cave, perhaps one where both people and animals lived. The precise location is less important than the lowliness of the Messiah's birthplace. The Gospel-writers make it clear that the Christ-child was born in conditions of poverty, which many in the modern Western world find difficult to envisage.

Had he come in majesty and splendour there would have been throngs clamouring to accommodate him. As it was, he came in lowliness and none found room for him.

All too often we repeat the mistake. He comes to us today in the persons of our needy brothers and sisters. As John Chrysostom, fourth-century bishop of Antioch, never tired of reminding his congregations: 'Neglect him not when naked; do not neglect him perishing outside with cold and nakedness. . .for he that said, 'This is my body'. . .is the same person who said, 'You saw me hungry, and did not feed me.'

It is a relief to turn away from Santa Claus, reindeer, the Holly and the Ivy and all the rest of the mythological unreality under which we have buried the historical account of the birth of Jesus.

We humans have a way of 'snatching fantasy from the jaws of truth'. The Gospel-writers, by contrast, tell their story without resorting to adjectives. It is told in restraint and simplicity. Their account may be considered under three headings.

Arranging the birth

There is a problem in relating the biblical story to the known history of the period. Jesus was born during the reign of Herod the Great (37–4BC), which was before Quirinius became governor of Syria (AD6–9), in whose time the registration is said to have taken place. However, there are too many unknowns to allow us to dismiss Luke as a careless historian. There may have been a lengthy process of registration which began in Herod's reign and ended at the time of Quirinius' appointment as governor. Whatever the precise details, the striking feature is that the story of Joseph and Mary undergoing registration for taxation is thoroughly consistent with the established practice within the empire. So it was that, without knowing anything about it, arrangements for the birth of Jesus

▲ Shepherds took a very low place in the society of Gospel times, so it was unexpected that Jesus' birth should be announced to them. But then so much in this story goes beyond what could ever have been predicted.

were being made in the offices of the rulers of the day. God was all the time managing his affairs and working out his purpose.

As we have noted, Jesus was born during the lifetime of Herod the Great. This means that he must have been born earlier than 4BC, the year of Herod's death. Matthew's reference to the slaughter of male children up to two years old suggests that we must date the birth of Jesus at the latest at 6BC. Thus when the year 2000 comes it will really be about 2006.

Announcing and acknowledging the birth

Luke records the angel Gabriel's announcement to Mary that both her conception and the boy to be born will be supernatural: 'The angel answered, "The Holy Spirit will come upon you, and the power of the Most High will overshadow you. So the holy one to be born will be called the Son of God"'.

After the birth has taken place an announcement is made by 'a company of angels' to a group of Judean shepherds. There is a strange incongruity in so heavenly a display of glory being seen by a few

humble shepherds. In the ancient world shepherds belonged to a class of despised persons. In fact there was a legal regulation which would not allow the evidence of a shepherd to be heard in court. So it is a reversal of human expectation that shepherds should appear in such a mighty story. Yet it was not incongruous in God's sight. He has little regard for human opinions.

It is interesting to notice the prominence of angels surrounding the birth of Jesus. Throughout the central part of the Gospel story we hear

▲ Bethlehem today is a place of pilgrimage, with bells and grotto. When Jesus was born it was a minor Judean town. But the prophet Micah had predicted that here the Messiah would be born.

practically nothing of angels. It is at the beginning and at the end that they appear. The appearance of these supernatural beings has the effect of characterizing the birth and resurrection accounts as unique. Although taking place in the course of history, they are of a different texture from ordinary history. The presence of angels is a pointer to the fact that we are moving in an area where the mystery of God among humanity is at work. (No doubt the angels of the Bible are very different from those which appear on our Christmas cards!)

In addition to the shepherds we are told by Matthew that there were 'Magi'—astrologer-priests—who paid homage to the Christ-child. (He does not say there were three!) These visitors followed what may have been a freakish conjunction in the heavens. It is noteworthy that in 7BC there was a triple conjunction of Jupiter and Saturn, a phenomenon which occurs once in 805 years. In February, 6BC, Mars moved past them, too, forming a triangle in the sky. It is pure scepticism to dismiss the reference to the 'star' in view of this information.

Not all acknowledged the birth in a positive way. Herod was alarmed at the thought of a possible rival and resolved to destroy the child. Joseph and Mary fled with him to Egypt where they may well have had relatives or friends, since there were at least as many

The Messiah

The title *'Messiah'* is our transliteration of a Hebrew word which means 'anointed'. Translated into Greek it is *Christos*, from which we get 'Christ'.

Among the Jews there was more than one idea of what the Messiah would be and do. In the Old Testament much is said, especially in the prophets, about the coming 'messianic age' which offered material bliss to the people of God. Little, however, is said about the Messiah himself. It was usual to speak of God as the one who was to bring in the golden messianic age. Occasionally the Old Testament does refer to the Lord's Messiah and in time this became a technical term to refer to the one who would be God's chosen instrument in the deliverance of his people.

This development becomes more pronounced when we turn to the literature of the period between the Testaments. The hope of the coming Messiah took many different forms, but the dominant idea was of the perfect successor to King David, who would establish an earthly kingdom for the people of Israel and banish Israel's enemies. In the Jewish expectation at this period, then, the Messiah was to be a political agent, but with a religious bias.

Clearly different groups among the Jews of Jesus' time visualized the coming of the Messiah in different ways. Priestly groups like the desert community of Qumran looked for a priestly Messiah. Nationalist groups looked for a political deliverer. There is little doubt that popular opinion leaned heavily towards the expectation that the Messiah would deliver the Jewish people from the oppressive yoke of Rome.

Certainly the Gospels make it clear that the time of Jesus was a time of heightened expectation. Luke records the confusion of the populace over whether John the Baptist was the Messiah. The fourth Gospel indicates that there was confusion in the minds of some people in Jerusalem because of the tradition that the Messiah's origin would be unknown, whereas Jesus' origin was known. These and other verses from the Gospels make it clear that Jesus' ministry was carried out against a background of popular expectation which carried a variety of ideas about the Messiah.

But what did Jesus himself think? According to the Gospels he seems to have been reticent to acknowledge himself publicly as the Messiah. In view of the political overtones the term had acquired this is not surprising. To announce himself as the Messiah would have been to invite misunderstanding. Every Jew who heard the term would be thinking in terms of eventual rebellion against Rome, and of the great day when the Jewish empire would replace the Roman.

But Jesus did not reject the true understanding of the Messiah. Mark reports his words about giving a cup of water 'in my name because you belong to Christ'. Again, he raised no objection to the use of the term by Peter (Mark 8:29) or by Caiaphas (Mark 14:61), though in each case he went on to show that they did not understand it in the same way that he did. Some scholars have argued that in reality the historical Jesus never thought of himself as the Messiah. Passages in which Jesus enjoins his disciples to secrecy about his mission are said to be Mark's way of explaining why Jesus said so little about being the Messiah. But this theory founders on the solid fact that Jesus was crucified because he claimed to be the Messiah. This is what so angered the Jewish religious leaders.

One reason for Jesus' reluctance to be called the Messiah, then, was that the idea was wrongly understood. He believed he was the Messiah, but not of the kind most people expected.

But there may be an even deeper reason. Jesus was often indirect and veiled in teaching about who he really was. He was bound to be so in the very nature of the incarnation itself. The incarnate Son of God could never be obvious. The mystery of his person could be penetrated only by faith.

Jesus clearly recognized that Peter was using more than human deduction or intuition when he acknowledged him to be the Messiah (Matthew 16:17). It was God-given faith that enabled Peter to see this. For many others it remained a closed secret. They were not even conscious that they were in the presence of a mystery. They knew Jesus only 'after the flesh'. But this hidden-ness of the Messiah is within God's purpose. It calls forth the sort of faith which is a response to who Jesus really is, rather than to some preconceived notion of him. It leaves men and women free to make a personal decision.

The Gospels' secrecy about the title 'Messiah' is bound up with the way in which Jesus came to be a suffering and humiliated servant of God, the very opposite of the Messiah people expected.

▲ The adult Jesus would probably not have remembered Bethlehem. But he would certainly have remembered Nazareth, where he grew up and learnt the carpenter's trade.

Jews living in Egypt as there were in Palestine at this time.

The childhood of Jesus

Jesus was brought up in Nazareth in Galilee. He must have been reared in some degree of poverty, for when presenting their firstborn son to God Joseph and Mary brought a pair of doves as their offering. For those who could not afford a lamb, doves were a substitute.

As the years passed other children were added to Jesus' family. The names of four other boys in the family are recorded—Joses, Simon, James and Jude. Sisters are mentioned but unnamed.

The restraint of the Bible's account of Jesus' childhood contrasts vividly with the spate of childish stories which were later current in the 'apocryphal' Gospels. Luke makes two general statements about Jesus' childhood. He records his development, both physical and mental; he was notable for his strength and wisdom. It is unlikely that Jesus received the 'higher' education available in his day. For this reason he was despised as ignorant and unlearned by some who knew him.

Luke also tells us that Jesus found favour with God and men. His religious development would have begun with his mother's early influence. She was often mystified by things that he said and did. His childhood was also marked by obedience to his parents.

He was known as the carpenter or the carpenter's son; all male Jews were expected to learn a trade. Some of his most telling illustrations refer to instruments made in a carpenter's shop, such as the plough and the yoke.

Luke alone mentions an incident during the thirty years that Jesus spent in Nazareth: the visit to the temple in Jerusalem when Jesus was twelve. After the Passover festival he was left behind. To their astonishment, his parents found him consulting the Jewish leaders. All who listened were amazed at his astuteness. In reply to the mild rebuke of his parents, Jesus posed the question, 'Do you not know

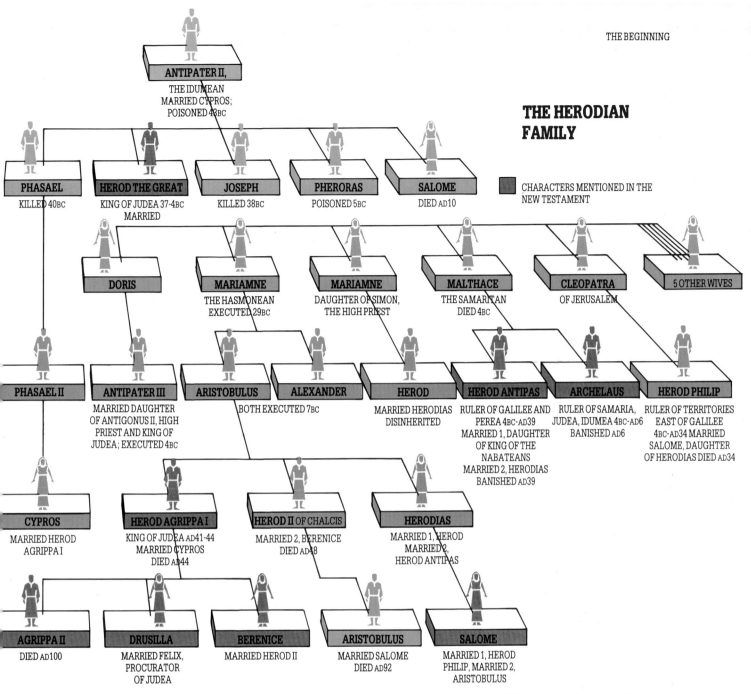

THE HERODIAN FAMILY

■ CHARACTERS MENTIONED IN THE NEW TESTAMENT

ANTIPATER II,
THE IDUMEAN
MARRIED CYPROS;
POISONED 43BC

PHASAEL
KILLED 40BC

HEROD THE GREAT
KING OF JUDEA 37-4BC
MARRIED

JOSEPH
KILLED 38BC

PHERORAS
POISONED 5BC

SALOME
DIED AD10

DORIS

MARIAMNE
THE HASMONEAN
EXECUTED 29BC

MARIAMNE
DAUGHTER OF SIMON,
THE HIGH PRIEST

MALTHACE
THE SAMARITAN
DIED 4BC

CLEOPATRA
OF JERUSALEM

5 OTHER WIVES

PHASAEL II

ANTIPATER III
MARRIED DAUGHTER
OF ANTIGONUS II, HIGH
PRIEST AND KING OF
JUDEA; EXECUTED 4BC

ARISTOBULUS

ALEXANDER
BOTH EXECUTED 7BC

HEROD
MARRIED HERODIAS
DISINHERITED

HEROD ANTIPAS
RULER OF GALILEE AND
PEREA 4BC-AD39
MARRIED 1, DAUGHTER
OF KING OF THE
NABATEANS
MARRIED 2, HERODIAS
BANISHED AD39

ARCHELAUS
RULER OF SAMARIA,
JUDEA, IDUMEA 4BC-AD6
BANISHED AD6

HEROD PHILIP
RULER OF TERRITORIES
EAST OF GALILEE
4BC-AD34 MARRIED
SALOME, DAUGHTER
OF HERODIAS DIED AD34

CYPROS
MARRIED HEROD
AGRIPPA I

HEROD AGRIPPA I
KING OF JUDEA AD41-44
MARRIED CYPROS
DIED AD44

HEROD II OF CHALCIS
MARRIED 2, BERENICE
DIED AD48

HERODIAS
MARRIED 1, HEROD
MARRIED 2,
HEROD ANTIPAS

AGRIPPA II
DIED AD100

DRUSILLA
MARRIED FELIX,
PROCURATOR
OF JUDEA

BERENICE
MARRIED HEROD II

ARISTOBULUS
MARRIED SALOME
DIED AD92

SALOME
MARRIED 1, HEROD
PHILIP, MARRIED 2,
ARISTOBULUS

that I must be in my Father's house?' His sense of communion with God as Father and his compulsion to do his will did not suddenly occur to him at the age of thirty. It developed, through adolescence to maturity. After this incident, Luke passes by the next eighteen years.

Baptism, then the wilderness

Matthew, Mark and Luke each begin their record of Jesus' public ministry with an account of his baptism and wilderness temptation.

It has often appeared strange to Christians that Jesus should have anything to do with a baptism which was explicitly said to be for the forgiveness of sins. Surely he had none? The rugged ascetic, John the Baptist, hesitated to carry out the rite. But Jesus answered him, 'Let it be so now; it is proper for us to do this to fulfil all righteousness.' In this event Jesus was already beginning to identify with sinful men and women. The long shadow of the cross reached back to the beginning of his ministry, or, as someone has commented, the baptism was 'a dummy run for Calvary'.

There are two unique features associated with Jesus' baptism—a vision and a voice. This double testimony was not public. The purpose of the event was mainly for Jesus himself. It marked God's seal on his special mission. The Spirit descended on him in a dove-like way. Now that he was about to begin

▼ **Machaerus (main photo) was on a hill top east of the Dead Sea; there John the Baptist was executed.**
▼ **Herodium was in the hills south of Jerusalem. These** were just two of several fortresses built by Herod the Great, and furnished with the ultimate in Roman refinement.

The Temptations

In his popular book *The Screwtape Letters*, C.S. Lewis writes, 'there are two equal and opposite errors into which our race can fall about the devils. One is to disbelieve in their existence. The other is to believe, and to feel an excessive and unhealthy interest in them. They themselves are equally pleased by both errors and hail a materialist or a magician with the same delight.'

Jesus' temptation in the wilderness can only have been derived from the personal report of Jesus, and this must mean that Jesus believed in a personal agent of evil. The Gospel writers are not relating a symbolic representation of a psychological conflict: this was a real spiritual encounter.

The Gospels tell us that Jesus went straight from God's declaration that he was his 'own dear Son' to the most vicious counter-attack of the enemy. Details of the kind of temptations which came to him are given only by Matthew and Luke. Three aspects of Jesus' life and character enabled him to survive this ferocious attack.

■ **Jesus loved God.** His deep God-centredness shines out from this whole narrative. The devil struck at the very roots of Jesus' self-awareness. God, the

▲ The Judean wilderness is a place of stony hills. Here Jesus spent forty days preparing for his ministry, and was tempted to approach it in false ways.

Bible tells us, cannot be tempted. But Jesus was tempted. The writer to the Hebrews spoke of him as 'one who in every respect has been tempted as we are, yet without sinning'. He laid aside any divine immunity to temptation. His conflict with evil was utterly real.

The devil tried to deflect Jesus into an understanding of who he was and what he had come to do that was quite contrary to the one God had given him. He has been declared the Son of God; how is God's Son to set about the work his Father has given him?

The first temptation related to food. A Son of God might use his power to alleviate his own hunger. But God had taught Israel in the wilderness that there are things more important than food. A son must accept his Father's scale of values.

In the second temptation (using Matthew's sequence), the tempter took Jesus to the Holy City, to a pinnacle of the Temple. If from this point Jesus were to cast himself down in order to be miraculously saved it would have a spectacular impact on the crowds. The devil misquotes scripture to lure Jesus from the path of unquestioning trust in his Father. Jesus counter-attacks with scripture that expressly forbids forcing God's hand in this way.

The third temptation focused on Jesus' mission to establish God's rule in the world. The devil would give him the kingdoms of the world without a fight if Jesus would disown God and worship the tempter instead.

Jesus saw each of these temptations as attacks on his relationship with the Father—to disobey him, to tempt him and to disown him. The whole story highlights Jesus' total devotion to God his Father.

■ **Jesus submitted to the Bible's teaching.** His experience was in this way common to all who are tempted: he had the same weapon of defence, summed up in the formula 'It is written'. What stood written in the Old Testament was what showed Jesus how his love for God should be expressed in precise practical and moral terms. What scripture said, God said. It was inconceivable to Jesus that he should love God and disregard the Bible. The same should apply for his followers today. Those who face temptation without adequate knowledge of the Bible give the advantage to the tempter.

■ **Jesus resisted the devil.** In fact he rounded on him (or 'it') with indignation, 'Away from me, Satan!' There was no argument or negotiation, only instant rebuke. This surely is a major secret of victory in Christian living. It is the little compromises which lead to the big falls. And Jesus was going to show no compromise in his battle with the power of evil.

his ministry Isaiah's prophecy was being fulfilled: 'The Spirit of the Lord shall rest upon him'.

Equally remarkable is the heavenly voice: 'This is my Son, whom I love; with him I am well pleased'. There is no suggestion that Jesus needed a heavenly voice to confirm who he was. The heavenly voice was expressing pleasure in the beginning of the Messiah's mission. God's appointed man was moving into action. But before the echo of the Father's voice had died down in the ears of Jesus, the devil challenged it.

The Father's baptismal words proclaimed Jesus' double destiny. First, that he would reign as God's Son. But, before that, he would suffer and die as God's servant. The devil offered Jesus a short-cut compromise. He offered glory without suffering.

But Jesus was so focused on God that it was inconceivable he should compromise with the devil. Obedience to God characterized his whole ministry, and it was fitting that so striking an example of his obedience should be seen right at the start.

The Virgin Mary

Mary holds a place of great honour in Christianity. She was available for God in a unique way. As Christian piety developed over the centuries, she became a focus of people's devotion: who better than a mother to understand people's pain? In Roman Catholic devotion, Mary is thought of as queen of heaven and chief of intercessors. But the Protestant tradition is cautious of anything that may distract attention from the central place of Jesus himself. All agree, however, that Mary has high dignity as a great servant of God.

▶ An ancient pilgrim medallion found in St John's Basilica, Ephesus.

▲ A Byzantine icon in St Sophia, Istanbul.

▶ A painting of Virgin and child from the seventeenth-century Moghul period in India.

▲ Mary at the foot of the cross, from a window in Norwich Cathedral, England.

1. JESUS' BIRTH AND CHILDHOOD

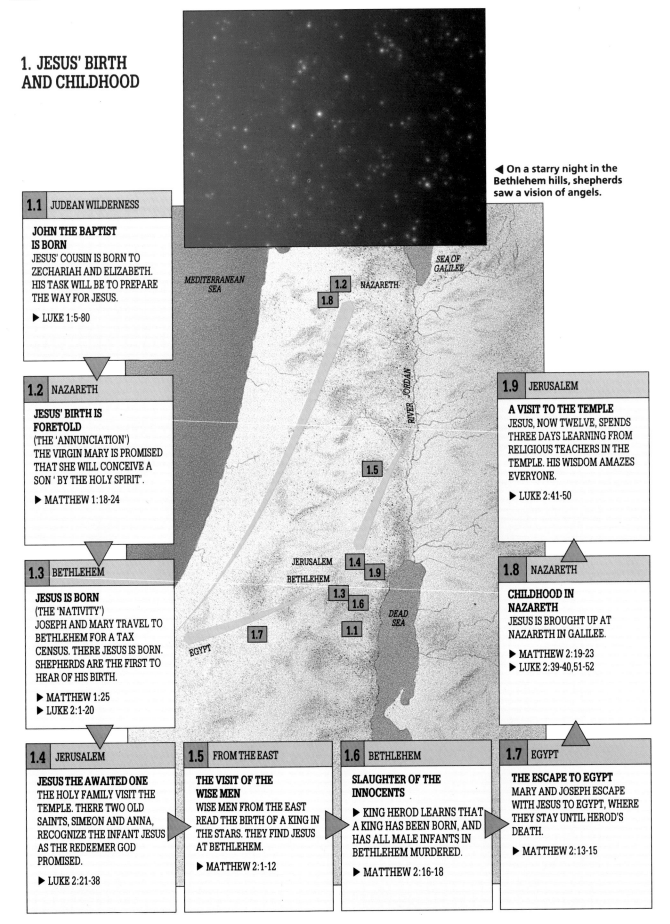

◄ On a starry night in the Bethlehem hills, shepherds saw a vision of angels.

1.1 JUDEAN WILDERNESS

JOHN THE BAPTIST IS BORN
JESUS' COUSIN IS BORN TO ZECHARIAH AND ELIZABETH. HIS TASK WILL BE TO PREPARE THE WAY FOR JESUS.

▶ LUKE 1:5-80

1.2 NAZARETH

JESUS' BIRTH IS FORETOLD
(THE 'ANNUNCIATION')
THE VIRGIN MARY IS PROMISED THAT SHE WILL CONCEIVE A SON ' BY THE HOLY SPIRIT'.

▶ MATTHEW 1:18-24

1.3 BETHLEHEM

JESUS IS BORN
(THE 'NATIVITY')
JOSEPH AND MARY TRAVEL TO BETHLEHEM FOR A TAX CENSUS. THERE JESUS IS BORN. SHEPHERDS ARE THE FIRST TO HEAR OF HIS BIRTH.

▶ MATTHEW 1:25
▶ LUKE 2:1-20

1.4 JERUSALEM

JESUS THE AWAITED ONE
THE HOLY FAMILY VISIT THE TEMPLE. THERE TWO OLD SAINTS, SIMEON AND ANNA, RECOGNIZE THE INFANT JESUS AS THE REDEEMER GOD PROMISED.

▶ LUKE 2:21-38

1.5 FROM THE EAST

THE VISIT OF THE WISE MEN
WISE MEN FROM THE EAST READ THE BIRTH OF A KING IN THE STARS. THEY FIND JESUS AT BETHLEHEM.

▶ MATTHEW 2:1-12

1.6 BETHLEHEM

SLAUGHTER OF THE INNOCENTS

▶ KING HEROD LEARNS THAT A KING HAS BEEN BORN, AND HAS ALL MALE INFANTS IN BETHLEHEM MURDERED.

▶ MATTHEW 2:16-18

1.7 EGYPT

THE ESCAPE TO EGYPT
MARY AND JOSEPH ESCAPE WITH JESUS TO EGYPT, WHERE THEY STAY UNTIL HEROD'S DEATH.

▶ MATTHEW 2:13-15

1.8 NAZARETH

CHILDHOOD IN NAZARETH
JESUS IS BROUGHT UP AT NAZARETH IN GALILEE.

▶ MATTHEW 2:19-23
▶ LUKE 2:39-40,51-52

1.9 JERUSALEM

A VISIT TO THE TEMPLE
JESUS, NOW TWELVE, SPENDS THREE DAYS LEARNING FROM RELIGIOUS TEACHERS IN THE TEMPLE. HIS WISDOM AMAZES EVERYONE.

▶ LUKE 2:41-50

MEDITERRANEAN SEA

SEA OF GALILEE

NAZARETH

RIVER JORDAN

JERUSALEM
BETHLEHEM

DEAD SEA

EGYPT

2.2

BORN OF A VIRGIN?

There was nothing unusual about the birth of Jesus. His mother went through the pain and labour and eventual joy that mothers the world over have gone through. It was all very normal and natural. But the manner of Jesus' conception —now that, according to the Bible, was very different. It was abnormal and supernatural. This is what Christians mean when they speak, somewhat misleadingly, of the 'virgin birth'.

The evidence for the virgin birth

According to both Matthew and Luke, the two evangelists who write about it, when Mary became pregnant it was not because of the usual process of fertilization. You and I were conceived when two people made love. This did not happen in the case of Jesus. Both Gospel-writers are quite un-ambiguous. Matthew records the angel saying in a dream, 'Joseph, son of David, do not be afraid to take Mary home as your wife, because what is conceived in her is from the Holy Spirit.' Luke tells us that the angel Gabriel reassured Mary with the words, 'The Holy Spirit will come upon you, and the power of the Most High will overshadow you. So the holy one to be born will be called the Son of God.' In both these passages the action of the Spirit is being thought of in creative rather than in sexual terms. Just as God created the human race in its beginning so, too, Jesus, a new starting-point, a new departure in the history of humanity, is brought into being in a unique way.

Apart from Matthew and Luke there is no other direct biblical evidence for the supernatural conception of Jesus. But there are significant indirect

▲ A stained-glass window in the chapel of Winchester College, England, depicts a Jesse tree. The allusion is to Jesus' descent from 'the tree of Jesse', father of King David, in whose line the promised Messiah was to be born.

references which should not be overlooked in the writings of both John and Paul. John, for example, claims that Jesus 'came from above', 'came down from heaven', 'was sent by the Father' and 'came into the world'. All these phrases are certainly consistent with the idea that Jesus was supernaturally conceived. Again, Paul in writing of Jesus coming into the world uses unusual vocabulary. So in Galatians chapter 4 verse 4 he writes, 'But when the right time finally came, God sent his own Son. He "came" as the son of a human mother. . .' In spite of some modern translations, Paul does not use the same word for Jesus being 'born' which he uses later in the chapter of the birth of Ishmael and Isaac. It would appear that in this passage Paul wants to avoid the suggestion that Jesus had a human father on earth.

It is therefore false to say that the only witnesses to the virginal conception are a handful of verses in the infancy narratives of Matthew and Luke. The references in John and texts such as Galatians 4:4; Philippians 2:7 and Romans 1:3 cannot simply be set aside as of no significance.

Granted, then, that the New Testament writers speak of the 'virgin birth', the next question we must ask is, how do they understand it? Did they consider themselves to be writing sober history or is there a legendary or symbolic component in their writing? Some scholars have argued that Matthew was not intending to write a purely historical narrative, but that he freely expanded and embellished his sources, particularly by weaving in ideas from the Old Testament. It is claimed that a 'mixture of history and non-history' was a familiar form of Jewish literature in his day.

But it is difficult to see how much myth-manufacturing could take place in a Jewish context such as Matthew represents. The very idea of an incarnation was something quite foreign to Jewish thinking. As Michael Green has commented, 'If you had looked the whole world over for more stony and improbable soil in which to plant the idea of an incarnation you could not have done better than light upon Israel! They would not happily have invented an idea so apparently contrary to their beliefs.' The Jews had had hammered home to them that there was one God, and no 'runner-up'!

Far from being imaginative creations out of Old Testament narratives, the birth stories bear all the marks of being records of what actually happened. There is no suspicion in them of the plainly folk-religious elements which exist in the stories of the Buddha's birth or in the so-called 'apocryphal' Gospels.

Careful scholars have been impressed by both the differences and the agreements in the accounts of Matthew and Luke. It appears from the differences that Matthew and Luke composed their narratives from quite different and independent sources. Some

Mary's Song

A hymn given to Mary when she visited her cousin Elizabeth. Mary was carrying Jesus; Elizabeth expected the birth of John. The song, often known as the Magnificat, is found in Luke chapter 1 from verse 46.

My soul proclaims the greatness of the Lord;
  my spirit rejoices in God my saviour;
for he has looked with favour on his lowly servant,
  from this day all generations will call me blessed;
the Almighty has done great things for me,
  and holy is his name.
He has mercy on those who fear him
  in every generation.
He has shown the strength of his arm;
  he has scattered the proud in their conceit.
He has cast down the mighty from their thrones,
  and has lifted up the lowly.
He has filled the hungry with good things,
  and the rich he has sent away empty.
He has come to the help of his servant Israel,
  for he has remembered his promise of mercy,
the promise he made to our fathers,
to Abraham and his children for ever.

scholars go on to conjecture that the first Gospel goes back ultimately to Joseph while the third Gospel goes back to Mary. They argue that many elements in the common core between them (and especially the virginal conception) are matters of such a private family nature that the only source which we could have is one of these two.

This account of the origin of the sources may well be correct but it is important to recognize that we have arrived at the stage of hypothetical reconstruction. Such claims lie outside our scientific control. But we have said enough to show that the writers did not mean to pass on a legend. They were passing on an account of what actually happened.

Why is the virgin birth important?

The importance of this doctrine lies in what it tells us about Jesus, rather than in what it tells us about his mother (see *The Virgin Mary*). She is to be honoured and esteemed. He is to be worshipped and adored. This doctrine interlocks with other New Testament truths concerning the nature of Jesus.

▲ **The Church of the Annunciation in Nazareth was built to commemorate the angel's visit to Mary,** **when she was told that the son to be born to her would 'be great ... called the Son of the Most High'.**

Simeon's Song

When old Simeon saw the infant Jesus being presented in the temple, he recognized God's chosen saviour. This short poem greeted the event. Known as the Nunc Dimittis, it comes in Luke chapter 2 from verse 29.

Lord now you let your servant go in peace;
    your word has been fulfilled.
My own eyes have seen the salvation,
    which you have prepared in the sight of every people;
a light to reveal you to the nations,
    and the glory of your people Israel.

■ **Jesus is fully human.** Plainly the 'incarnation'—the Son of God becoming the man Jesus—presents human reason with a problem. How can one person be at the same time both perfect man and perfect God? But our understanding of this problem is helped by carefully considering the manner of Jesus' birth. He was born quite naturally, which emphasizes his full humanity. But he was conceived supernaturally, which is only imaginable if we believe also in his divinity.

■ **Jesus was also God.** The virginal conception does not prove the divinity of Jesus. But it is in keeping with that fact. How else could the eternal Son become a man?

Nevertheless it must be admitted that we are moving in an area where the mystery of God among humankind is at work. There is no need to be afraid of admitting that the human mind cannot always keep up with God. How did Jesus return from his historical presence among men and women to the eternal presence of his Father? That too (the ascension) is not something we can understand scientifically. So also must the moment of his breaking into our history remain outside our historical understanding.

2.3

JOHN THE BAPTIST

John the Baptist and Jesus were almost exact contemporaries, John being some six months older. Luke's Gospel takes great care to explain how they were related through their mothers, Mary and Elizabeth. Both were to become preachers of immense significance. But their ministries were very different.

The boys cannot have had much, if any, contact for, as Luke informs us, John 'lived in the desert until he appeared publicly to Israel'. This public appearance came as a result of a specific call from God to preach repentance and to baptize. The evangelist, in true historian's form, is very specific about the time of that calling: he gives the year of the reign of the Roman emperor, Tiberius, the name of his governor in the province, Pontius Pilate (a link confirmed by the 'Pilate-stone' discovered near Caesarea some thirty years ago), he tells us the name of the Tetrarch of Galilee at the time, Herod, mentions two other tetrarchs and finally indicates the holders of the office of high priest. This method of briefly summarizing the historical and local-political setting of a particular event had been well established among historians since the great Thucydides four centuries before. Depending on the particular calendar used, late AD27 or early 28 are thus the most probable dates for the beginning of John's public ministry.

But Luke goes one step further: the Baptist's public appearance is more than a simple historical event. It is closely connected with God's saving grace in Jewish history. John is likened to the prophet Isaiah's prediction: 'The voice of one crying in the desert.' By coming from the desert like Elijah, John could be seen as the second Elijah who was to come (Jesus himself described him as such). And John underlined this prophetic link by wearing the simple clothes, made of camel's hair with a leather belt, also worn by Elijah.

His mass appeal was unprecedented: he did not have to go to the people, they came to him. And those who responded to his preaching by repenting, he baptized. The exact place where he performed his baptisms is still under debate. Three places are mentioned in John's Gospel: 'Bethany on the other side of the Jordan', thought to have been in a wadi leading eastward from the river Jordan, at the level of Jericho; a place where he baptized 'in the early days', which Rainer Riesner has identified with Batanaia (Bashan in the Old Testament); and further north-east, at Aenon near Salim, some eight miles to the south-east of Scythopolis (Beth-Shan).

John was more than a charismatic preacher of repentance. He proclaimed that 'the kingdom of heaven is near'. That is why repentance is needed: only the repentant sinner will have a part in this kingdom. Jesus, after his own baptism by John, takes up the same proclamation: 'Repent, for the kingdom of heaven is near.' Even the Sadducees and Pharisees, heavily attacked by John, came to repent and to be baptized. He tells them insistently that they will have 'to produce fruit in keeping with repentance'. (The third important group, the Essenes, are not mentioned. Their view of baptism was different: they performed regular, ritual self-baptisms, after careful initiation, in their own closed community.)

John knew that his baptism by water was only preparing the way for someone else. Someone would come, he said, who would baptize 'with the

Holy Spirit and with fire'. When this man came to him, he recognized him: it was Jesus. John publicly proclaimed him to be 'the Lamb of God', 'the thongs of whose sandals I am not worthy to untie'. This messianic language was further underlined when John insisted that Jesus surpassed him 'because he was before me'. After a brief conversation in which John protested that it was he who should be baptized, not Jesus, John baptized Jesus, and his action marked the official, public beginning of Jesus' ministry. The next day, he met Andrew, Peter and Philip who were soon afterwards to become his first disciples in Galilee.

John continued his own ministry after Jesus had travelled back to Galilee. He moved to Aenon near Salim and later back into the territory of Herod Antipas who had him arrested. This was for two reasons. According to a contemporary Jewish historian, Flavius Josephus, Herod feared a kind of sedition from John's mass following. And also John had dared publicly to denounce the adultery Herod had committed with Herodias, the wife of his brother Philip. John was taken to the fortress of Machaerus, east of the Dead Sea. Here, the machinations of Herodias prevailed over Herod's own attitude towards John, which was a mixture of fear and admiration. The famous story of 'Salõme' and her dance ends with John's beheading.

From prison, John had sent disciples to Jesus to find out if he really was the Messiah. Jesus' evident preparation for suffering rather than triumph, for martyrdom rather than judgment, was so unexpected that confirmation seemed necessary. And Jesus provided this in a characteristic way, by pointing to all those aspects of his ministry which the prophets had predicted of the Messiah. More than that, Jesus went on to praise John publicly, saying that there had never been 'anyone greater than John the Baptist'. Thus John is greater than Elijah, greater even than Moses. He was the last of the prophets, truly linking the Old Covenant with the New.

We do not know what happened to John's followers after his death. Some will have continued to practise John's form of baptism; we hear of them at Ephesus later in the New Testament. In later centuries, their teaching may have influenced the baptismal sect of the Mandaeans. In the middle ages, Christians in a world of violence and strife rediscovered John's unique role as a preacher of repentance: in 1099, Crusader Knights founded an order in Jerusalem, dedicated to care for the weak, the sick and the poor, and to the defence of the faith. They called it the Knightly Order of the Hospital of St John of Jerusalem.

2.4

JESUS THE TEACHER

About five centuries before Jesus' time, the Jews returned to their homeland from exile in Babylon. In the years following, many pious Jewish groups emerged which organized themselves to study the writings of the Old Testament. So that they could hold services away from the Temple in Jerusalem, they used to meet in ordinary houses. Later, houses were specially constructed for this purpose, and these 'synagogues' are increasingly being excavated by archaeologists today. In Capernaum and Magdala, places where Jesus preached, the remains of synagogues of the first century AD have been discovered.

The main part of the synagogue service was the reading from the Books of Moses and the Prophets. These readings were then interpreted. In New Testament times each adult Israelite was allowed

actively to participate in the synagogue service. And so that ordinary working people could read and interpret the Scriptures, the synagogues were affiliated to simple schools. The servant of the synagogue used the ancient writings to teach boys to read and write. Special value was placed on learning by heart, as it was in most ancient theories of education. The scrolls were also accessible to adults for further study beyond the sabbath service. The synagogues began a form of popular education. In the years before Christ was born there was in Judaism the first known attempt in history to introduce compulsory education, though this did not in fact materialize until 300 years later.

Jewish parents who took their religious faith seriously felt it a duty to have their sons instructed in the Old Testament. After receiving his first instruction from his foster father Joseph, Jesus probably went to a synagogue school. His disciples would have received the same upbringing.

From the words he uses, Jesus clearly knew large parts of the Old Testament by heart. Jewish teaching offers him an important background, not only for his school education but also for his public ministry. If the Gospels give us a reliable record of his words, then this is primarily linked to his work as teacher. As a teacher Jesus had much in common with other teachers of his time. But there were also characteristic differences—differences not only in the content of his message, but also in his approach.

The Jewish teacher

The famous Jewish historian, Flavius Josephus, who lived at the end of New Testament times, called

▼ **These students at Yeshiva Seminary in Israel are learning from an age-old tradition of interpreting** God's Law. The Jewish rabbis of Jesus' time taught groups of disciples. But Jesus taught a new message in a new way.

Jesus 'a teacher and wise man'. The Gospels also show that Jesus was regarded as a teacher by his contemporaries. The form of address, *Rabbi*, proves this. Matthew, Mark and John keep this word in Jesus' own Aramaic mother tongue for *Rabbi* was the usual, respectful form of address at that time for a teacher. But in New Testament times it did not imply academic study or an official title as teacher of Old Testament Law. The word is only used in this way in Judaism today, and Jesus was not a Rabbi in this modern sense. The trained scribes, however, did recognize him as someone with whom they could discuss the finer points of the Law. Ordinary people turned to him again and again with questions of interpretation.

Jesus' role as teacher became even clearer as he gathered a circle of students around him. The Greek New Testament word for 'disciples' has its linguistic roots in the Hebrew for 'to teach'. A main duty of Jesus' closest associates was to learn from him. Even the Babylonian Talmud has, independently of the Gospels, preserved the recollection that Jesus had students.

In common with other Jewish teachers, Jesus

▲ This synagogue at Capernaum dates from later than Jesus' time, but beneath it have been found remains of the first-century building which Jesus attended. Here he taught the people 'as one who had authority'.

referred to the Old Testament in his teaching. And we hear again and again in the Gospels that he preached in the synagogues. One such account, recorded in Luke's Gospel, is the most concisely detailed description of a synagogue service which we have from the first century AD.

The sayings of Jesus, particularly in the first three Gospels, are usually very short. Even longer sections of speech, like the Sermon on the Mount (found in Matthew chapters 5 to 7), are collections of short sayings linked with somewhat longer parables. Here we see the influence of Jewish teaching, which relied primarily on imprinting on the memory. Like other Jewish teachers, but with his own special mastery, Jesus summarized the main points of his teaching in short, weighty sayings.

To make his words easier to learn by heart, Jesus also used another resource of Jewish education. He borrowed the favourite style of Old Testament

The Twelve

At a certain point in his ministry, Jesus grouped around him twelve specially selected disciples. Some scholars have speculated that this central core of twelve only arose after Jesus' death. But this now seems unlikely. Jesus himself called them together, and the reason was probably the so-called 'Galilean crisis'. After a period of apparently successful preaching Jesus must have recognized that his call for people to turn back to God was not really being acted on.

By choosing twelve disciples, Jesus maintained his claim on all Israel, for the number symbolizes the twelve traditional tribes of Israel. This inner group represented a remnant of the Old Testament people of God, a remnant faithful to Jesus and a sign of hope for the future. But Israel herself had largely rejected Jesus' message, and the twelve disciples would be instrumental in the judgement on Israel, as witnesses on Jesus' side.

After the Galilean crisis, the persecutions by the prince of the province, Herod Antipas, were intensified. Jesus, like the prophet Isaiah before him, withdrew into his closer group of disciples. Just before his trial in Jerusalem, Jesus gave them a special

instruction. He revealed things to them, which he had only expressed in veiled terms until then. He acknowledged that he was the Messiah, but said this would demand suffering. He explained the meaning of this suffering to the twelve at the last supper.

The twelve are listed at four points in the New Testament (see Matthew chapter 10, Mark 3, Luke 6 and Acts 1). They agree on eleven names: Simon, called Peter, and his brother Andrew, the two sons of Zebedee, James and John, Philip, Bartholomew, Thomas, Matthew, James the son of Alphaeus, Simon the zealot and Judas Iscariot. Only one name differs: Matthew and Mark list a Thaddeus, but Luke speaks of Judas, the son of James. This can perhaps be explained if this Judas was called only by his surname after Jesus' resurrection, in order to distinguish him from Jesus' betrayer.

After the resurrection the group of twelve formed the core, and even the first leadership, of the early Christian community in Jerusalem. Recalling the time when Jesus had sent them out to preach, the twelve also were called 'apostles', from the Greek word for 'to send'. But other early Christian missionaries

also bore this title. The twelve ensured continuity when the time came to spread Jesus' teaching after Easter as well. They were able to bear witness to Jesus, because they were with him from the outset.

Judas' place was taken by another disciple, Matthias, who had followed Jesus from the beginning. This restored the number of apostles to twelve—an important symbol while they were preaching the message of a New Israel to their fellow Jews.

When James, the son of Zebedee, died a martyr's death in the year AD43 under Herod Agrippa II, no one else was added. The

▲ On this ancient ivory 'pyxis' (box or container) is carved a relief showing Jesus teaching his disciples.

mission to the gentiles was beginning to take first place, there was less need for the symbolism of the twelve.

poetry, where two sentences often reflect each other. Here is an example from Jesus' own teaching: 'Whoever wants to save his life, will lose it. Whoever loses it for my sake, will gain it.'

A saying such as this makes a deep impression when it is first heard. The ability of his first disciples to retain the words of Jesus was further helped by rhythm and rhyme. These can no longer be discerned in our modern English translations, but can be clearly seen when Jesus' words are translated back into Aramaic or Hebrew. We all know that a poem can be retained much more easily

than prose, and the Old Testament prophets had already condensed key statements of their message into poetic sayings.

Jesus' words could also be easily remembered as he used a wealth of gripping stories. His parables stand out because of their unforgettable pictures. Parables such as the Prodigal Son or the Good Samaritan stay with us long after we first hear them. Even highly sceptical researchers, those who doubt the authenticity of much of the New Testament, consider the greatest part of Jesus' parables to be genuine. And they believe that most of the parables

2. JESUS' MINISTRY BEGINS

2.1 JORDAN VALLEY

JOHN PREACHES AND BAPTIZES
JOHN THE BAPTIST PREACHES. SOME PEOPLE REPENT, AND HE BAPTIZES THEM IN THE RIVER JORDAN.

▶ MATTHEW 3:1-12
▶ MARK 1:1-8
▶ LUKE 3:1-18
▶ JOHN 1:19-28

2.2 RIVER JORDAN

JESUS IS BAPTIZED
JESUS ASKS JOHN FOR BAPTISM. THE HOLY SPIRIT COMES ON HIM.

▶ MATTHEW 3:13-17
▶ MARK 1:9-13
▶ LUKE 3:21-22

2.3 JUDEAN WILDERNESS

JESUS IS TEMPTED
FORTY DAYS' FASTING IN THE WILDERNESS; JESUS IS TEMPTED BY THE DEVIL.

▶ MATTHEW 4:1-11
▶ MARK 1:12-13
▶ LUKE 4:1-10

2.4 GALILEE

JESUS BEGINS TO PREACH
HE IMMEDIATELY DECLARES THE HEART OF HIS MESSAGE.

▶ MATTHEW 4:12-17
▶ MARK 1:14-15
▶ LUKE 4:13-15

2.5 GALILEE

JESUS CALLS DISCIPLES
HE INVITES PETER AND OTHERS TO FOLLOW HIM

▶ MATTHEW 4:18-22
▶ MARK 1:16-20
▶ LUKE 5:1-11
▶ JOHN 1:35-51

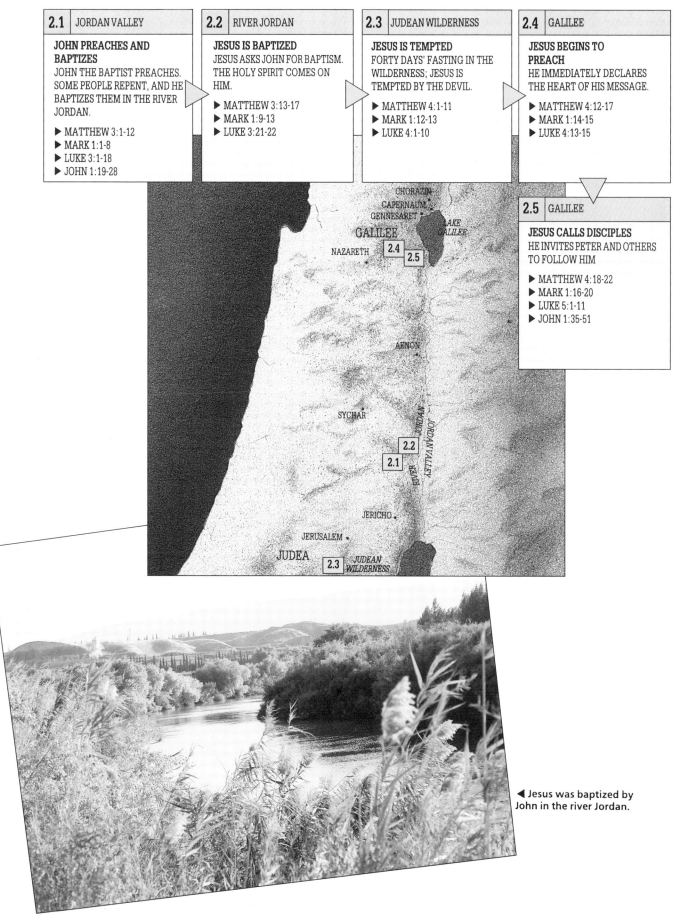

CHORAZIN
CAPERNAUM
GENNESARET
GALILEE
LAKE GALILEE
NAZARETH
2.4 **2.5**

AENON

SYCHAR

RIVER JORDAN
JORDAN VALLEY
2.2
2.1

JERICHO

JERUSALEM
JUDEA
2.3 JUDEAN WILDERNESS

◀ Jesus was baptized by John in the river Jordan.

Communicating Jesus

How did they do it? How could a handful of Christians communicate the good news of Jesus so effectively? But somehow they did. The new religion—one of so many competing in the Roman Empire at the time—became within a mere three hundred years the best known and most influential of the faiths.

With hindsight, we may detect three good reasons:
▪ **They followed a command of Jesus himself**;
▪ **They were careful in their strategy**;
▪ **They had the spirit of sheer practical inventiveness**.

The command of Jesus, recorded at the end of Matthew's Gospel, came as what we call the Great Commission: to 'make disciples of all nations'. The first disciples and their circle began that task when they simply started telling others what they had seen and learned. It was a 'word-of-mouth' enterprise. Sometimes there were thousands of listeners, as in Jerusalem at Pentecost; sometimes, as in the case of Peter and Cornelius, it happened in front of a household of perhaps twenty; sometimes, as with Philip and the Ethiopian 'Chancellor of the Exchequer', only four eyes witnessed it.

Most of these people became communicators in turn, conveying the message they had heard. Many of those who had heard the Pentecost sermon would have returned to their home countries, spreading the news (and we must keep in mind that they had all heard Peter's words 'in their own languages'). Others were in positions of influence and authority, such as the Roman centurion Cornelius, through whom the gospel would have reached Roman soldiers and fellow officers, or the Ethiopian, who would have had direct access to the

◀ ▲ **The advent of printing, together with translations into the common languages, made the Bible available to the people. This title page is from the English 'Great Bible', published in 1539. Before then, manuscripts of the Bible had all to be copied by hand. The printed word had now become the greatest medium of communication.**

court back home. Thus in the very beginning we can see how ordinary people, Jews and non-Jews alike, members of the imperial power and high-ranking politicians of foreign countries came to hear the message of Jesus. Within years, even within months, these very few disciples had managed to reach far beyond the confines of Jerusalem or Galilee.

At the same time, others had already begun to write down what they had seen of Jesus' ministry. Someone like Matthew, a trained tax-collector, would almost of professional necessity have been able to write short-hand—an ancient technique known to us from historical documents from Rome, Palestine and Greece. . Historically speaking, it is quite possible that he had made shorthand notes of what Jesus did and taught, including above all such extended texts as the full version of the Sermon on the Mount, which we find only in his Gospel. So the first Christians had both oral and written source material at their disposal when they decided to write comprehensive books, 'Gospels', which would be sent to areas beyond the everyday reach of the apostles themselves. (There is considerable dispute about exactly when this transition finally took place, which is discussed in the chapter *The Witness of the Gospels*.)

All the evidence now at our disposal suggests, however, that within the lifetime of the first generation of the apostles and their disciples, the gospel news had been spread both orally and in writing. Even without the Gospels there were letters, by Paul and others, preparing the ground and explaining the message. Letters, in those days, were a much more important form of communication than they are today: like the Gospels they would be read out aloud, passed on, copied, redistributed. When it comes

to strategy, Luke, among the first generation of Christian writers, is perhaps the best example. He dedicated his two books, his Gospel and the book of Acts, to 'his Excellency' Theophilus, a high-ranking Roman. In antiquity, the dedicatee of a book would undertake to have it copied and distributed at his cost. Thus, at one stroke Luke had found an influential Roman convert to Christianity who would willingly cover the expense of spreading his writings.

This ingenious, practical attitude was highlighted again at the end of the first century when the Christians began to use the book-format, the 'codex', instead of the more cumbersome scroll. Codex-type writings had been known before, but it was the Christians who developed this into a format which would then eventually be copied by others. There were at least three good reasons for this change. The codex was cheaper, since one could write on both sides of the papyrus. It was easier for reference: one did not have to unroll a whole scroll to find a passage but could leaf through the codex pages much as with a book today. And it was space-saving: where one scroll each was needed for, say, Luke's Gospel and Acts, now all four Gospels and Acts could fit in one handy codex. This was soon to prove useful in times of persecution: a few smallish codices were easier to hide, to store away or to send off quickly than the considerable number of voluminous scrolls which would otherwise have been required.

Right from earliest times, then, Christians were expert communicators. And against this background, Christians have always felt the impetus to improve their techniques of communicating Jesus. In the mid-fifteenth century, printing with moveable types was invented by a Christian, and the first book ever to be thus printed was the Bible. One of the two

▲ **The tradition of illuminated Gospel texts perhaps reached its summit in the Celtic Lindisfarne Gospels. This is the title page of Matthew.**

inventors of radio was a Christian (the other one, interestingly, was a Jew).

Writing, printing, using wavelengths have for a very long time been seen as accessories to the spoken word in communicating the message of Jesus. The same Christian who invented the radio technique later founded Radio Vatican.

At the other end of the scale, Christians have often jealously tried to reserve the use of these media for themselves, and guard them against anything that smacked of anti-Christian tendencies. Thus, the 'Index of Prohibited Books' was very effective for centuries in preventing certain publications from being printed or sold. On radio, certain types of programming simply did not reach the airwaves; they were not even produced. It is only in this century, broadly speaking since the invention of television, that Christian censorship has begun to disappear. And at roughly the same time Christians have ceased to be at the forefront of new communication techniques. New developments in television, such as cable and satellite programming, have happened and are happening without any apparent Christian influence. Christians are rather

desperately trying to catch up, sometimes not quite knowing if they really want to catch up at all.

It is true, of course, that we still have great masters of the archetypal Christian form: oral communication. It is also true that a considerable number of extremely effective books and radio programmes, and even the occasional inventive television production, still originate from Christians, from highly professional contributors to the public as well as to the private media (compare the article *Jesus and the Modern Media*). The techniques of preaching, of writing, of radio and television producing can be learnt at Christian colleges and institutions. The knowhow is there for the asking.

But there is a striking phenomenon: at the end of the twentieth century communicating Jesus has become, again, the same minority enterprise it was in the first centuries. At a time when, in Western Europe at least, 'Christianity' and 'the church' are on the verge of becoming elements of national folklore rather than the salt of society, the example of the communicative inventiveness of the very first Christians is a challenge to be met.

were first spoken in the world of rural Galilee.

The parables, like the other words of Jesus, are also steeped in allusions to the Old Testament. At the same time they pick up experiences, accurately and lovingly observed, from the everyday world of Jesus' audience. The picture of two women at a corn mill, the astounding growth of the mustard seed, a net full of different fish, were examples which even simple people in Galilee could immediately understand. But the parables also point to a deeper statement on the dawning of God's reign announced by Jesus. Those listening could often discover the deeper meaning of the parable if they thought about it longer. In the story known to us as the parable of the sower, Jesus described how seed took root on different soils. Only a quarter of the seed came up, which was definitely the experience of farmers on poor private land in Galilee. But how could the extension of the kingdom of God be compared with largely unsuccessful sowing? Anyone who thought about this would recognize that Jesus was describing

the effect of his preaching. He was giving an invitation to people to come back into God's kingdom; some would accept and be changed people, but many would not.

Many of Jesus' words contain, even if sometimes concealed, a claim of authority. It is an authority which goes far beyond that of any other Jewish teacher. Jesus differed from contemporary scribes: he preached not only in the synagogues, but also in the open air. As a prophetic preacher who wanted to turn people's lives around, he needed to reach as many people as possible, even those such as tax collectors and prostitutes who were outside the religious community. But the differences from other Jewish teachers are not restricted to practical matters. They go deeper.

The Messianic teacher

It was strange how Jesus personally tied the group of his disciples to himself. If a Jewish student had been

▼ The medieval Ecternach Bible is an example of the 'paupers' Bibles', quite common at the time. These were picture Bibles, telling the stories – as here the parable of the labourers in the vineyard – to those who could not read.

▼ In his parable of the sower, Jesus spoke of seed falling among thorns, which grew up and choked the plants. This is like people whose faith is choked by 'the worries of this life, the deceitfulness of wealth and the desires for other things'.

receiving instruction from a teacher for some time, he was passed on to another so that he could extend his knowledge. Finally, he would become a teacher himself. But it was quite different with Jesus. 'You are not to be called Rabbi,' he once said to his disciples, 'for you have only one Master'. Jesus expected his followers to be ready even to die for his sake, a demand which was acceptable in Judaism only for God and his law. Plainly the authority of Jesus' teaching lay not just in its content, but also in the person who gave the teaching.

Followers and opponents alike increasingly asked one question: 'Who is this who teaches with [direct] authority [from God] and not as the scribes?' Because Jesus never relied on the authority of another teacher. Indeed, he was able to put his own word even above that of the Old Testament. Speaking of the teaching handed down by Moses, he dared to say, 'You have heard that it was said to the people long ago. . . But I say to you. . .' Was this arrogance, this claim to direct spiritual authority?

Many Jews expected that the coming Messiah would possess the wisdom of God in abundance, and would also pass it on to others. But Jesus did not even praise the wise and discerning, but the foolish and the weak. How could he be the Messiah?

Even John the Baptist was at one point not secure in his judgment of Jesus. From prison he asked, 'Are you the "one who was to come" or should we expect someone else?' By the 'one who was to come' he meant the Messiah. Jesus did not answer the question directly, but for those familiar with the holy scriptures his words offered a clear Yes. 'Go back' he said to the enquirers, 'and report to John what you hear and see: the blind see, the lame walk, the lepers are cured, the deaf hear, the dead are raised. . .' The signs predicted by Isaiah for the messianic time were being fulfilled through Jesus. Indeed, he was the promised messianic good news in person, for through his preaching 'the Good News is preached to the poor'. And then Jesus added a final warning: 'Blessed is he who does not fall away on account of me!' Jesus preached the message of the messianic age; he healed the sick and told the crowds he would be the final judge of all. John could draw his own conclusions.

The words of Jesus were therefore not the expressions of any other Jewish teacher, however great. They were the words of the Messiah; they had the highest authority: 'Heaven and earth shall pass away, but my words will not pass away.' Such words as these could not be ignored or forgotten. Jesus said that at the last judgment a person's destiny would be determined by them: 'Whoever is ashamed of me and my words in this adulterous and sinful generation, the Son of Man will be ashamed of him when he comes in his father's glory with the holy angels.'

Anyone who, like the disciples, believed Jesus' claim, could do no other than engrave the most important of his sayings on their minds. And Jesus' teaching method served to imprint them even more firmly.

He would have quite consciously taught the disciples many sayings. For example, he would have taught them the prayer which we now know as the Lord's Prayer. The disciples would have learnt Jesus' words by heart, before going out by themselves to proclaim the message in nearby towns and villages. Wherever they preached they were asked for the authentic words of the one who sent them. According to the ancient Jewish law on messengers they should not teach their own ideas, but keep to: 'He who listens to you, listens to me. . .' The disciples also naturally began to recount the miracles

▼ On the road from Jerusalem to Jericho stands this inn, perhaps near the spot where stood the inn to which, in Jesus' parable, the Good Samaritan took an injured traveller. This story has sounded echoes in many generations, evoking a response of caring for our neighbour.

Jesus' Recipe for Happiness

As he began his Sermon on the Mount, Jesus described the character of a disciple in the famous 'Beatitudes'. They are to be found in Matthew chapter 5 from verse 3.

Blessed are the poor in spirit,
　for theirs is the kingdom of heaven.
Blessed are those who mourn,
　for they will be comforted.
Blessed are the meek,
　for they will inherit the earth.
Blessed are those who hunger and thirst for
　righteousness,
　for they will be filled.
Blessed are the merciful,
　for they will be shown mercy.
Blessed are the pure in heart,
　for they will see God.
Blessed are the peacemakers,
　for they will be called sons of God.
Blessed are those who are persecuted because of
　righteousness,
　for theirs is the kingdom of heaven.

Blessed are you when people insult you, persecute you and falsely say all kinds of evil against you because of me. Rejoice and be glad, because great is your reward in heaven, for in the same way they persecuted the prophets who were before you.

and actions of Jesus in memorable forms. We can expect that some sympathizers in towns also made written notes on Jesus' prophecies for their own private use. Papyrus provided relatively cheap writing material. Some of the accounts which make up our Gospels were formed while Jesus was still teaching. They are not all products of post-resurrection faith.

But the resurrection itself had far-reaching effects on the teaching which Jesus had given. Its claim was now clearly and finally confirmed by God himself. Along with the accounts of Jesus' suffering and rising again, the record of his own words was the first Christian community's most important possession. The apostle Paul tells us that new converts received instruction in the tradition of Jesus. The early Christians strived to pass the message on faithfully, which explains to a great extent the agreement between the Gospels. But the Christians also understood that Jesus' words were not for one small group, but needed to be passed on beyond Palestine. They had to translate, paraphrase obscure expressions, and sometimes omit misleading statements. Here lies an explanation for the differences we find in the Gospels. But, at the beginning of the Gospel record stood not Christians with a fanciful imagination, but Jesus the messianic teacher.

Jesus and the Modern Media

'You're kidding! The modern media are 2,000 years too late!'

Correct, in one sense. It is almost a contradiction to talk of Jesus in relation to the modern media. After all, there is no videotape, film-footage or quarter-inch sound recording of the man Jesus who lived two thousand years ago in Palestine. There are only a small number of written documents left by his immediate followers (the earliest of those written some thirty years after his death). Given that the modern media are usually about actuality— give us the blood, the tears, or at least the family photographs— then on first glimpse it would appear that Jesus doesn't stand much of a chance.

But think back over the last few years. The debate on women priests, the authenticity or not of the Turin Shroud, the portrayal of Christ in Martin Scorsese's film The Last Temptation, all have been covered avidly by the secular media. And in the process hundreds of millions of people have literally been forced to think about some aspects of the historical Jesus. It might not be the coverage some of us like, but the secular media can still be interested in Jesus.

But what of the modern media being used to speak of Jesus in a more overt way—in what is known as 'religious broadcasting'? The tele-evangelists in the United States have their own channels on cable and satellite; there are the world-wide Christian radio stations; and there is religious broadcasting on national network television and radio stations through-out most of the West.

Religious broadcasting is rather a dull-sounding word to describe opportunities that encourage people to think of life in what could be called a three-dimensional way. It represents an attempt to raise the 'spiritual' in life to a level equally as important as any other dimension of modern living, and it does this in a number of ways using documentary, worship and the presentation of different views and teachings.

How different things are today from a century ago. Pictures of the latest disaster can be bounced from a mobile earth station on the ground thousands of miles into space, to a satellite circling the globe, and then back to whoever wants the pictures for their evening news bulletin—and all this in less than a second. Our horizons are so much bigger than in any previous generation, and our demands for information, for facts, are unprecedented. Such fast technological development offers amazing opportunities to people who want to communicate Jesus. For centuries the gospel was promoted through writing, painting, preaching to those within ear-shot. Then along came radio, followed by television, and suddenly there was a whole new discipline to master. Here was the possibility for a preacher to address millions of people at one time, where previously a life-time's preaching would yield, at the very most, hundreds of thousands.

On hearing about the possibility of broadcasting church services, a former Dean of Westminster in England was appalled that a man could conceivably listen to radio worship in a bar—and with his hat on too! And today we have our own hesitations. Are we losing sight of Jesus in the sea of technology or can we catch glimpses of what previously was hidden? Is Jesus at work in the cutting room, in the studio, through the lens? Or is he being fragmented into almost unrecognizable pieces as the eye used to slick commercials is fed a neatly-packaged Christ?

So long as we recognize these dangers, who is to say that Jesus cannot be found in the apparatus of satellite, radio waves and television sets?

On Sunday mornings in Britain, there is a unique venture in broadcast worship. A programme called This is the Day, adapted by Norwegian television and available in the Netherlands and Belgium via cable, is produced by the BBC. It is a live outside broadcast from a viewer's home anywhere in Britain or Northern Ireland, and on occasion has come from a lighthouse, a hospital, even a prison. Via the screen it aims to reach out to people in their own homes, so that by following the readings, lighting a candle, joining in the prayers, and breaking bread, they are united in worship. The programme has come to mean a lot to people who ▶▶

▼ **Radio is the most widely-used communications medium in the developing world. Millions of homes have their transistor.**

Christians have learnt to use radio to teach the message about Jesus.

are housebound, or who for whatever reason feel unable to attend church worship. Roughly a third of the programme involves prayer based on letters or phone calls received from viewers. The prayer-requests cover the whole gamut of human life— problems with relationships, sickness, bereavement, depression.

This is something different from a relay of a traditional act of worship from a church, where with the best will in the world the viewer is a spectator of other people's worship. Here television is being used for intimate, one-to-one communication with viewers at home, as full participants in an unseen viewing congregation.

There is also another important contrast with a lot of Christian television. Here the Jesus-image of the programme-maker is secondary; foremost is the

space for the viewer at home to worship and to pray for the concerns of other viewers as expressed in the letters.

This problem of Jesus-image is a recurrent one. There are a number to choose from. The American teleevangelists present Jesus complete with credit-card number and telephone prayer-line. The image available in many countries comes through conventional acts of worship from any one of a number of Christian denominations. And the image via documentary from Latin America presents Jesus as a freedom fighter struggling for justice and peace. Today as always, each of us makes our own image of Jesus.

In the United States—years ahead of the rest of the world in cable and satellite technology—the plethora of conflicting Jesus-images available raises big questions

for the rest of the world about to undergo similar technological change. Jesus is a multi-million-dollar business and the message is available any time of day or night—just press the right button.

What comparison is there between the Jesus of 2,000 years ago who angered the authorities, fed the hungry, healed the sick and spoke of new life and forgiveness, and this slick, commercialized gospel, where human need is measured in dollars and where you 'have only to reach out and touch the TV set and you will be healed'.

This question of image is crucial to understanding Jesus and the modern media. These powerful images affect us deeply. But are they useful, or are they destructive? Do they help us know more of Jesus, or do they hide him behind someone else's perception? Am I prepared to admit that

▲ **Christians today use song as one method of passing on the gospel. Singing can work alongside preaching, conveying the emotional impact of the message.**

people have images different from mine, or do I go all out to get my own cable channel and sell only my own Jesus-image?

One of the good things about public service broadcasting, as found in the national broadcasting networks of many countries, is that it does just what the word implies: it broadcasts in the true sense of the word, it does not 'narrow-cast'. The openness and diversity expressed through such religious broadcasting ought to be a reason for celebration. Unfortunately, the commercial pressures operating in new communication technology result in carving up the airwaves between competing gospels,

and the image of Jesus is fragmented.

Perhaps the question comes down to this. How would the man Jesus have used the world of the modern media had he been conducting his earthly ministry today? Would he have appeared on chat shows, been interviewed on news programmes, and so made his message available to the widest possible audience? Or would he have been forced to set up his own cable channel to speak only to his own followers or the random channel-switcher? Would he have used these media at all?

I believe he would have found a way, and that the modern media's interest in Jesus has to be considered good news. Here is an opportunity that has been denied all but the most recent generations. God's gift to us of creativity can now be used to present the claims of Jesus to the whole of the modern world. And as the ever increasing number of letters in response to programmes shows, there are now new avenues open to that mystery which television cameras will never capture fully—the power of God to work deeply in the lives of men and women.

▲ **The twentieth-century communications media – newspapers, radio, television – have made it possible for news to pass round the world within hours of it happening. In the first centuries it took longer. But Christians still found imaginative ways to communicate the news about Jesus.**

2.5

JESUS THE MIRACLE-WORKER

For many readers the most striking features of the Gospel accounts of Jesus' life are his miracles. Matthew, Mark, Luke and John all regularly portray Jesus as having the power to heal illnesses, cast out evil spirits from the demon-possessed, and overrule the forces of nature by a single spoken command. Why did miracles play such a central role in Jesus' ministry? At least four main reasons emerge from the pages of the New Testament.

■ **Jesus worked miracles in response to people's faith in him.** A Roman army commander pleaded with Jesus to heal his servant. He expressed confidence that even if Jesus would only speak a word from a long distance away, then the servant would be cured. Jesus complied and then marvelled aloud, 'I tell you the truth, I have not found such great faith even in Israel'. Or again, a woman who had been haemorrhaging for twelve years reached out in a large crowd to touch Jesus' cloak, thinking, 'If I just touch his clothes, I will be healed.' Jesus identified the one who had touched him, pronounced her well, but then made it clear that there was no magic in his clothes. 'Your faith has healed you,' he said.

Still, Jesus did not heal every one of his followers of all their infirmities. If anything, the impression we get is that miracles were the exception to the rule, or they would have stopped being miracles. Matthew understands Jesus' ministry of healing as a fulfilment of Isaiah's prophecy: 'He took up our infirmities and carried our diseases.' Isaiah made this prophecy as part of his description of God's 'suffering servant' who would die to pay the penalty for the sins of humanity. So we get the impression that as people trust in Jesus to save them from

God's punishment for their *spiritual* sickness (disobeying God's commands), they can also expect him at times to free them from physical maladies. But it is unfair to conclude that he must always grant bodily healing when requested. Jesus refuses to be 'put in a box'. Even during his lifetime, when asked to prove himself by working a miracle he refused.

■ **Jesus often worked miracles to instil faith in him where little or none was present.** After stilling a storm on Lake Galilee, he chastised his

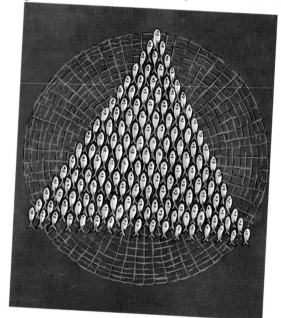

▲ This Indian 'mandala' painting – 'It is the Lord', by Jyoti Sahi – pictures the 153 fish miraculously caught on the day the apostles met the risen Jesus on the shores of Lake Galilee.

disciples for their lack of faith and for their fear. The miracle forced them to confront the question, 'Who is this? Even the wind and the waves obey him!'. On another occasion Jesus healed a paralyzed man to justify his claim to be able to forgive his sins. Again the bystanders marvelled at his authority. In a pair of remarkably parallel miracles, Jesus guided his disciples to extraordinary catches of fish on Lake Galilee, to illustrate how they would be 'fishing' for human followers. The first happened when Jesus first called Peter to become a disciple; the second accompanied Peter's reinstatement after he had denied even knowing his Lord. It is as if Jesus was saying in each case, 'I am the one who will provide for all your needs; trust me and me alone.'

John's Gospel emphasizes this 'evangelistic' aspect of Jesus' miracles most of all. Only John specifically labels them 'signs'—pointers to Jesus' identity. He clearly expects that anyone reading his Gospel will be challenged by the accounts of the miracles to believe in Jesus as God's unique Son, the one who is the only 'way and the truth and the life'. Yet John also tempers his enthusiasm for Jesus' wonder-working with a caution. Though the miracles are meant to awaken faith in Jesus, they should not become crutches which people require in order to

▲ **Jesus healed people because he cared about them, and also as a sign that God's kingdom had come. Christian medical work in today's world has the same twin motives.**

believe. So when 'doubting Thomas' refused to acknowledge that Jesus had risen from the dead until he personally saw and touched him, Christ replied, 'Because you have seen me, you have believed, blessed are those who have not seen and yet have believed'. Miracles can encourage faith but faith should not be dependent on them.

▪ **Jesus sometimes worked miracles out of sheer compassion for those in need.** Before multiplying the five loaves and two fishes to feed the 5,000, Jesus 'had compassion on them, because they were like sheep without a shepherd' (that is, they were leaderless). Later, when two blind men cried out for Christ to heal them, the Gospel-writers make a similar observation: Jesus had compassion on them and restored their sight. In the most famous example of all, when Jesus learned of the death of his dear friend Lazarus, he went to the tomb and wept. Immediately before the miracle in which Jesus brought Lazarus back to life, John tells us that Jesus was 'deeply moved in spirit and troubled'.

This compassion contrasted with many Jewish laws and rituals which prohibited certain kinds of people at certain times from experiencing God's goodness. Jesus frequently worked miracles which deliberately violated Jewish laws about not working on the sabbath, or not touching 'unclean' people (such as lepers), or not associating with those who were not Jewish. He bluntly repudiated the notion popular in some Jewish circles about all illness being God's punishment for sin. Sometimes God permits ill health to afflict a person for a while, sometimes because a greater good will result later when that person is healed. So, when the disciples asked Jesus

▲ The most widely-reported Gospel miracle is Jesus feeding 5,000 people from five loaves and two fish.

These are known as St Peter's fish; their large mouths could carry a coin (see the story in Matthew 17:27).

whether a certain man's blindness stemmed from his own sin or from his parents' sin, he responded, 'Neither. . .but this happened so that the work of God might be displayed in his life'.

■ **Jesus worked miracles to back up his teaching that the 'kingdom of God' (God's new society) was coming through his life and work.** This is perhaps the most important reason for the miracles. After John the Baptist was imprisoned, he began to

MIRACLES JESUS WORKED

▲ At the Pool of Bethesda, crowds of sick people awaited a miracle. Jesus healed a lame man there.

▲ It was prophesied that when the Messiah came 'the lame would walk'.

▲ When Jesus calmed a storm on Lake Galilee, the disciples asked 'Who is this? Even the winds and waves obey him!'

HEALINGS	■ MATTHEW	■ MARK	■ LUKE	■ JOHN
A LEPER	8:2-3	1:40-42	5:12-13	
A CENTURION'S SERVANT	8:5-13		7:1-10	
PETER'S MOTHER-IN-LAW	8:14-15	1:30-31	4:38-39	
TWO GADARENES	8:28-34	5:1-15	8:27-35	
A PARALYSED MAN	9:2-7	2:3-12	5:18-25	
A WOMAN WITH A HAEMORRHAGE	9:20-22	5:25-29	8:43-48	
TWO BLIND MEN	9:27-31			
A MAN DUMB AND POSSESSED	9:32-33			
A MAN WITH A WITHERED HAND	12:10-13	3:1-5	6:6-10	
A MAN BLIND, DUMB AND POSSESSED	12:22		11:14	
A CANAANITE WOMAN'S DAUGHTER	15:21-28	7:24-30		
A BOY WITH EPILEPSY	17:14-18	9:17-29	9:38-43	
BARTIMAEUS, AND ANOTHER BLIND MAN	20:29-34	10:46-52	18:35-43	
A DEAF-AND-DUMB MAN		7:31-37		
A MAN POSSESSED, SYNAGOGUE		1:23-26	4:33-35	
A BLIND MAN AT BETHSAIDA		8:22-26		
A WOMAN BENT DOUBLE			13:11-13	
A MAN WITH DROPSY			14:1-4	
TEN LEPERS			17:11-19	
MALCHUS' EAR			22:50-51	
AN OFFICIAL'S SON AT CAPERNAUM				4:46-54
A SICK MAN, POOL OF BETHESDA				5:1-9
A MAN BORN BLIND				9

NATURE MIRACLES				
CALMING THE STORM	8:23-27	4:37-41	8:22-25	
WALKING ON THE WATER	14:25	6:48-51		6:19-21
5,000 PEOPLE FED	14:15-21	6:35-44	9:12-17	6:5-13
4,000 PEOPLE FED	15:32-38	8:1-9		
A COIN IN A FISH'S MOUTH	17:24-27			
A FIG-TREE WITHERED	21:18-22	11:12-14,20-26		
A CATCH OF FISH			5:1-11	
WATER TURNED INTO WINE				2:1-11
ANOTHER CATCH OF FISH				21:1-11

BRINGING THE DEAD BACK TO LIFE				
JAIRUS' DAUGHTER	9:18-19,23-25	5:22-24,38-42	8:41-42,49-56	
A WIDOW'S SON AT NAIN			7:11-15	
LAZARUS				11:1-44

question Jesus' credentials. He sent messengers to ask Jesus if he were really the 'coming one' the Jews had been awaiting. Jesus replied by telling the envoys to remind John of the miracles and to encourage him to continue believing.

As pointers to God's new society which Christ was establishing, the miracles often had symbolic value. Jesus turned water into wine at a wedding party not to promote drunkenness but because wine symbolized the festive spirit which his presence and the arrival of the kingdom merited. Again, Jesus sent a 'legion' of demons into a herd of pigs, who then rushed off the edge of a cliff to their deaths, not because he was an animal-hater but vividly to illustrate the doom of Satan and his demons, which the arrival of the kingdom makes certain. As Jesus elsewhere exclaimed, after hearing about exorcisms performed by his disciples, 'I saw Satan fall like lightning from heaven'. God permits the devil a limited amount of mischief in the present age, but the day of his dominance is past. All that remains for the devil is limited guerrilla activity until the day

▲ The first miracle John records happened at a wedding, when Jesus turned water into wine. This early painting of that wedding at Cana is in the catacomb of St Peter and St Marcellinus in Rome.

▲ Many Christians believe that Jesus still heals people miraculously today, in answer to prayer. This paralyzed man began to walk at a service at Lourdes in France.

arrives when Jesus triumphantly returns to earth at the end of human history as we know it. This future coming of God's kingdom was vividly foreshadowed by a temporary, brilliant transformation of Jesus' appearance, seen by three of the apostles, which is commonly known as the transfiguration.

Miracles since Jesus' time?

As well as Jesus' own miracle-working, the Gospels describe how he authorized the twelve apostles to work similar wonders in his name. These they performed not only while Jesus was alive but also after his death and resurrection, during the early years of the church's history. The New Testament does not specifically say whether or not subsequent generations of believers expected similar powers, but there are reasons to believe they should have. Others besides the twelve performed miracles during the earliest years of the church (Paul, for example, and Philip the deacon).

Paul spoke of miracles and healings as 'spiritual gifts' alongside other gifts such as teaching and administration. The latter still exist in the church, so presumably the former should too. We should therefore expect Jesus today to continue to work miracles, from time to time, through certain Christians. But that does not mean that all modern-day claims to the miraculous are to be believed. Some can be proved fictitious; others are the product of human deception; a few may even be demonically induced. But despite the fakes and the failures, Jesus is still spiritually alive today, and his miracle-working power is still with us.

PART 3

THE GREAT TEACHER

What did Jesus teach? What makes his words so penetrating
and so memorable, even for us centuries later?

This, the longest of the investigation's six stages,
spells out eleven key themes of Jesus' teaching. It also gives
examples, culled from 2,000 years of Christian living, of how his
teaching has been put into practice.

CONTENTS

SPECIAL FEATURES

Three central events
The parables of Jesus
Advocate of the young
Ignatius and the exercises
Jesus and women
The Imitation of Christ
The Christian tradition of prayer
The neighbour
Law and love
Francis of Assisi
The second coming
Jesus and the painters

3.1

THE KINGDOM OF GOD

Jesus introduced his mission in Galilee with the 'slogan': 'The time has come; the kingdom of God is near. Repent and believe the good news!' According to the Gospels it was his first recorded proclamation. But what did he mean by 'the kingdom of God'? And what did those who heard him make of it?

'Kingdom' suggests to most people either the place or the people over whom a king rules. Here 'kingdom' is a concrete 'thing', which can be identified and pointed out. But the basic meaning of the Greek word *basileia* (and of the Hebrew and Aramaic words which lie behind it) is more

dynamic—it refers to the fact of someone reigning, of acting as a king.

So the 'kingdom of God' really means 'God reigning', 'God in control' or, as one scholar has paraphrased it, 'God in strength'. It is a way of talking about God's power, his sovereignty. It points us to the situation where God has his way, and his will is done. So in the Lord's Prayer the phrases 'your kingdom come' and 'your will be done' are really different ways of saying the same thing. They both ask for God to be acknowledged and obeyed as king.

In 'kingdom of God' the focus falls not on the kingdom but on God. The phrase tells us something about what God is doing; it is not about a thing called 'the kingdom'. In fact the New Testament hardly ever speaks simply of 'the kingdom', but almost always of 'the kingdom of *God*' (or 'of heaven', which is Matthew's more Jewish way of saying the same thing). 'The kingdom' is no more meaningful on its own than 'the will' or 'the power' might be! We can avoid this sort of misunderstanding if instead of the familiar phrase 'the kingdom of God' we speak here of 'God's kingship'.

God as king

The Old Testament assures us that God is king. The world is his, because he made it. The prophets reflect on God's sovereignty in human affairs; no one, ultimately, can resist his will. Again and again the psalms rejoice that 'the Lord reigns'.

◄ **Leo Tolstoy (1828–1910) came to his own form of Christian belief. He believed that Jesus' teaching was** meant to transform human societies, and that people should refuse to co-operate with any evil system.

And yet the world does not seem always to be under God's control. People go their own way, and even seem to challenge God and get away with it. God may be king by right, but he does not always seem to be so in fact.

And so the belief grew up that one day God would act decisively in the affairs of the world to reassert his kingship. 'Then', wrote the prophet Zechariah, 'the Lord will be king over all the earth; on that day there will be one Lord, and his name the only name'.

These complementary themes (that God is sovereign, yet he promises to re-establish his authority in the future) are both presented in the Old Testament. Kingship is an eternal fact, and a hope for the future. And both these aspects continue to be expressed in later Jewish literature. The actual phrase 'the kingship of God' does not occur very frequently either in the Old Testament or in later Jewish literature (certainly not with the frequency with which Jesus used it). But there can be little doubt that a Jew of Jesus' day would have

▲ Desmond Tutu, Archbishop of Cape Town, has become internationally known as someone who tries to bring Jesus' teaching about the kingdom of God to bear on the deep racial problems of his own country.

3. THREE CENTRAL EVENTS

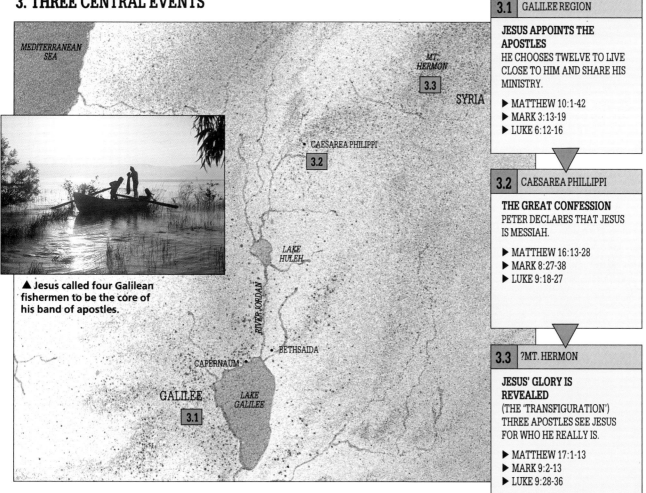

▲ Jesus called four Galilean fishermen to be the core of his band of apostles.

MEDITERRANEAN SEA

MT. HERMON

3.3

SYRIA

• CAESAREA PHILIPPI

3.2

LAKE HULEH

RIVER JORDAN

• BETHSAIDA

CAPERNAUM •

GALILEE

LAKE GALILEE

3.1

| **3.1** | GALILEE REGION |

JESUS APPOINTS THE APOSTLES
HE CHOOSES TWELVE TO LIVE CLOSE TO HIM AND SHARE HIS MINISTRY.

▶ MATTHEW 10:1-42
▶ MARK 3:13-19
▶ LUKE 6:12-16

| **3.2** | CAESAREA PHILLIPPI |

THE GREAT CONFESSION
PETER DECLARES THAT JESUS IS MESSIAH.

▶ MATTHEW 16:13-28
▶ MARK 8:27-38
▶ LUKE 9:18-27

| **3.3** | ?MT. HERMON |

JESUS' GLORY IS REVEALED
(THE 'TRANSFIGURATION')
THREE APOSTLES SEE JESUS FOR WHO HE REALLY IS.

▶ MATTHEW 17:1-13
▶ MARK 9:2-13
▶ LUKE 9:28-36

recognized it as picking up an important aspect both of his belief about God and of his hope for the future.

A prayer used regularly in the synagogue since pre-Christian times runs, 'May God make his kingship rule in your lifetime and in your days and in the lifetime of the whole house of Israel, speedily and soon.' When Jesus proclaimed, 'God's kingship has arrived', his Jewish hearers would have recognized a familiar note.

Jesus believed that God's kingship would be established through his ministry. But how? Such language would suggest different things to different Jewish hearers. Some would think of an ethical and spiritual reformation based on obedience to God's law, others of the military restoration of Israel to its former glory and political independence. And some would hope for a more comprehensive divine 'invasion', leading to a new heaven and a new earth.

But Jesus used the phrase 'God's kingship' so often, and in such a variety of ways, that any attempt to tie its meaning down to any one viewpoint will not do justice to his range of language. God's kingship, Jesus tells his hearers, is coming soon. It has already come upon you, is among you; you can enter it, or be shut out from it. It is preached, it is prayed for, it is to be sought, its mystery is revealed; it is seized, and suffers violence; it is taken away from some and given to others. It belongs to children and the childlike, to the poor in spirit and the persecuted; it will soon be seen to have come with power.

These form only a selection from the baffling range of expressions Jesus used about God's kingship. Sometimes he used parables to explain what God's kingship was like, but here too different subjects are touched on. Some parables spoke of the preaching and power of the gospel, others of people's response to it. Some considered the convert's experience or obligations as a disciple on earth, others the rewards and punishments beyond this life.

This means that we must not try to define God's kingship in terms of any particular situation or objective. It is a general term for all that God wants to accomplish, as it is focused in the words and deeds of Jesus. It is any situation where 'God reigns' and his will is done.

Now and not yet

New Testament scholars used to argue whether Jesus spoke of God's kingship as something still in the future or as the rule of God already present since he himself had brought it. We can now see that this is an inappropriate question. It assumes God's kingship refers to some particular time or situation. But that is not so.

We have seen in the Old Testament both that God *is* king, and yet the full exercise of his kingship remains to be completed. Jesus brought the fulfilment of that hope; now God's kingship was

▼ These Romanian Christians live and worship on the front line between the kingdom of God and the power of a state deeply opposed to spiritual values.

▲ Several of Jesus' parables describe the powerful growth of God's kingdom. A mustard seed is tiny, but when planted it grows into 'the largest of garden plants and becomes a tree'.

established, and people could begin to experience it in a new and final way. But even now there remained something to look forward to, and to pray for. That is why the Lord's Prayer contains both the assured statement, 'Yours is the kingship', and the prayer 'May your kingship come'.

Some of Jesus' parables speak of God's kingship gradually spreading in the world. Like yeast in dough, it needs time to take effect. It may appear now as small as a mustard seed, but that seed will grow into a striking shrub. No one can observe or hasten the process, but like the growth of a seed it takes its own course and the harvest will follow.

So Jesus' establishment of God's kingship must work itself out, as the preaching of the gospel extends its influence throughout the world. It is indeed already powerfully present, but its full effect will not be seen until all people everywhere acknowledge God as king.

Israel and the kingship of God

The Jews who heard Jesus preaching about God's kingship would have understood him first of all in nationalistic terms. Israel was the special people of God. And while God was indeed the king of all the earth, it was through his people Israel that they

expected his kingship to be exercised. There must be a special place for Israel. Jesus' disciples initially understood him in this way, and even after the resurrection they were still asking, 'Lord, are you at this time going to restore the kingship to Israel?'

But Jesus' vision of God's kingship was much broader than theirs. It is summed up in his praise for the Gentile centurion, whose faith he declared greater than any in Israel. 'I say to you that many will come from the east and the west, and will take their places at the feast with Abraham, Isaac and Jacob in the kingdom of heaven. But the sons of the kingdom will be thrown outside, into the darkness, where there will be weeping and gnashing of teeth.' Jesus said that when God's kingship is established the Jewish patriarchs would remain at the head of the table. But the guests would include many who were not from Israel, and those born to be subjects under God's kingship might find themselves outside, in the place they had thought reserved for the Gentiles.

Another parable depicts the official leaders of Israel as defaulting tenants of God's vineyard. It

PARABLES JESUS TOLD

▲ In Jesus' parable of the wise and foolish bridesmaids, everything hung on who had enough oil for their lamps.

▲ Just as the tiny mustard seed grows into a big plant, so the kingdom of God grows explosively.

▲ In the parable of the sower, some seed was 'choked by thorns'.

▲ Jesus said, 'There was a man who had two sons...'

	MATTHEW	MARK	LUKE
A LAMP UNDER A BUSHEL	5:14-15	4:21-22	8:16;11:33
HOUSES ON ROCK AND ON SAND	7:24-27		6:47-49
NEW CLOTH ON AN OLD GARMENT	9:16	2:21	5:36
NEW WINE IN OLD WINESKINS	9:17	2:22	5:37-38
THE SOWER	13:3-8	4:3-8	8:5-8
MUSTARD SEED	13:31-32	4:30-32	13:18-19
WHEAT AND TARES	13:24-30		
LEAVEN (YEAST)	13:33		13:20-21
HIDDEN TREASURE	13:44		
A PEARL OF GREAT VALUE	13:45-46		
A DRAG-NET	13:47-48		
LOST SHEEP	18:12-13		15:4-6
TWO DEBTORS (UNFORGIVING SERVANT)	18:23-34		
WORKERS IN THE VINEYARD	20:1-16		
TWO SONS	21:28-31		
WICKED TENANTS	21:33-41	12:1-9	20:9-16
AN INVITATION TO A WEDDING FEAST; A MAN WITHOUT A WEDDING-GARMENT	22:2-14		
THE FIG-TREE AS HERALD OF SUMMER	24:32-33	13:28-29	21:29-32
TEN 'BRIDESMAIDS'	25:1-13		
THE TALENTS (MATTHEW); THE POUNDS (LUKE)	25:14-30		19:12-27
SHEEP AND GOATS	25:31-36		
SEEDTIME TO HARVEST		4:26-29	
CREDITORS AND DEBTORS			7:41-43
THE GOOD SAMARITAN			10:30-37
A FRIEND IN NEED			11:5-8
A RICH FOOL			12:16-21
ALERT SERVANTS			12:35-40
A FAITHFUL STEWARD			12:42-48
A FIG-TREE WITHOUT FIGS			13:6-9
PLACES OF HONOUR AT THE WEDDING-FEAST			14:7-14
A GREAT BANQUET AND RELUCTANT GUESTS			14:16-24
COUNTING THE COST			14:28-33
A LOST COIN			15:8-10
THE PRODIGAL SON			15:11-32
DISHONEST STEWARD			16:1-8
A RICH MAN AND LAZARUS			16:19-31
A MASTER AND HIS SERVANT			17:7-10
A PERSISTENT WIDOW AND AN UNRIGHTEOUS JUDGE			18:2-5
A PHARISEE AND A TAX COLLECTOR			18:10-14

concludes: 'the kingdom of God will be taken away from you and given to a people who will produce its fruit'. This is followed by a picture of God's kingship as a great feast, and again the expected guests are replaced by those they would have despised. God's kingship, then, is not the special preserve of any favoured group; it is open to all who respond in faith to Jesus. It offers no place to those whose only claim on God is that they happened to be born into the right family.

The demands of God's kingship

In Jesus' parable of the vineyard, the new tenants are those who will 'produce its fruit'. The parable of the feast concludes with the sobering picture of one of the unexpected guests who is thrown out when he is found to be unsuitably dressed for the occasion. There are obligations for those who come under God's kingship.

Jesus pictured the response to God's kingship in terms of the man who sells all he has to acquire a hidden treasure. He spoke of a collector of pearls who sells his whole collection to gain the finest pearl of all. No other loyalty, not even the natural ties of the family, must be allowed to get in the way. 'Leave the dead to bury their own dead, but you go and

▲ In Jesus' story of the labourers in the vineyard, the tenants end up killing the owner's son. He taught that the coming of God's kingdom sometimes brings conflict.

▲ This ancient oil lamp reminds us of Jesus' story of the wise and foolish bridesmaids, some of whom ran out of oil for their lamps. We are to be ready when God's kingdom fully comes.

proclaim God's kingship... No one who puts his hand to the plough and looks back is fit for God's kingship'.

To be a subject of God is not a matter of a cosy sense of belonging, but of a radical demand which leaves no part of life unaffected. No aspect of our daily living falls outside God's concern; no relationship is outside the scope of his will. When God is king, his subjects are responsible only to him.

Jesus as king

Jesus proclaimed God as king. But underlying this proclamation, both then and now, is a growing awareness that Jesus himself is more than just the herald of God's kingship. It is through his work that that kingship is being established, and he is more than just one subject among others.

In Matthew's Gospel this idea becomes explicit in language about the 'kingship of the Son of Man'. The vision in the prophecy of Daniel of 'one like a son of man' to whom universal and everlasting kingship would be given lies behind Jesus' habit of referring to himself as 'the Son of man'. So he can speak of a future time when the Son of man will 'come in his kingship' and weed out all evil from his realm, when he will 'sit on his glorious throne' and all nations will be gathered before him for judgment.

So Jesus is not just the 'king of the Jews', the one who comes to lead God's people as their Messiah. He is the universal King who decrees judgment and blessing in the world to come. The kingship of God finds its fulfilment in the kingship of the Son of man.

▲ In the kingdom of God everyone belongs. Jesus did the unthinkable when he touched lepers. And Christians are still in the forefront of leprosy work.

3.2

THE CALL TO FOLLOW

Disciples were common in the world of Jesus' day. The word disciple means learner or student, and there were three ways in which people commonly thought of them. Many regarded themselves as disciples of Moses because they studied and followed his teaching. There were also popular living teachers and interpreters of Moses' law whose lectures could be attended by those who could afford it. These might be known as disciples of that rabbi if they accepted and professed his teaching and way of life. In addition, there were those who entered into a formal relationship with a rabbi to be his full-time student-trainees. These entered into a kind of apprenticeship which involved living with the rabbi and following him around wherever he went. In effect they became his servants for the term of their training, with the one exception that no disciple was required to take off his rabbi's sandals or wash his feet. This would have reduced him all the way to the level of a slave.

Jesus' disciples

Jesus was recognized as a disciple-gatherer from the very beginning of his ministry, when he was in Judea with John the Baptist. John and Jesus worked alongside each other at the Jordan River, calling the people to return to God, and baptizing those who were willing. It was not long before Jesus was baptizing more people than John, and although Jesus did not ask these people to believe in him, they were seen by the authorities as his disciples because they were responding to his teaching. Jesus also had a growing band of helpers in this period of his ministry who no doubt considered themselves as his special disciples. However, they must have come and gone as the demands of their families and their work allowed, because when Jesus came to Galilee to begin his real life's work he found some of the

▼ The carved relief on this sarcophagus shows Peter and Paul being taken off to martyrdom in Rome. Jesus, depicted in the centre, had warned that his followers might receive the same treatment as he did.

disciples who had been with him in Judea back at their fishing.

The new ministry in Galilee was quite different to what had gone before. There was no more baptizing, no more preparing people for the arrival of the Messiah. Instead Jesus made the dramatic announcement that the kingdom of God was at hand, and he called people to repent, believe and enter in. Great crowds flocked to hear him, and wherever people received his message and welcomed him he appears to have accepted that they should see themselves as his disciples.

One of the things that distinguished Jesus and John the Baptist from the traditional rabbis was that they preached openly to the masses, without even the control and respectability of a school-house. In this they more resembled the preachers of revolutionary violence who had been active in the previous generation, which is one reason they were held in suspicion by the authorities.

But the real uniqueness in Jesus' ministry in Galilee was that he never tried to organize or identify or isolate those who believed in him from those who did not. He saw it as his task to invite all Israel into God's kingdom; the business of separation was not his interest at that point. Consequently it was the people themselves who decided whether they were his disciples, and people were constantly moving in and out as Jesus' words and actions drew them or offended them.

The twelve

From among the many who listened to him Jesus still needed a group of special helpers. Early in the Galilean period he called certain individuals to a closer and more constant service and Mark informs us simply that Jesus approached two pairs of brothers, Peter and Andrew and James and John, when they were at work in their fishing partnership. He commanded them, 'Come and follow me, and I will make you catch people.' They left everything and followed him, obviously into a full-time work. Matthew the tax-collector was called in similar fashion from his tax-office, and later, as the crowds were growing larger, Jesus spent a whole night in prayer and then chose others to complete the group of twelve. He called the twelve 'apostles', which means 'commissioned agents'. Their task was 'to be with him and to be sent out to preach and to heal'. They were apprentices, training to go out and cast their nets for a human catch. Jesus had come to win a kingdom for himself and its subjects had now to be attracted and won.

Advocate of the Young

No generation has ever faced a world that appears more discouraging, hopeless and dissatisfying than today's young people. They see themselves inheriting a legacy of overwhelming problems that they did not create—high national debts, ecological crises, economic disparity, famine, unemployment, warfare... And so they feel disillusioned with a careless and selfish adult generation. Today's young people are the first group of human beings who have never known a single day free from the threat of nuclear holocaust. Many wonder if they will live long enough to die a natural death.

They are often disillusioned, too, with the effects of the scientific and technological revolution, which can be impersonal and dehumanizing. Science and technology have failed as saviours of humanity and the environment, and have not offered a comprehensive explanation of human reality. This dissatisfaction can lead to exploring alternative spiritual experiences through various occult practices, experimenting with psychic powers and oriental mysticism. Many pop songs affirm the empty frustration and lonely yearning for significance that this young generation feels.

It is not surprising, then, that modern young people have a strong sense of alienation and futility. This has forced them to grope for significance and affirmation from the only apparent source within their world: their friends. Friendship with peers is the strongest influence and highest source of enjoyment in their lives. Involvement in the major institutions of society—school, government, church—has been abandoned in favour of the opportunity to experience the warmth of belonging and peer-group intimacy.

It is easy to understand why young people are delighted when they discover that the Jesus of the New Testament is willing to become their personal friend and advocate. To realize that Jesus Christ, the God of the universe, is in control of human history

Children from Africa and Korea, teenagers from Britain – young people in today's world face particular pressures. The call to follow Jesus comes to the young as powerfully as to their elders.

gives reassurance and a new optimism that peace and justice will some day prevail in a world that appears completely awry. To discover that Jesus offers the personal interest and affirmation of a listening friend in an impersonal world provides a welcome relief from the many substitute and unfulfilling pursuits.

Unfortunately, this message of emancipation is not always communicated clearly. In previous generations young people perceived and responded to Jesus as he was taught by the religious tradition of their own culture. A person's initial religious beliefs usually became permanent convictions through the influence of parents and society. But now the revolutionizing impact of technology, particularly in communication and transport, has changed all this. Information about other ways of thought is rapidly available and most societies have anyway become cultural mosaics. So today's young people have enhanced understanding of

other religious traditions. Many countries around the world have adopted the Western emphasis on religious tolerance, so that in Singapore, for example, all major religions are now taught within the public school system. So it has become easy to accept Jesus as one of many gods to appease in order to obtain health and wealth. This growing global pluralism has had a twofold effect: in previously closed countries, people have been introduced to Jesus, while in countries formerly thought of as Christian he has simply become one of many possible options.

In North America, with the deliberate separation of church and state, most young people do not attend church. They think of Jesus Christ as some ancient and remote religious figure occasionally mentioned on television or in movies. Many Western young people no longer know the real story of Christmas and Easter. Despite the fact that a high percentage of young people still indicate that they believe in God—90 per

cent according to a recent Canadian survey— comparatively few attend church. The curious few who do investigate church meet a bewildering proliferation of denominations; many rate church as dull and irrelevant.

So despite the many young people who have found the friendship of Jesus, the majority still miss out on the good news. Perhaps the failure is more than one of communication. Don Posterski has written, 'Today's teenagers need advocates...adults who will champion their cause.' Many young people will only be drawn to consider Jesus' invitation to friendship when they meet adults who give them living pictures of Jesus the advocate.

Ignatius and the Exercises

Ignatius of Loyola (1491–1556), a Spaniard, was the founder of the Society of Jesus (the Jesuits), which played an important part in the Catholic Reformation and is still highly active today. Ignatius first followed a military career, but he determined to become a soldier of Christ. He went into retreat at Manresa (1522–23), and his meditations and mystical experiences at that time formed the basis for his *Spiritual Exercises*, which were complete by 1535. They became the major instrument in forming Jesuit spirituality. In later times many other Christians besides the Jesuits have also found them valuable.

The *Exercises* provide instructions for a month of intensive, supervised retreat. The main aim is to discover and commit oneself to God's particular will for one's life, or to renew such a commitment. The method consists in a series of meditations leading into prayer. Two fundamental meditations are on the Kingdom of Christ and the Two Standards. In these the participant receives the call of Christ the King to enlist in his service and to fight against Satan. Jesus is seen to be engaged in a battle against evil which is not yet finished. So he wants his loyal friends and servants to fight with him now.

They learn how to do so by meditating on the life and sufferings of Jesus, in which he fought against Satan and triumphed over him through the cross. Meditations on 'the mysteries of the life of Christ' occupy a large part of the *Exercises*. Ignatius here follows the method of meditation on Gospel stories which had been developed in the late middle ages. Participants are to imagine each episode in the life of Jesus with all possible vividness and concreteness, as though they were present. They should visualize the place and the people, listen in on the conversation, and try to have the right emotional and moral responses to what is going on. In this way they allow themselves to be affected by the life of Jesus and begin to order their own lives under its influence.

By involving themselves in the life of Jesus in this way the participants are not only remembering the past history of Jesus. They are also meeting the living Christ. Each meditation therefore ends with a 'colloquy' (conversation), sometimes with God or with the Virgin Mary, but most often with Christ—'as one friend speaks to another, or as a servant speaks to his master'. The participants talk over with Jesus the matters affecting their own lives which have arisen from their meditation on the life of Christ.

Through the *Exercises* the participants commit themselves to imitating Christ, which means following him in his way of fighting for his kingdom by humility and suffering. But this also means fighting *with* the living Christ as his

▼ **These Jesuit missionaries in seventeenth-century Japan paid the ultimate price. Every Christian century has had its martyrs.**

intimate companion in battle: 'He who wants to be my companion has to labour with me, so that, following me in suffering, he may also follow me into glory.' So Ignatius, by means of his military metaphor, turns the traditional themes of the imitation of Christ and the friendship of Christ strongly in the direction of active *service* for Christ in the world.

The spirituality of the *Exercises* is primarily one of service through love. The participants, contemplating the crucified Christ, realize their own sinfulness and the extent of Jesus' love for them. Their response is always to ask, 'What *more* can I do for Christ?'

▶ **Ignatius Loyola, seen in a painting by Rubens, founded the Order of Jesuits.**

▲ Disciples are called to make other disciples. This group of Christian 'wandering minstrels' use street drama to invite people to follow Jesus.

When Jesus travelled from town to town announcing the arrival of God's kingdom he was accompanied by the twelve and other disciples who included several women who cared for the group out of their private means. (We see this in Luke chapter 8 verses 1 to 3.) There were to be two developments from this pattern:

■ **Something less than a year after his arrival in Galilee Jesus split the twelve into six pairs,** invested them with his own authority to heal and cast out evil spirits, then sent them out into all the towns and villages to carry the news that the kingdom of God was arriving. They were to do exactly what he was doing, but over a larger area.

■ **As his ministry in Galilee came to a close he called and commissioned seventy-two others and sent them ahead of him into Judea to do the same task.** The Gospels do not tell us what became of this group after their task was done. They probably returned to their homes in Galilee and were no doubt among the many hundreds to whom Jesus appeared there alive after his resurrection.

The twelve and their women supporters remained a close-knit group around Jesus until the last days. But on his arrest even the twelve deserted him. Some of the women stayed by the cross while he was dying, and these women were the first witnesses of his resurrection. Then came six weeks during which the disciples saw him frequently, and he took up teaching them again in readiness for their new task. On the day of Pentecost, endowed with the supernatural power of the Holy Spirit, they began the work for which Jesus had trained them, netting 3,000 new believers in their first catch!

Answering the call

Not all disciples were called in the way Jesus called the twelve. Many were attracted by his teaching and followed him of their own accord. Some, however, he confronted with a specific command to leave what they were doing and follow him. These people had either to obey or disobey; there was no third option.

Matthew simply left his place at the tax-office and went off to be with Jesus; in so doing he entered the kingdom of God. A rich nobleman was commanded to sell his possessions and come and follow Jesus, but he refused. Jesus made it clear that in refusing him this man was refusing God's kingdom.

The authoritative way in which Jesus dealt with people was virtually without parallel; the only resemblance to it was the way in which in the Old Testament God had from time to time called certain people to be his prophets. It was this assumption of authority—in teaching, exorcism, forgiving, healing, and now calling people to himself—that made people ask, 'Who is this man?' In the end it made the disciples realize that he could only be the Messiah, and ultimately God himself, become a man.

The Gospel-writers relate these particular episodes of Jesus calling people to follow him as models of what discipleship entailed in their own day. The same happens in our day. For with the resurrection and the coming of the Holy Spirit it is now possible for all Christians to be with Jesus constantly. When they hear the gospel they receive it as his authoritative call to come to him and to follow him with an absolute commitment throughout the whole of their lives. By studying his word, the Bible, they can hear and learn his teaching, observe and imitate his life, and understand and join his work and mission.

The disciples, the kingdom and the cross

When people came to him and followed him Jesus regarded them as already being in the kingdom of

God. Whenever people joined him he celebrated. He was criticized for not being more serious about his religion, but he answered that when a wedding feast was in progress it was unthinkable to be solemn and fasting. The wedding feast he spoke of was the coming of God to dwell with his people. When people came to him or when he came to people it was the same as them being reunited with God. When people are reconciled with God, their King, the kingdom of God becomes a reality.

Thus the call to follow Jesus was and is a tremendous privilege. When a rich young ruler refused to abandon his wealth and follow Jesus, he turned his back on a wonderful opportunity and walked away from the kingdom he had come seeking. When Jesus invited himself to the home of Zacchaeus, that tax-collector was so overwhelmed at his generosity and so conscious of the privilege that he gave away half his possessions. (The story is an instructive example; see Luke chapter 19 verses 1 to 10). Many people today regard Jesus' call to follow as a terrible threat; but others grasp it as the most marvellous gift.

Jesus' call was absolute and exclusive. It was all or nothing and no half-heartedness was possible. One man asked Jesus if he could bury his father before he followed him. Jesus told him to leave the dead to bury their own dead; his task was to proclaim the kingdom of God. Someone else wanted to go and say goodbye to his family, but Jesus said no; there could be no looking back for those who took up God's work. When he was on his way to Jerusalem knowing that the cross awaited him there, he warned the enthusiastic crowds that unless they took up their own crosses and followed him they could not be his disciples. His obedience

was leading him to death, and unless they were prepared for the same commitment they should not trouble themselves any further about being his followers. He urged them to count the cost before they got too involved because following him to the end might mean death.

Little has changed since in this respect. Wherever Jesus and his cause is, there the true follower must be, and as then so now, his cause is often unpopular. In 1937 a German Christian, Dietrich Bonhoeffer, wrote: 'When Christ calls a man he bids him come and die.' In 1945 he was hanged by the Nazis for his opposition to Hitler. The call to follow was and is an unlimited and unqualified call. Jesus told his disciples to pray 'lead us not into temptation', which means, 'do not let us be tested to the limits'. This means we are not meant to be tested to the extreme every day. Nevertheless there come times when everything must be put on the line, as happened for Jesus.

But as well as the testing of exceptional circumstances, every day Christians find themselves in situations where their own desires and fears dictate one thing and Jesus' word commands another. Every day there are little deaths to be died and no Christian knows when God might call on her or him to go all the way. Nevertheless, following Jesus with such commitment, even when it leads to death, does not end in death. Beyond death lies resurrection. Even the 'little deaths' of self-denial lead to 'resurrection' experiences here and now, while giving way to fears and evil desires leads us into deeper darkness. It is Jesus' solemn promise to guard and protect all who follow him and 'raise them up on the last day'.

3.3

REPENT AND BELIEVE

If Jesus was not just an ordinary man but the one sent by God as his 'special agent' to put things right in the world, how should we react to him? Jesus chose the words 'repent' and 'believe' to describe the way he hoped that people would respond to him and to God.

The central core of Jesus' message is summed up at the beginning of Mark's Gospel in three simple sentences: 'The time has come, the kingdom of God is near, *repent* and *believe* the good news!'

Jesus was saying, 'The time which the Jewish prophets dreamed about has come at last! God has begun to do something very significant to establish, or re-establish, his authority in the world. This is the good news I have come to announce, and it is through me that it is all going to happen. If you believe this you must be prepared to change your minds and look at life in a completely different way from now on, or "repent".'

For the first disciples of Jesus, therefore, 'believing' meant much more than believing in the existence of God. It meant believing that Jesus had been sent into the world to establish the kingdom of God and trusting him as God's representative on earth. 'Repenting' meant more than feeling sorry or guilty about wrong things done in the past. It meant accepting a complete change of world-view and of lifestyle. And it is exactly the same today: repentance and faith go together like two sides of a coin, one total response to the challenge of Jesus.

'What shall we do?' was the question put to John the Baptist while he was preparing the way for the coming of Jesus. He gave some very specific examples of what repentance and faith in Jesus would mean in daily life: 'The man with two tunics should share with him who

has none, and the one who has food should do the same.' When tax collectors asked what they should do, he replied: 'Don't collect any more than you are required to.' And to soldiers he said: 'Don't extort money and don't accuse people falsely—be content with your pay.'

As a sign of their willingness to repent and believe, many people were baptized by John in the River Jordan. As they went into the water, they confessed the things in their lives which they realized had to be put right. (We see this in Luke 3:1–18.)

Living pictures of repentance and faith

What is involved from the human side in repentance and faith? The well-known parable of the Prodigal Son told by Jesus gives a clear picture. In this story the younger son insults his father deeply by demanding his inheritance while his father is still alive, and then goes off 'into a far country'. When he has spent all his money and lost all his friends, he is reduced to the humiliating task of feeding pigs. At this point, we are told, 'he came to his senses and said, "All my father's hired workers have more than they can eat, and here am I about to starve! I will get up and go to my father and say, 'Father, I have sinned against God and against you. . .'"' When he does return home, his father runs out to meet him and welcomes him. The parable presents a powerful picture of how God, instead of punishing us in the way that we really

▶ People can be called to repent and believe in many ways. These visitors to London have been approached by a street evangelist.

deserve, forgives us and welcomes us into his family when we turn to him in repentance and faith. (Read the story in Luke 15:11–32.)

But God also has his part. Two other parables, which Luke sets alongside the Prodigal Son story, give some idea of what God's role is. In the first, a shepherd leaves his ninety-nine sheep safe in the fold, and goes out to look for one lost sheep until he brings it back joyfully on his shoulders. In the second, a woman sweeps her whole house to find one of the ten valuable silver coins which were part of her dowry. When she eventually finds it, she invites her neighbours to celebrate with her. In these two parables Jesus speaks about a God who takes the initiative in winning our love and is overjoyed when we turn to him in repentance and faith: 'I tell you, there will be more joy in heaven over one sinner who repents than over ninety-nine respectable people who do not need to repent.'

As well as these illustrations in the parables, the Gospels record many examples of people who were changed when they came under the influence of Jesus. Zacchaeus, for example, was a dishonest tax collector. When he met Jesus and began to believe in him, he was determined to change his ways: 'Look, Lord! Here and now I give half my possessions to the poor, and if I have cheated anyone out of anything, I will pay back four times the amount'.

A prostitute anointed the feet of Jesus at a dinner party as her way of showing gratitude and devotion to Jesus for the change he had brought about in her life. The religious leaders criticized Jesus for allowing an immoral woman to be so demonstrative towards him. But his answer was, 'I tell you. . .the great love she has shown proves that her many sins have been forgiven.'

A middle-aged woman who had been ill for many years had such confidence in Jesus that she believed she would be healed if only she could touch him, even while he was surrounded by a crowd of people. When she did so and was healed, Jesus commended her faith: 'Daughter, your faith has healed you.'

An officer in the Roman army had the same kind of faith to believe that Jesus could heal his sick servant. He sent a message to Jesus saying there was no need to come to his house: 'Just give the order, and my servant will get well.'

Not everyone, however, had such a strong and clear faith. Once when Jesus said, 'Everything is possible for the person who has faith', a father who had brought his son to be healed felt very inadequate. All he could say was, 'I do have faith, but not enough. Help me to have more!' (Mark 9:23–24 tells the story.) In spite of the weakness of his faith, his son was healed.

It is important to notice at the same time that the

▲ Mass rallies, such as this Toronto meeting addressed by Billy Graham, leave people in no doubt that the message of Jesus requires a response.

▲ The Parthenon looks down on Athens, where Paul said to the worshippers of an unknown deity: 'Now God calls people everywhere to repent.'

Gospels are not 'success stories' of vast numbers of people believing in Jesus. In fact they give many examples of people who did *not* believe. One rich young man could not take the step because he was not prepared to give Jesus priority over his wealth. Others who were invited to become followers of Jesus decided that loyalty to their family or their work made it impossible to commit themselves to following him. And many of the religious leaders were more concerned about their reputation with their colleagues than about their relationship with God.

Why believe?

In the twentieth century people need to know reasons why they should believe. In the first century it was no different. John's Gospel uses the word 'believe' ninety times, and gives several case studies of people who believed, and of others who did not believe in Jesus. After Jesus' conversation with a woman from a village in Samaria, for example, we are told that people in the village believed in Jesus 'because of his words'. The way he taught about God and the claims he made about himself were enough to convince them.

For others, however, it was the combination of his teaching and his miracles which led them to believe in him. Jesus worked many miracles—turning water into wine, feeding the 5,000 with five loaves and two fish, healing a man who had been blind from birth, raising Lazarus from the dead. These were not acts of magic to impress simple people. They were miracles, which made people wonder. 'Healing, multiplying food and raising the dead are surely things that only God can do. So if Jesus is doing things that only God can do, he must have a very special relationship with God.'

But the greatest miracle of all was the resurrection. Seeing Jesus' grave clothes in the empty tomb convinced the apostle John that Jesus had been raised from death. Doubting Thomas, however, was not prepared to believe the reports he heard from the other disciples, but demanded evidence that he could see for himself: 'Unless I see the marks in his hands and put my finger where the nails were, and put my hand into his side, I will not believe it.' When Thomas did later see the risen Jesus for himself, he expressed his complete surrender and commitment to him: 'My Lord and my God!' (Read the story in John chapter 20: verses 25 to 28.)

John goes on to explain that he wrote his Gospel with special emphasis on Jesus' miracles in order to

▲ At Ostia Antica a road called the Decumanus Maximus carried traffic to Rome's seaport. The system of Roman roads made it possible for early Christian preachers to travel throughout the empire.

help his readers come to the same faith in Jesus: 'Jesus did many other miraculous signs in the presence of his disciples, which are not recorded in this book. But these are written that you may believe that Jesus is the Christ, the Son of God, and that by believing you may have life in his name.'

John sums up the significance of faith in Jesus in this well-known verse which many regard as one of the best and most complete summaries of the Christian gospel: 'God so loved the world that he gave his one and only Son, that whoever believes in him shall not perish but have eternal life'.

3.4

CONVERSION AND NEW BIRTH

We convert dollars into sterling, or gallons into litres; and builders convert a barn into a cottage. In these cases 'conversion' means turning an object into something completely different. The literal meaning of the word, however, is simply 'turning'. This is why the word is also used to describe any major change of belief (conversion to a different religion, for example, or to a different ideology), or a change of practice ('I've been converted from a meat-eater to a vegetarian'). When used in a Christian context, 'conversion' refers to the complete reorientation of people's lives which takes place when they turn to Jesus and begin to trust him as the final revelation of God.

If the word 'conversion' focuses attention on *our* part in turning to God, 'new birth' is an expression which draws attention to *God's* part in the whole process. When people turn to Jesus and become Christians, they feel that they are making the decision. But when they look back on what has happened, they begin to realize that God has been at work in bringing them to faith. The idea of 'new birth', therefore, expresses the conviction that God has taken the initiative in bringing them into his family. Just as a baby does not do anything to bring itself into the world, so in the same way Christians feel that they have contributed little or nothing to the radical change that has taken place in them.

Our part: conversion

If our lives are set in a certain direction, listening to the message of Jesus will involve a complete reorientation of our lives. From now on Jesus becomes our focus, and our minds are set on finding out what God wants us to do and how he wants us to live.

Jesus referred to this process of turning round: 'I tell you this: unless you *turn round* and become like children, you will never enter the kingdom of heaven.' Entering the kingdom of God and becoming a Christian involves a drastic turn around in our attitudes to ourselves, to others and to God. The whole of our personality is involved in this turning—our mind, our will and our emotions. And such a conversion comes about through repentance (a complete change of mind and heart and turning away from wrong) and faith (believing the good news about Jesus and trusting him).

It may take a long time for someone to believe in

True Devotion

The search for reality has always been a deeply-rooted longing of the human heart. Many have sought it through long prayers, meditation and self-denial. Sashi, a Hindu from Mauritius, was born into a Brahmin family. He prayed to the gods and goddesses from early childhood.

'I was told that spiritual progress depended on intense *bhakti* (devotion). I used to pray fervently, hoping that the gods would answer my prayers. Years later, I read the story of Sri Ramakrishna who worshipped the image of goddess Kali so intensely that it became alive and talked with him. This convinced me

that real *bhakti* could only happen when the devotee could communicate with a living God. The worship of lifeless images became like children playing with a toy. I continued to practise intense yoga, meditation and strict discipline, but it was the simple prayer of a Christian woman from Edinburgh that finally arrested me. As she prayed, I felt there was a presence in the room and an extra-ordinary sense of peace.'

The Child in the Midst

George MacDonald was a great Victorian fantasy writer, to whom C.S.Lewis has acknowledged a deep debt. He had eleven children of his own, and often wrote for children. He was struck by the occasion when Jesus wanted to challenge those who misunderstood the kingdom of God. Jesus set a child in the middle of them, and said, 'Unless you turn and become like children, you will not enter the kingdom of God.' MacDonald preached about this event:

'God is represented in Jesus, for God is like Jesus: Jesus is represented in the child, for Jesus is like the child. God is therefore childlike. In the true vision of this fact lies the receiving of God in the child. . . Our Lord became flesh, but was already man. He took on the form of man. In the same way, he could never have been a child if he had ever ceased to be a child. Childhood belongs to the divine nature.'

◀▲ When a dispute arose over who would be great in God's kingdom, Jesus used a child as a living example: 'Unless you turn and become like little children, you will never enter the kingdom.' What is it about children that makes them models for entering the kingdom?

Jesus fully. Probably this was the case for many of Jesus' first disciples. But sometimes there is a sudden change of direction. Paul the apostle is a vivid example of someone dramatically changed by a spiritual encounter with Jesus even after he had died and risen again. It is worth reading the story in Acts chapter 9.

God's part: new birth

When Christians look back on the way they came to faith, they can remember the people who helped them and the things that made them change their minds. They cannot forget how they worked through their doubts and questions, and how they made the decision that changed the direction of their lives. Before this process started, it was as if

God did not exist for them—or, if he did, had little or no effect on their lives. So what is there to explain the radical change that has taken place?

The phrase 'new birth' comes from a remarkable conversation Jesus had with Nicodemus, a religious leader. (Read the story in John chapter 3.) It is simply one way of expressing that it is God who takes the initiative when people become Christians. It is like being born all over again—but this time in a spiritual rather than a physical way. There is no change in the personality, but a Christian begins a new kind of life, living with a power given by God's Spirit. And just as every baby is born into a family, so every new Christian becomes a member of the family of God, the church.

The two sides of the process—conversion and

A child is baptized, and so are adults – in a river near Brest Litovsk in the Soviet Union; in the sea on Samoa. Baptism pictures cleansing and new life in Christ.

Jesus at the Frontier

John Smith has been described as the most unusual preacher in the world. In the 1970s, he became an apostle to Australia's outcasts. John never stops observing, watching people and movements; no day is ever dull.

'Every newspaper, every song makes me think, laugh or cry. Jesus did that all the time. He was asked a question and noticed a local fig tree growing nearby, so he used that image.'

John believes in the importance of thoughtful Christianity, of a faith built on strong foundations: 'The gospel liberated me. It gave me a reason to think, a reason to be, a reason even to go through pain in order to find the reason behind things. I am thrilled with that, every work of art I see, every film I watch, I find myself more filled with a sense of wonder and delight of the meaning of life. . . . If one is a lover of one's fellow human beings, then the pains and struggles of the great minds of the Universe are of enormous importance.'

new birth—are well expressed in baptism. Those who are baptized as adults are publicly confessing their new faith and their rejection of all that is evil. The water illustrates how God washes away their sin and forgives all that has been wrong in their lives; it is like drowning and then coming back to life. When the children of Christian parents are baptized as babies, they obviously cannot express their own faith. The whole ceremony for them, therefore, dramatizes even more clearly that it is God who is responsible for all that is involved in becoming new Christians.

Since everyone who believes in Jesus experiences new birth, it is unfortunate that the expression 'born-again' has come to be attached to Christians who have experienced a particular kind of conversion or belong to a particular group within the church. Even if Christians experience a very gradual conversion, they are, in the language of the New Testament, 'born-again'. And even if they have been brought up in a Christian family and have never known a time when they did not believe, they have experienced 'new birth'. What matters is not the manner of conversion but the reality of being 'turned towards God' and the promise of God to give new life.

3.5

JESUS THE LIBERATOR

The air must have been electric. Jesus had just read to his townmates at Nazareth a passage from Isaiah setting forth the task of the long-hoped-for Messiah:

The Spirit of the Lord is upon me, because he has anointed me to preach good news to the poor. He has sent me to proclaim release to the captives and recovering of sight to the blind, to set at liberty those who are oppressed, to proclaim the acceptable year of the Lord.

With the eyes of all fixed on him, Jesus made the stunning announcement: 'Today this scripture has been fulfilled in your hearing.'

As we read the story in Luke chapter 4, we find that wonder and incredulity broke loose: 'Is not this Joseph's son?' The carpenter's boy who played around and kicked the dust with the rest of the village kids proclaimed himself to be the fulfilment of Israel's hope of liberation from the bootheels of colonial Rome and the restoration of the kingdom to the ruined house of David. They were shocked by the incongruity between the humble and gentle artisan before them and the lordly political Messiah they had been waiting for.

The response of the people of Nazareth is not unlike our own sense of ambiguity about Jesus. What kind of liberator is he? Some see him as a rather detached, super-spiritual figure whose kingdom is certainly not of this world, but some radicals have appropriated him as a patron saint for revolutionary struggles. In many parts of the Third World today, liberation movements find force in an alliance with church elements who see in Jesus a stalwart for the poor and oppressed.

What are we to make of this tension between Jesus as a harmless idealist fit to be martyred and Jesus the subversive?

The Gospels certainly show us that Jesus did not suit Israel's expectations of a Messiah, since they looked more for a political saviour coming in a blaze of fire and glory than for a suffering servant. And yet his own career and self-understanding were marked by a focused concern for the poor and marginalized and a consciousness that in the end he had authority over rulers and powers.

The great reversal

As soon as Jesus' birth was announced, Mary foresaw that his coming would mean a great reversal. The song she sang when she visited Elizabeth is full of it: putting down the mighty from their thrones and exalting those of low degree, filling the hungry with good things and sending the rich away empty. Jesus on Palm Sunday, riding a lowly ass into the gates of Jerusalem to shouts of 'Hosanna in the highest!' dramatizes to us the upside-down nature of the kingdom he has come to usher in, a strangely unorthodox order in which the first is last and the poor and dregs of society find themselves as guests at the messianic feast. It is a kingdom where the lost sheep is infinitely valuable, and where there is more joy over one sinner who repents than over ninety-nine righteous who need no repentance.

To redress the plight of the poor is central to Jesus' vision of what he had come for. In his brief career he spent much time among them, healing the sick and preaching the good news of hope: 'Blessed are you poor, for yours is the kingdom of God.

Blessed are you that hunger now, for you shall be satisfied. Blessed are you that weep now, for you shall laugh.' While he refused to crank out feeding miracles as if he were primarily engaged in social welfare, he was still moved to feed the hungry crowds whenever there was need.

In a similar way, Jesus rubbed elbows and went about eating and drinking with 'tax-collectors and sinners', people who were on the wrong side of the politics and morals of that time. He braved the sneers of the crowd in going in as house guest of Zacchaeus, a notorious tax agent of the hated colonizing empire. He refused to satisfy the self-righteous blood thirst of a mob about to stone a woman caught in adultery by pointedly raising the bleak fact of universal guilt: 'Let him who is without sin cast the first stone.'

Such decisive solidarity with the outcast of society is also seen in Jesus' dealings with women, as the special feature shows.

In both his life and teaching, Jesus showed a clear bias towards the small people who are swept to the sidelines, oppressed and rendered helpless by

▲ **A Bedouin woman and her children beg for money in Jerusalem. The gospel of**

Jesus speaks of liberation from all forms of oppression – economic as well as spiritual.

structural imbalances in society. While his work of forgiveness was for all, he saw that his messianic calling involved shifting the balance of justice and power in human life.

The reluctant subversive

One reason some people were attracted to Jesus lay in his political promise. Some who attached themselves to him had sympathies with the 'zealot option', a violent overthrow of Roman rule and a return to a more pristine allegiance to Israel's God and his law. 'We had hoped that he was the one to redeem Israel', was the sad and disappointed feeling

Overleaf **The slums of Glasgow's Gorbals in the 1940s were a hard place to grow up. The message of**

salvation in Jesus touches every aspect of our lives. His aim is to make us whole people.

of the disciples after the crisis of his death.

Yet at various points in his career Jesus very clearly dissociated himself from attempts to make him king and enlist him on the side of those who favoured armed resistance. He would withdraw to the hills whenever the crowds, impressed by the signs that he did, became unduly enthusiastic and combustible. In answer to Pilate's question, 'Are you the King of the Jews?', he denied its political connotations: 'My kingship is not of this world.'

How do we account for Jesus' being perceived as a threat to Caesar even while he consistently disclaimed political ambitions? What was it about the kingdom he brought in that laid him open to charges of sedition?

As we all know, Jesus once said 'Render to Caesar what is Caesar's and to God what is God's'. But if we want to understand what he meant we

◀ **Jesse Jackson's 84 and 88 presidential campaigns succeeded in mobilizing black and poor Americans. His theme was that those whom society has marginalized can make their voices heard. The idea that everyone counts is a deeply Christian one.**

▼ **Young people join in a protest against racial discrimination. The new society to which Jesus pointed treats all men and women as brothers and sisters in the same human family.**

▲ Orphans of the war in Kampuchea dig the foundations of their own orphanage, in a project devised by a Christian relief organization. The mission of Jesus reaches the poorest people on earth.

should look at how he actually lived. He was careful to be subject to human authority: paid the temple tax, obeyed his parents. But he was also conscious of operating under a higher power. He must go about his father's business, as he told his distraught and anxious parents. Driven by an inner sense of mission, he was impervious to external threat and serenely confident of control over his own life: 'No one takes it from me, but I lay it down of my own accord. I have power to lay it down, and I have power to take it again; this charge I have received from the Father.' God was the authority over every part of Jesus' life.

While clearly spiritual, God's kingdom is such that it undermines all despotic claims to human loyalty. When Pilate, provoked by Jesus' silence, parades his authority, 'You will not speak to me? Do you not know that I have power to release you, and power to crucify you?', Jesus replies, 'You would have no power over me unless it had been given you from above'. Following this lead, his own disciples, pressed by Jewish authorities to desist from preaching about him, displayed the same unflinching courage: 'We must obey God rather than men.'

Jesus' kingship is in truth 'not of this world', but it is exercised in the world and so encroaches on the once-absolute power of rulers. Jesus as 'the Messiah' may be dismissed by Pilate as a harmless crank out to give the Jewish priestly establishment a run for their money, but Jesus as 'king of the Jews' is a threat to imperial authority, a fact recognized with rare unanimity by all anxious parties, civil and religious. This was the focus of apprehension among the chief priests and pharisees huddled in council: 'What are we to do? For this man performs many signs. If we let him go on thus, everyone will believe in him, and the Romans will come and destroy both our holy place and our nation.' It was also the charge brought against him before the Roman governor: 'He stirs up the people,' shouted the priests. 'We have no king but Caesar.' The prospect of being damaged by insinuations of disloyalty to Caesar finally broke Pilate's hesitations, and undid his already wobbly sense of justice.

The lynching rabble spoke more truth than it knew with the insight that 'everyone who makes himself a king sets himself against Caesar'. Jesus' unambiguous acceptance of homage in his triumphal entry to Jerusalem signalled a challenge to the powers that be that here at last is 'the King who comes in the name of the Lord'. To owe allegiance to him would necessarily make a person less completely loyal to the Caesars.

A liberating spirit

'For freedom Christ has set us free,' wrote Paul. In Jesus, God's kingdom of freedom and righteousness has invaded human history and is bringing power to break every force and every institution which can hold us in captivity.

Today, wherever Jesus is preached and a community of people experiences solidarity in guilt and forgiveness, a new social ethic emerges where the weak, the outcast and the dispossessed take priority and find themselves at centre stage. Individual men and women and large historical movements equally derive inspiration from the lofty ideals and invincibility of spirit afforded by commitment to a King higher than Caesar. The sense that government has its limits and that the poor, the women and ethnic minorities should have equal access to the rewards and opportunities of the social system is but one of the benefits modern society derives from the presence of the kingdom of God. Jesus inaugurated it 2,000 years ago, and it is still changing the face of the earth.

3.6

BEING MADE WHOLE

A woman used to racial prejudice and the barriers of her sex, slinking along in the dead hours of the day to draw water from a well, finds herself in conversation with a surprisingly friendly male chauvinist Jew. He offers to make her drink deep, to quench the thirst of soul that has made her insatiably loose, groping about for a slippery satisfaction that has eluded her even after five husbands and a current live-in flame. Touched by the uncanny insight into her needs, she forgot her water jar and could not restrain herself from speaking to the people of her city, 'Come see a man who told me all that I ever did. Could this be the Messiah?'

A corrupt tax-collector is overwhelmed at finding himself host to a man who invites himself to his house in spite of social disapproval. Moved by the acceptance of someone whose presence both shames and softens the sharp practices of his past, he stands up from his table and declares, 'Behold, Lord, the half of my goods I give to the poor; and if I have defrauded anyone of anything, I restore it fourfold.'

What has come into the lives of these and many other people who tell stories of having met Jesus?

Jesus himself has his own word for it: 'Today salvation has come to this house,' he tells Zacchaeus the tax-collector. The twisted, obsessive thing that has gripped Zacchaeus' life and led him to a vicious and wearying round of money-grubbing and shady dealings has been broken. In its place is a conscience made tender and grateful by the experience of forgiving acceptance.

'Salvation' today to many people means getting on board a ship in the afterlife, an eternal security system that has little to do with the problems of our

▲ A young man with Down's Syndrome gets the beat going. Everyone, whatever their disability, has something to contribute to the rest of us. Being made whole involves both giving and receiving.

world and our daily struggle to keep body and soul alive in the face of scarcity and relentless assaults on integrity. But throughout the Bible we are told that 'being saved' is more than an abstract pardon that grants access to a world beyond this one. It is deliverance from all that hinders wholeness, a present reality that is transforming human life.

Images used to describe the total nature of this experience range from being 'born again', and passing from death to life, to entering a 'kingdom' and possessing a land. It is an internal, spiritual rebirth as well as a social and political belonging. It makes those who are in it heirs of this earth. In Luke chapter 4 verse 18 Jesus announces his

▶ **To be whole includes taking on board the teaching of Jesus. To study the Gospels and make them part of us is just as practical as any social action.**

The Power of the Powerless

In 1969, David Jenkins, then an academic but now Bishop of Durham, addressed a World Council of Churches consultation on Theology and Development:

'How seriously do we have to take Jesus Christ as a real embodiment in historical conditions of the presence and power of the kingdom of God? The presentation of the New Testament is that when God gets down to work on earth in a personal and definitive way, he exhibits his power through powerlessness. The forsaken and crucified man is believed to be the Christ of God. The New Testament is built on the conviction that Jesus is the way God works. The ultimate power which is capable of establishing the kingdom of God, is the love of God which exhibits its power as powerlessness.

'Although this is difficult to believe and even more difficult to live up to, as clearly it involves the Cross from the beginning of history to its end, it might be the only hope of establishing a kingdom of love in which all people might be really fulfilled. Power as we know it always involves counter-action and counter-effects. Oppression forces either despair or revolt. Revolution produces counter-revolution. In personal terms, only the soft answer turns away wrath (sometimes). Wrath creates new waves of resentment.

'If we are ever to get to a state of equilibrium in which all are fulfilled in each other and each can enjoy all (a creative kingdom of love), then there must be a power at work which will absorb powerful power rather than counter power with power. Christians believe that there is such a power, the power of God embodied in Jesus Christ. The question remains how does this affect our attitudes to the 'powerful' sort of power i.e. power as the world and its institutions, including the churches, know and practise it?'

The Gospel For All Races

In a meeting in Brixton, south London, in 1988, evangelist Billy Graham addressed a cosmopolitan crowd of 1,300 people. He spoke with the specific intention of making himself understood to black citizens living in the area. Until recently, they have remained unreached in Britain by crusades of his kind. He said, 'Jesus came from a part of the world that touches Europe, Africa and Asia, and his message is for the whole world.' Having preached an identical sermon to a primitive tribe and to a student audience in Oxford, and seeing the response of people in both groups recognizing the saving power of Jesus, Graham believes he has evidence that 'the gospel's message is universal'.

No Chauvinist

Jesus was born into a society with a low and restricted view of women. He did not campaign for women's rights, but he did treat women with a challenging graciousness which was and still is in the truest sense liberating. In the words of Dorothy Sayers:

'Jesus was a prophet and a teacher who never nagged at women, never flattered or coaxed or patronized. He never made jokes about them. He never mapped out their sphere for them, never urged them to be feminine or jeered at them for being female. He had no axe to grind, and no uneasy male dignity to defend. He took them as he found them and was completely unselfconscious.

'There is no act, no sermon, no parable in the whole gospel that borrows its pungency from female perversity. No one could possibly guess from the words and deeds of Jesus that there was anything "funny" about a woman's nature.'

A Jew finds Jesus

Michele Guinness, in her book, *Child of the Covenant*, describes how her own family as Jews perceived Jesus. They visualized him as a cold, lifeless statue with glazed eyes and a pitiful expression. Jesus was seen as the gentile god; an idol created by the church to satisfy the imaginations of those poor Christians who could not believe in anything invisible. In sharp contrast, and against all odds, Michele wanted to hear more about the real Jesus. As she weighed up the evidence for herself, she concluded that Jesus was unique and one of the most dynamic people who had ever lived.

As she read about him for the first time in John's Gospel, she says:

'Jesus Christ lived for me. This was no remote historical character of two thousand years ago, but someone who was vibrantly alive now in the present. He became as real to me as the people whom I sat next to every day in the bus. He was utterly unique, totally compelling.'

Every word that Jesus spoke mattered, not just because they made sense out of the world and human nature but because they spoke directly to her as an individual. The more she pursued her relationship with Jesus, the more she found in him the completion of all that made her a Jew. Without doubt she had found her Messiah.

---

messianic platform; he speaks of it as 'good news to the poor', proclaiming release to the captives, recovering of sight to the blind and liberty to those who are oppressed. His death on the cross forgives people's sin, yet also redeems the entire creation groaning for release from its bondage to futility and decay. In his work and teaching, salvation is a wide thing, holding together what are often thought of as opposites:

▪ **It is personal and cosmic.** When he delivered a man controlled by a 'legion' of demons, Jesus showed his power not merely in dealing with the classic symptoms of a person deranged—unusual strength, seizures, multiple personality and a morbid preoccupation with death—but also with the cosmic powers that had possessed him. (This story is found in Luke chapter 8 from verse 26.) The struggle for integration in human personality is here seen against the wider backdrop of a power confrontation in the cosmos.

Jesus saw his exorcisms as an invasion of Satan's evil empire. Defeat of the powers in a human being is a sign of the encroaching presence of his kingdom: 'If it is by the finger of God that I cast out demons, then the kingdom of God has come upon you.'

▪ **It is spiritual and physical.** When a paralyzed man was brought to him Jesus offered him forgiveness first rather than healing. Jesus with unerring insight had diagnosed the man's physical condition as having a spiritual cause. With efficient authority he lifted the burden of guilt, which at once showed itself in the man taking to his feet. (Read the story at the start of Mark chapter 2.)

▪ **It is individual and social.** Zacchaeus must have been a terribly lonely individual, despised by society for his fraudulent and traitorous profession. To this self-enclosed isolation Jesus broke in with the warmth of his fellowship, calling him by name to come down from his tree. (The account comes in Luke chapter 10.) Jesus' gesture melted the man's acquisitive hardness into unstinting contrition, and from the arid desert of alienation restored Zacchaeus to community and a sense of social responsibility.

▪ **It has to do with both personal experience and relationships.** The Samaritan woman hardly knew what Jesus was getting at. (For this story turn to John chapter 4.) His talk of water sounded almost magical, considering he had nothing to draw water with and great forefather Jacob could only manage a deep well. But she was willing to try, until he touched a sore spot: 'Go call your husband. . .' She had no husband; that part at least was true at the moment. The man, however, was frighteningly acute: 'You are right, for you have had five husbands, and he whom you now have is not your husband. . .' Embarrassed, she shifted to safe theological questions on worship and the Messiah. Jesus was insistent and pointed: 'I who speak to you am he.'

It took time for the woman to understand that behind the series of her failed loves was a thirst— deep, vast, wild as the open spaces where her desires had wondered unabated. Face to face with

Jesus and Women

Women had a wider importance in the life and ministry of Jesus than is usually appreciated. Most people focus on Mary, his mother, yet the biblical writings reach much wider. They point to his relationship with a specific group of women who were among his closest followers. They show his concern to communicate with all women by using language which included them. We read how he dismisses many of the stereotypes of his day, and addresses women fundamentally as people. We see a Jesus who tells an outcast woman that he is the Messiah, and gives her and others the task of spreading his good news. This Christ who affirms women also rebukes many men, including his closest friends, when they despise what the women have to say or share.

Jesus related to many women during his life, and in doing so often cut across cultural barriers and social taboos. A woman with period problems, a Samaritan divorcee, a Canaanite woman, a woman who was found committing adultery, and a poor widow all found a voice in his concern and compassion. A woman who burst in on a private party to wash and perfume Jesus' feet braved hostility and flouted public opinion to be near him. But Jesus reinforced her love and faith, speaking against the men who dismissed and sneered at her. Jesus, then, treated women with dignity, and he was careful to address them in his teaching. Frequently he drew on women's lives and experiences in the

stories he told and the metaphors he used, talking of baking bread, sweeping the house for lost coins, patching clothes, or nursing children.

Jesus also had close relationships with some women, one of whom of course was his mother. But this relationship was a rich and complex one. Once he allowed her to persuade him to perform a miracle, when he turned water into wine at the wedding at Cana in Galilee. On other occasions he insisted that God's will came before any family relationship. His last concern before he died in terrible pain was that his mother should be cared for, and he committed her wellbeing to one of his trusted and most loving friends.

Other women as well as Mary his mother are recorded among his disciples. Some are mentioned by name: Mary and Martha of Bethany, Mary Magdalene, Susanna, Joanna, as well as those who were simply called 'the other women'. Some of these women supported him financially. Some provided their home for him whenever he needed it. Others travelled with him, even on the arduous journey from Galilee to Jerusalem. These women had a very important place in Jesus' ministry. Mary and Martha feature many times, once in a dispute over domestic roles, where Jesus affirmed Mary the learner, rather than Martha who fretted about the housework. At another time, when Jesus brought their brother Lazarus back to life, it was Martha to whom he first drew close and talked

about himself as 'the resurrection and the life'.

The women followers were with him at the very end of his life. They had travelled with him on his final journey. They watched in torment while he was crucified, and were there faithfully to anoint his body two days after the burial. They were the ones who saw the empty tomb, and heard the message of the angel that he was alive. Mary Magdalene was one of the first disciples to see the risen Christ, and the women were given the task of spreading the good news, and of telling others of the resurrection.

Not surprisingly, Jesus' impact on the lives of women did not stop with those who surrounded him during his lifetime, or those active in the New Testament church. Throughout the ages many women have discovered through him that dignity and humanness which those early women knew, but which other people often deny them. Christian women have been among the world's greatest pioneers and reformers. They have been campaigners, hymn-writers, authors, doctors and missionaries.

▲ Jesus had a place of honour for women in his following. In contrast to the usual practice of downgrading women, he treated their concerns with great seriousness.

Many have also suffered imprisonment, torture and even death, because they have not been prepared to give up their faith in Christ. Now, as then, women have found in Jesus their wholeness and their liberation.

him in whom all longing finds fulfilment, the woman drank deep of his offer of life and spilled it out to whoever among the people of her city would care to hear.

Filling our emptiness

The wholeness Jesus brings has a total finish, making people not just better but new.

In many poor places today there are the sick and the infirm with no access to medical help. Tribal groups and post-technological societies experience life like sweet, frail music that cannot still the quiver of fear before unseen powers that lurk underneath a stone or behind the ectoplasmic mist that swallows in darkness the neon lights of the city. Many are driven into a narrowed life of acquisition, or tortured by some dark deed haunting from the past.

Jesus in the Philippines

Corazon is a slight, giggly wisp of a woman who, as the old folk would say, is 'gifted'. In her town every one comes to her—the sick who need her healing touch, the heartbroken women frayed by poverty and philandering husbands, the curious who are attracted by magical power. In the old days she would be classed with those dancing, ecstatic women in trance called *babaylan*, priestesses who lead the community in its cultic festivals. Except that her rather hard common sense makes her look a bit too sober for the part.

'It is his work altogether,' she says, smiling shyly at the wonder of a cataract vanishing, or a rotting piece of cancerous tissue being restored. 'And sometimes, the Spirit merely tells me to write a prescription,' which she did once for a man suffering supposedly from cirrhosis of the liver. It turns out that he was getting the wrong medication, as do many of the poor in rural areas who have access only to quack doctors. The God of mercy had stepped in where human error and economic deprivation had bound a man to continual suffering.

Corazon is but one of many today who through the power of Jesus bring good news to the poor.

And Jesus is also in the business of healing heart-break and the breakdown of relationships. A famous folksinger relates how, after knowing Jesus, she began to feel a need to seek out her estranged husband. An opportunity came for her to sing in Hongkong where he was then living. Unknown to her, he too had been experiencing the initial stirrings of faith and searching for a way of getting his life together again. Brought to the conviction that the way forward was to put his family back together, he ventured to send feelers to his wife about the possibility of seeing her. The meeting was not without tears as he was offered to reconcile. Quite moved and touched, she received him back. Today they have added another child to the brood which used to feel orphaned, rent asunder by the pain of their alienated parents.

In the face of the poor's powerlessness, against fear of demons and the powers that rule the cosmos, in the cutting edge of failure and loneliness and alienation, Jesus brings power for good, and power for newness of life. By his victory on the cross, he has provided a way to wholeness to all who seek forgiveness for the sins of their broken past.

Christ the Healer

Charnwood is a school where handicapped and able-bodied children are brought together. Its founder has written:

'Most of those whose children come to Charnwood know little if anything initially about its basis as a Christian charity, although over the years there has been a steady trickle of people who after many months have encountered God personally. The Bridges' story is one example. Their three-year-old daughter, Joanne, had been diagnosed as having a malignant brain tumour. She had already spent nine months of her short life in hospital, having radio therapy and extensive treatment which left her almost blind. When she came to Charnwood, she had little stick-like legs, scant hair, sightless eyes and cried almost continuously. Gradually the legs began to strengthen, the sight returned and the crying stopped. Joanne's mother had called for a priest to give her child a final blessing when the doctors had told her she was going to die. By committing Joanne to God's care, seeing the faith of another mother in hospital coming to terms with her dying child and after weeks of Christian care at Charnwood, Kathy and her once sceptical husband John both came face to face with Christ the healer, whose active presence in the life of their daughter had spoken powerfully beyond their greatest hopes and dreams.'

▼ Charnwood is a school in England which brings handicapped and able-bodied children together.

The Lotus Children

Liz Nunn is no ordinary woman. Having worked with young people in Britain, she visited India and encountered in India's cities thousands of children with no homes or education, who had little choice but to grow into adulthood as beggars and tricksters. Acting as Christ's agent across the continents, Liz has since established the Society of Friends for the Lotus Children because, like the lotus flower which has its roots in the mud on the bed of the lake, these children have their roots and bed down in the filth of the city streets. Liz believes that, with help, they too could reach up and blossom beautifully in the light. This initiative aims to bring hope and growth. Hope that, in tomorrow's world, children with no one and nothing except their self-respect may find growth to maintain themselves and be socially accepted citizens living their lives to the full.

Despite the growing affluence and the overflow of goods, some parts of the world suffer what the psychoanalyst Carl Gustav Jung calls 'the central neurosis of our time': emptiness.

To such as these Jesus is able to bring not just power to heal, but power for good. In a world where evil seems strong and forces of good always vulnerable, his risen life is giving power to people who were once conscious of fear before the more obviously powerful forces of injustice. Those broken and made bitter by failed relationships find forgiveness within themselves because they know themselves forgiven. People feeling the pointlessness of a machine-driven existence are liberated by finding in Jesus a return to the poetry of a higher cause.

Through the knowledge of the Son, the ability to 'see life whole and to see it steadily' is within our grasp. The many scattered pieces of our lives are put together, and the breakdown of adequate explanations for the meaning of our lives finds reintegration in him in whom 'all things hold together'. As the psalmist puts it, 'In your light we see light': or, as the late C.S. Lewis once remarked: 'I believe in God in the same sense that I believe that the sun has risen; not because I see it, but because by it I see everything else.'

The Gospels tell us that when Jesus died there was darkness on the land. The earth shook, the tombs broke open and the bodies of many saints who had died were raised to life. These are signs to us that in the death of Jesus the conflict with evil powers that his kingdom had provoked has been resolved in a cosmic upheaval whose liberating tremors we now feel.

Then as now, salvation and wholeness come to us as we respond to Jesus: 'He who is not with me is against me, and he who does not gather with me scatters.'

3.7

'WHEN YOU PRAY'

For Jesus, prayer was not merely addressing God. It was an atmosphere in which both God and people could engage in a far-reaching process of mutual self-discovery.

Though he occasionally delivered formal teaching on prayer, Jesus spent most of his time interacting with people. As he mingled with them, he helped them mature spiritually and personally as they began to see things from a new perspective—that of the Kingdom of God which he had come to announce.

Yet it was precisely because of Jesus' close and meaningful commitment to God, and his distinctive understanding of prayer, that he was able to do this so effectively.

To grasp something of Jesus' understanding of prayer, we need to take a closer look at his home and cultural environment. For prayer was supremely important in the life of every Jewish family in first-century Palestine—just as it is today.

A striking feature of the Bible's story is that in it, God is always communicating with people. In the first pages of the Old Testament, Adam and Eve talk with God, and he speaks with them. Later, as the nation of Israel is forming, Moses and God communicate with each other face to face as friends.

Though the precise forms and contents of prayer changed over the centuries, the Jewish people were always certain that God was available to them and would take great delight in their prayers. Sometimes they used written prayers, such as those in the Old Testament book of Psalms, as part of their worship services. At other times, prayer was the vehicle through which men and women could share their deepest feelings with their God. Jeremiah and other prophets prayed this way while agonizing about the

▲ Mount Athos, on the coast of Greece, has long been a centre for meditation on the Jesus prayer, as a way of growing in union with him.

ministry to which they were called.

By the time of Jesus, corporate prayer was a part of everyday life for the people of Palestine. This had come about partly as a result of the development of the synagogue as a place to worship. After the exile in Babylon (586–539 BC), worship underwent many far-reaching changes. The fact that the temple had been destroyed was serious enough, though it was subsequently rebuilt. But as Jewish people were

▲ To know about Jesus is important. To know him in relationship lies at the heart of faith. Prayer is how such a relationship is built.

scattered all over the world following this catastrophe, the majority could not worship regularly at the temple in Jerusalem anyway. Since some things—such as sacrifice—could take place only in the Temple, Jews the world over made it an ambition to celebrate at least one of the great annual festivals in Jerusalem. But everyday worship had to centre on the things that could be done in distant places. Prayer was one of these, and before long it came to occupy a central position in the life of the synagogues that sprang up as local centres of worship and culture everywhere that Jewish people lived.

The synagogue was not the only place where believers could pray regularly. Prayer was also a regular feature of daily life in the average Jewish home. No doubt Jesus regularly joined with others in prayer in private homes, as well as when he visited the synagogue. Home prayer often resembled synagogue prayer. For example, following the pattern of the 'benedictions' used in synagogue worship, family prayer often focussed on God's glory, acknowledged in worship and thanksgiving.

The Gospels suggest that Jesus regularly spent time in prayer. Luke in particular emphasizes how every significant occasion in his life—from conception to ascension—was accompanied by serious prayer. But the other Gospels also stress Jesus' attention to prayer. He conducted his entire ministry in the conscious awareness of God's presence, so that God's will should be paramount in all that he did. And prayer was the key to that.

According to Luke 11:1, it was Jesus' own example in prayer that led the disciples to ask him to teach them to pray too. In response to that, Jesus gave them the pattern of what we often call 'the Lord's Prayer'—but which in reality is 'the Disciples' Prayer'. This is found in two versions in the Gospels, a shorter one in Luke (11:2–4) and a more extended one in Matthew (6:9–13).

Matthew's version is better known to most people

today. It has a more structured, poetic form, and was no doubt the one the earliest Christians remembered and used in worship. Indeed, Matthew sets it in the Sermon on the Mount in a broader context of teaching not only about prayer but about other forms of worship too. Giving money to the poor, prayer and fasting—these were three main ways in which Jewish people in Jesus' time might worship God. There was nothing wrong with any of them. All were commended in the Hebrew scriptures. But it was very easy for these forms of worship to draw attention to the worshipper's dedication, rather than to centre on God himself.

That is why Jesus not only suggested words which his disciples might use when they prayed, but also outlined some important principles about how they should use them.

■ **Prayer is for God**, he told them. An obvious enough fact, you may think—but look at the example of the 'hypocrites' who stood self-consciously on street corners and prayed so that everyone would praise their devotion. These 'play actors' (for that is the meaning of the Greek word that lies behind the translation 'hypocrites') got their reward there and then: everyone applauded when the performance was finished. And that was all the reward they could expect!

Practising the Presence

Among the many who have come to a living faith in Jesus, there have always been some who have chosen a contemplative life. Brother Lawrence is a good example. Born in France, he was driven by an inner calling to become a lay brother among the barefooted Carmelites in Paris in 1666. His conversion, as an eighteen-year-old, was the result of seeing a dry and leafless tree on a midwinter day, standing gaunt against the snow. This stirred deep thoughts within him of the change the coming spring would bring. From that moment on, he grew and became strong in his knowledge and love for Jesus, seeking always to walk as in his presence.

For Lawrence there was no distinction between work and worship. He aimed to practise the presence of God wherever he was. 'The time of business does not differ with me from the time of prayer. In the noise and clatter of my kitchen, whilst several people are at the same time calling for different things, I possess God in as great tranquillity as if I were upon my knees at the blessed sacrament.'

Brother Lawrence was a humble man whose simple walk with God remains an inspiration and guide for all who seek, amid their busy and demanding lives, constant communion with Jesus.

The Face of the Lion

In his book *The Magician's Nephew*, fantasy author C. S. Lewis gives a powerful glimpse of what it would be like to look into the face of Jesus. The children in the story are just returning from the kingdom of Narnia to their home in London:

'Both children were looking up into the Lion's face. And all at once (they never knew exactly how it happened), the face seemed to be a sea of tossing gold in which they were floating, and such a sweetness and power rolled over them and entered into them that they felt they had never really been happy or wise or good, or even alive and awake before. And the memory of that moment stayed with them always, so that as long as they both lived, if ever they were sad or afraid or angry, the thought of all that golden goodness, and the feeling that it was still there, quite close, just round some corner or just behind some door, would come back and make them sure, deep down inside, that all was well.'

▶ C.S. Lewis was a literary scholar, but also a highly effective apologist for the Christian faith.

Jesus' teaching contains other stories making the same point. A notable example is his parable of the Pharisee and the tax collector who went into the temple together. The Pharisee was a regular visitor. He knew all the ropes—and told God so in a magnificent, if ostentatious, prayer. The tax collector, however, was quite unfamiliar with both the ritual and the jargon. All he could do was acknowledge his own inadequacies before God. Now, asked Jesus, who was in the right with God? His hearers would naturally applaud the religious expert. But no, it was the humble tax collector who put God in first place.

Our culture today is obsessed with individual rights, needs, achievements and rewards. Unfortunately, much that passes for prayer tends to reflect merely personal concerns with ourselves and our circumstances. But for Jesus, reflective contemplation of God and his greatness was always the starting point of true prayer. The Lord's Prayer begins by reflecting on God and his glory, the coming of his kingdom and its challenge, before moving on to the disciples' personal concerns.

■ **Prayer can be learned.** Another consequence of our culture's individualism is the way some people imagine that to be authentic, prayer must be the personal composition of the one who does the praying. Since few of us are skilled in putting words together, this can be rather a daunting prospect. But

▼ The abbey community of Iona, off the coast of Scotland, continues the Celtic spirituality of Columba its founder. Their faith combines a profound reverence for the earth's beauty with an earthy sense of realism about practical human life.

The Imitation of Christ

Many of the themes of late medieval devotion to the humanity of Jesus find classic expression in the book called *The Imitation of Christ*. This has become one of the most widely read of all Christian works.

It circulated (from about 1425) anonymously, because of its author's desire for humility. Most often the author has been thought to be Thomas a Kempis (1380–1471), and if not by him, it certainly comes from his circle. It is therefore a product of the so-called *devotio moderna* ('modern devotion'), a movement of spiritual renewal which originated in late fourteenth-century Holland.

The book is a manual of the spiritual life, intended primarily for members of a religious community. Its emphasis is very much on the interior life, on which it has much sound and wise advice. But the note of practical service of others, which was also a feature of the *devotio moderna*, is rather lacking.

The imitation of Jesus' life and intimate friendship with Jesus are recurrent themes. Humility and self-denial are the way in which Christians can follow Jesus on his way to the cross. Christ's love for Christians leads them to self-denial, and the more they deny themselves the more their love for Christ is freed from self-interest and becomes pure love for him. 'He who will lose his life will find it,' said Jesus. By renouncing self, Christians find themselves in Christ. Imitation of Christ in self-denial is the route to union with God.

The insistence that the Christian way is one of self-renunciation and suffering is balanced by the author's delight in fellowship with Jesus: 'When Jesus is with us, all is well and nothing seems hard; but when Jesus is absent, everything is difficult.' The Christian who turns from the world to the kingdom of God within him, finds that Jesus visits him there as a friend. He can converse with Jesus, who speaks to him in his heart. Accordingly, the longest of the four books of the *Imitation* is written as a dialogue between Christ and the Christian.

▲ **Central to Christian prayer is reflection on the Bible. Many people have put the Bible to the test of a lifetime's experience and found in it a well that never runs dry.**

of course Jesus gave a prayer as a pattern or model for his disciples to follow. Like everything else, even Jesus' prayer can become meaningless mumbo-jumbo when it is repeated mindlessly and without thought for either its words or its destination. But used sensitively, as a vehicle for true devotion, it can open new lines of approach to God himself.

■ **Prayer should be shared.** Notice that in the Lord's Prayer, everything is in the plural ('Give *us* this day...', 'as *we* forgive...'). When Jesus advised his hearers to go into a private place to pray, he clearly did not mean they should always pray alone. Praying discreetly and with due reverence for God does not necessarily mean praying in personal solitude. There is a time and place for that—Jesus himself occasionally retreated to be alone with God—but, in general, prayer is something to do with other people. Jesus clearly taught that prayer is not just for God. It is also for other people. Prayer opens our lives to new ways of relating to others, even as we open our lives to God himself.

Jesus encouraged his disciples to address God as 'Abba', the Aramaic word for 'Father' used in the home. This was something new. Jewish people occasionally addressed God as 'Father', but they did not use the familiar language Jesus used, and they normally did not say 'Father' at all without also referring to God's holiness and majesty. By addressing God as 'Abba', Jesus showed his openness towards God and his intimacy with him. It is this sense of openness towards God that is perhaps most characteristic of Jesus' teaching on prayer, and it is this emphasis on the close personal relationship between God and people that gives prayer such a distinctive nature in Jesus' ministry.

The Christian Tradition of Prayer

Prayer is central to religious life. It is natural to us, whether as a response to God's presence or as a call for his help. So all religions practise prayer. But in Christian prayer, the presence of Christ and the living relationship between him and the person praying create a unique faith, unknown in other religions.

Today there is great interest in 'spirituality'; prayer and meditation are matters of wide concern. So we all need to ask, what is the truth about prayer? Does it matter to whom we pray? Are our breathings in prayer real because of our sincerity, or is prayer valid only to the true God?

In one sense, we all pray. 'Let everything that has breath, praise the Lord,' said the psalmist. There is devout prayer in all the major religions. The apostle Paul quoted a Greek prayer in a sermon at Athens, but he went on to say that while such prayers had been acceptable before Jesus died and rose, now things were different. God has revealed his true nature in Jesus, who is the one mediator between himself and humanity.

So the unique element in Christian prayer is that it is prayed 'in the name of Jesus'. Jesus taught us to pray in his name, and in doing so Christians from the earliest days have laid claim to a personal relationship with God through the life, death and resurrection of Jesus. In prayer we are promised the help of the Holy Spirit, who prays in and through our hearts and minds, tuning us to God's will. 'No one can say Jesus is Lord,' wrote Paul, 'except by the Holy Spirit.'

In prayer we enter into the life of God the Trinity. Eternal communion is the inner reality of God himself, so in prayer we are invited to share in divine conversation. By his Spirit we become God's prayer partners in the most intimate way possible. God takes over our lives, so that in prayer we are taken outside of ourselves.

The classic way, then, of expressing how the early Christians prayed was to the Father, through the Son, by the Holy Spirit.

Daily prayer

The early Christians prayed both personally and in public, both 'liturgically' (using set words) and spontaneously. No liturgical prayers have been recorded from the first century, because prayers were preserved orally, but snatches of liturgy crop up repeatedly in the New Testament. The Lord's Prayer may itself have been used liturgically by Christians; it may have fitted into the daily Jewish *tefillah* prayer. Jesus taught his disciples to call God *Abba*, 'Father', but they also often prayed to Jesus as 'Lord'.

Christians were to be vigilant, expecting Jesus to return, and prayer was central to this. 'Watch and pray,' Jesus taught them. This constant watchfulness had two important results in their practice of prayer:

■ **Hours of prayer.** Part of their vigilance involved fixing regular days and hours for prayer. This was part of Jewish life, too, though not in a totally set way, any more than was Christian prayer at that time. There are many references to prayer at the third, sixth and ninth hours of the day. Clement of Alexandria, towards the end of the second century, writes of rising to pray at night, so maintaining a watchful attitude. Tertullian, in the same generation, encouraged regular times of prayer as a means of discipline, 'to drag one away from affairs to such duty'. Wednesdays and Fridays became days for fasting, with preaching in the afternoon; Sunday was for the eucharist, or Lord's supper.

■ **Prayer without ceasing.** Regular times, however, were not an end in themselves but a way of ensuring a constant prayerfulness. Clement of Alexandria, again, writes: 'We cultivate our fields, praising; we sail the seas, hymning. . .' Origen, in the next generation, spoke of 'the whole life of the saint as one integrated prayer'. It was an attitude to prayer that was to have a long continued influence in the Christian spiritual tradition, on the contemplative life of later Christian mysticism.

From these early Christian centuries we can see three important strands emerging, which were to become distinct spiritual traditions: **The 'Jesus prayer' tradition; The liturgical reciting of the Lord's Prayer; Meditative and contemplative prayerfulness as a way of life.**

The Jesus Prayer

'Lord Jesus Christ, Son of God, have mercy on me a sinner.' This prayer has a long history. 'Have mercy on me' goes right back to the Old Testament. In the New Testament it is the prayer of blind Bartimaeus, crying for Christ's help. 'Lord have mercy' is echoed frequently in the spontaneous, unstructured prayers of the Desert Fathers from the third and fourth centuries onwards. But the prayer in its present form was used at least from the sixth century in the monastery of St Catherine in Sinai. In the fourteenth century it was carried from there by the Abbot, Gregory of Sinai, to Mount Athos in Macedonia. Monks and others began to write down their reflections on the life of prayer and in 1782 a collection of these was edited and published in Venice as *Philokalia*, 'the love of the beautiful'. Before the end of that century, these were translated into Russian, and in this way the Jesus Prayer found its way into the monastic life of the Russian Orthodox Church, as it had done earlier into the Greek Orthodox Church. The Russian narrative of an unknown pilgrim, in the middle of the nineteenth century, spread the practice more popularly, and after 1930, when it was translated into English, French and German, the practice also became known in the West for perhaps the first time. Modern scholarship has now suggested that the invocation of a Jesus consciousness was taught by Nilus of Ancrya early in the fifth century, and by Diadochus of Photice a generation later. The motive of such practice is given as keeping guard upon our scattered thoughts, so that the mind becomes unified with the heart in the desire to love Christ, wholly so. But perhaps there have never been more practising the prayer, in the history of this tradition, than there are now.

Techniques of breathing and of posture have long been taught along with the Jesus prayer. They offer a way to explore inwardly, turning to God from the heart. But if the great emphasis is on physical techniques and constantly repeating the same prayer, there is a danger that the prayer may become no more than a 'mantra'. Those seeking genuine stillness of soul, undistracted by wandering thoughts or temptation, found in the Jesus Prayer a genuine cry for mercy, with tears of contrition, and learnt to pray, not by building a structure of thoughts, but simply by comtemplating God's presence.

Such prayer is a corrective to the modern mind-set of viewing God as a series of postulates, with a spectator's stance towards theological doctrines, not actually experienced. Practising the presence of Jesus in daily life ▶▶

▶▶ is more than thoughts in the head. It is also taking such thoughts into the 'heart', the centre of our whole being, so that we become comtemplatives in our whole demeanour as people before others, as well as before God. Then we can carry this inward serenity whatever we do, wherever we live, urbanite or solitary.

The Lord's Prayer

If the Jesus Prayer is typical of the Eastern tradition of stillness, the more liturgical recitation of the Lord's Prayer has been characteristic of the Western or Latin tradition. Tertullian wrote the first treatise on the Lord's Prayer. It is a beginning in the systematic treatment of the theology of prayer, as Christ taught us to pray. He writes also with the expectation that the faithful will keep a daily practice of three or four times of prayer. In fact if a Christian woman marries a pagan, she has to consider the practical issue of how she can sleep with a man when she has to rise at midnight to resume her prayers. Tertullian also saw that the Lord's Prayer provides a superstructure for all other prayers. Cyprian, in the third century, maintains that 'there is absolutely nothing passed over pertaining to our petitions and prayers' in this prayer. So we should first repeat it before we add our own personal requests. This will have a 'norming' effect on our own desires, and make them conformable to the revelation contained within the Lord's Prayer. This argument is repeated many times in later writings.

After the Peace of Constantine, in the fourth century, it became possible for local Christian communities to assemble together on a regular basis for their daily prayers. So Eusebius of Caesarea wrote that 'the pleasures of God are the hymns which are everywhere in the world offered in his church at morning and evening time'. This is the beginning of what scholars have called 'the Cathedral Office' that became the regular church attendance both in the East and the West. Augustine, in the generation after the Peace of Constantine, tells us of his personal practice: 'Day by day I rise, go to church, sing there a morning and an evening hymn, and sing a third and fourth in my house. Thus each day I bring a sacrifice of praise and offer it before my God'. The Council of Gerona, in Catalonia in the sixth century, directed that the Lord's Prayer should be added to the end of the morning and evening services, used daily. But it was slow in being accepted, for the Fourth Council of Toledo a century later criticized some priests who recited it only on Sundays. It appears that the recitation of the Lord's Prayer was more firmly established in the monastic tradition than in the services of the church. In the end, the great dominance of monasticism on the life of the churches supplanted the cathedral office altogether, and it became characteristic of the West that the cathedral service of the laity was eliminated by the effect of monasticism. Then, in addition to the more intensive daily routine of the four or more daily offices, the recitation of the psalter in the course of each week and other elaborations awed the laity from ever being able to share worship with 'the religious' on any common footing. Liturgical books of worship were elaborated and stabilized, so that the major part of the Roman liturgy created between the fourth and eighth centuries, with its liturgical year, biblical readings, chants and prayers, has remained substantially unchanged to the present century.

In the Gregorian Reform of the eleventh century, monastic liturgy was deliberately grafted with the life of the church. A broadly-diffused devotionalism was a mark also of the later Middle Ages, with the use of the rosary and the recitation of the Lord's Prayer, so that along with liturgy which was formal and collective, and contemplation which was personal and private, came devotions defined more by their objects of adoration—saints, relics, religious days, the Virgin, or the suffering Christ. Texts, paintings, sculptures became foci of devotion, but the whole ultimately generated such superstitions and corruptions that they became a major target of the reformers in the sixteenth century.

Singling out prayer as 'pure faith', Martin Luther reinstated the recitation of the Lord's Prayer, along with the Apostles' creed and the ten commandments as the daily mirror of the soul's devotions. The Christian should not only recite texts, but also enter into a true attitude of prayer. The only text that truly prescribed this, he argued, was the Lord's Prayer. 'A Christian has prayed profusely if he has prayed well the Our Father.' He recommended once more the daily habit of morning and evening prayer, though not as a matter of multiplying words, but of having 'a free heart disposed to pray'. Likewise John Calvin, while elaborating more theologically than Luther on the nature of true prayer, includes a commentary on the Lord's Prayer as the early Fathers did, adding that it also suggests that 'all our prayers to God ought only to be presented in the name of Christ'. The Puritans followed with scores of commentaries on the Lord's Prayer as the focus of their prayer life. No other period of history since the days of the early church, when the Lord's Prayer was taught to candidates for baptism, had so stressed the importance of this prayer, above all other prayers. But it went along with what was perhaps an over-emphasis on verbal prayer, in Protestant spirituality. So we need to conclude with another expression of prayer that is also expressive of devotion to Christ.

Meditation and contemplation

As we have seen, ceaseless prayer in the early church implied a meditative heart before God. Those who lived a life of meditation and prayer were frequently called, among the early fathers, 'Christ-bearers', since their constant meditation was on the life of Christ. So a homily of the late fourth century says: 'The heart is Christ's palace. . .There Christ the King comes to his rest.' This is no conflict between head and heart, for the heart is seen as the centre of the person, the inner being that is open in inexpressible ways to the direct encounter with God.

In the Western Monastic tradition, continuous prayer was exercised privately in the silence of the heart, combined with brief requests in the heart (*oratio*), meditative reading (*lectio*), and reflection on the Bible (*meditatio*). This last induced contemplation (*contemplatio*), and drew forth adoration of God for his deeds and words. Descriptions of this contemplative prayer become frequent in the lives of saints after the high Middle Ages, as a state of habitual prayer. From the eleventh century, beginning with the *Meditation and Prayers* of Anselm, a new genre of prayer develops that is highly personalized in the love and desire for God. So William of St Thierry prays with great candour, 'O Lord, when all is said and done, I am quite positive that, by grace, I do have in me the desire to desire you and the loving of you with all my heart and soul.' Those reading such texts as Richard of St Victor's *Mystical Ark* learnt of methodical stages of higher reaches of prayer, but these were more theoretical than practical. More immediate was the Franciscan spirit of contemplation, based on the personal rapture of Francis of Assisi at Mount La Verna, and the simplicity of his own prayers. His followers were henceforth called to the contemplative journey. As his interpreter Bonaventure could say: 'There is no other path but through the burning love of the Crucified.' But the great flowering of Christian mysticism occurred later, in the fourteenth and fifteenth centuries, with the various regional schools of contemplation.

The movement in the Low Countries called *Devotio Moderna* and associated with the Brethren of the Common Life, originated with Geert Groote, but became popularly associated with Thomas a Kempis, whose *Imitation of Christ* remained, next to the Bible, the most widely circulated book, with over two thousand editions. This led to currents of spiritual renewal elsewhere, such as the 'Friends of God' movement in southern Germany, and the piety of the later Pietist movement of the seventeeth and eighteenth centuries, as well as to the Carmelite and Franciscan renewal movements in Spain in the sixteenth century. But there were in England a whole series of more individual contemplatives. They did not create 'schools of contemplation', though their personal impact was great indeed. Richard Rolle, in the fourteenth century, had a love for Christ that shone through all his works. Best known is *The Mending of Life*. Walter of Hilton emphasized with Rolle that all true experience of God comes only through the love of Jesus. His work *The Ladder of Perfection* is a balance between the 'active life' of pursuing godliness

and the 'passive life' of contemplation. A related work, *The Cloud of Unknowing*, by an unknown author, is perhaps the most helpful and influential work on the discipline of contemplation in the English language, but the writer warns us it is not for the curious, only for those intent on loving God. Dame Julian of Norwich is becoming recognized as a contemplative in the tradition of Paul the apostle, leaving aside such niceties as the distinction between an active and passive life, and living wholly for Christ. In Spain, the golden age of spirituality was the sixteenth century, with such writers as Teresa of Avila, John of the Cross and Ignatius Loyola. These great writers speak of their encounter with God, and for Ignatius' *Spiritual Exercises* especially, meditations on the life of Christ continue to this day to be a living and transforming reality.

The central theme of so

▲ **Dame Julian of Norwich typifies the medieval mystical tradition. Her great emphasis was concentration on the love of God in Jesus.**

much meditative and contemplative prayer has been twofold:

■ **A deep devotion to the mystery of the Trinity.** Writers such as William of St Thierry, in his work *The Enigma of Faith*, emphasize that the Trinity is like an inexhaustible spring of water, something not to be discursive about, but the source of life-giving realities. He recognized the utter helplessness of words to convey the unspeakable majesty of God, as Father, Son, and Holy Spirit. Jan van Ruysbroek, a fourteenth-century Flemish mystic, also had had great influence on trinitarian devotion, accepting with the Greek Fathers that the soul's relation to God shares in the movements within the Godhead. In *The Divine*

Espousals he speaks of how the contemplative is caught up in the embrace of the Holy Trinity, to abide eternally at rest.

■ **Devotion to the incarnation of Christ.** This has been a controversial issue. Roman Catholic spiritual practices were alleged by Luther to be a way of establishing our merit before God, while reformers advocated trusting only in God's grace. The experience of conversion has tended to be the most convincing reality of the evangelical tradition, whereas the guidance of spiritual directors has been more the evidence given by Catholic spirituality. No one has written better of the experiences of prayer than Teresa of Avila, who also centred so deeply on the love of Christ.

Perhaps Christians today are looking to draw from all these traditions. Within an enriched spirituality of God the Trinity and a continuing belief in Jesus Christ as our unique Saviour and Lord, we may begin to see the importance of practising all forms of prayer. Perhaps we will become adepts at inner stillness, verbal prayer and contemplation on the life of Christ, without the divergences that have held these apart as separate traditions.

3.8

THE PEOPLE OF GOD

From start to finish, the Bible is about people. Its first pages focus on the relationship of people to the world in which they live, and on their relationship to one another and to God. The ancient stories of creation and the Garden of Eden emphasize that people find their true destiny in life not as isolated individuals, but in the context of a family and a community.

As we move on through the book of Genesis, it is not long before we meet Abraham and his partner Sarah. They are frequently mentioned in the New Testament as models of faith. But it is not their

▲ A Coptic priest conducts a service. Several million Egyptians follow this ancient tradition. The people of God comprise a rich kaleidoscope of nationalities and styles of worship.

personal piety for which they are remembered. It is the fact that they became the parents of a son—Isaac—through whom a great nation was to develop.

When we first meet them, both are old and childless. But through their faith in God, even those obstacles are overcome, and a son is born. Then, as the story develops and the history of the nation descended from Sarah and Abraham unfolds, we begin to discover why such a community is so important. There are pointers given in the Abraham story, which ultimately develop into three main areas.

Worshipping God

Modern Western thinking tends to be dominated by the needs and concerns of the individual. As a result, much Western Christianity focuses exclusively

▲ Protestants at En Lozere in France celebrate an outdoor communion. This service of breaking bread and sharing wine is at the centre of Christians' lives together.

on the relationship between individual believers and God. Nothing else appears to matter. Cultures in other parts of the world more easily acknowledge that none of us exists by ourselves. The Old Testament shares this view promising that 'God sets the lonely in families'. Faith, then, must make some kind of impact not only on individuals but on wider groups too. In some crucial ways worship of God himself is impoverished if it is an individual activity. It takes all of God's people to worship God adequately.

This is one reason why the Old Testament gives so much attention to the regular observance of the great religious festivals. They were a constant feature of the life of Israel and they were a reminder that the worship of God must affect the whole of life. The prophets often had to remind people that worship should be a vehicle to spread God's love throughout the community. Jesus reinforced this in his own teaching about the nature of true discipleship. 'Love God,' he said—but then he added, not as an afterthought but as a second fundamental rule, 'and love your neighbour as yourself.' At many points in his teaching he emphasized how love of others is not an optional extra, but is part and parcel of true devotion to God himself.

▲ Jesus' first followers included many whom society condemned.

▼ Refugee tribespeople, who have crossed the border from Burma to Thailand, are cared for in a Christian relief camp. People who follow Jesus are called to follow him in caring for the needy.

Creating a community

Our world today is full of lonely people. People who would love to be part of a community in which they can enjoy friendships with others. People who long for an atmosphere of mutual trust and respect, with the freedom to develop their own full potential as persons. Many of the revolutions in world history happened because people were searching for such an existence. And the establishment of Israel as a nation worshipping God was, in its day, a social revolution.

The story begins with the exodus. A band of dispirited slaves escaped from Egypt under the leadership of Moses, and eventually established a new way of life in their own land. The social overtones are obvious: a group of dispossessed, exploited and disadvantaged people are rescued from the power of totalitarian dictatorship and given their freedom. And this is something God has done! It reflects God's view of how things ought to be.

The same ideological battle was fought again once they reached their new land of Canaan. The people who already lived there were organized into small city-states by powerful rulers who frequently exploited their peasants and kept all the real power to themselves. But the escaped slaves had a different view, gained when they met with God at Mt Sinai and received his Law. They therefore set about the establishment of a different regime, characterized by justice and inspired by the example of God himself.

▲ Joyful worship is one of the main things Christians do together. Ever since New Testament times, his followers have worshipped Jesus as Lord.

Jesus also talked of the importance of community. He frequently described God's kingdom as a context in which people might find true personal fulfilment. There the outcasts of first-century society—people like tax-gatherers, women, prostitutes and the disabled—could find acceptance. And it was a place where disciples could love one another because they had experienced the love of God himself. For Jesus, people and their needs were of fundamental importance. They certainly took precedence over theology. This is what makes his teaching so attractive to many today. The South American writer Gustavo Gutierrez puts it like this: '. . .the gospel summons into being a people's church. A church which springs up from the people. . . We are called to build the church from below, from the poor, from the situation of the exploited classes, the excluded races, and the despised cultures.'

Sharing a vision

Abraham's task was to bring blessing into the lives of all nations. His family, and the nation that followed, were not selected because of any special virtues they had in themselves. They were to be a vehicle through which God's will could become a living reality in the lives of the whole human race. But at this point the story falls apart. Later generations of Abraham's descendants sometimes concluded that because God had chosen them, they must be better than everyone else. Yet the vision was never lost, and is repeated and reinforced in later Old Testament books.

Jesus placed this vision at the centre of his plan for his disciples. They were called to be with him, but only so they could be sent out to share the good news with others. The three years they spent with him were training for the larger mission in which they were later to engage. As we read the rest of the New Testament, we can see how that mission remained focused on God's original call to Abraham. They sought the development of a community of Christ's people who would reflect God's will in their life together.

3.9

THE WAY OF LOVE

▲ Jesus taught and practised a way of self-giving love. Mother Teresa of Calcutta is foremost among many who have adopted that way for life.

Ask someone who knows only a little about Jesus to sum him up, and somewhere in the answer will come that his message was love. If we comb through the four Gospels, we find that Jesus did not use the word 'love' very often. Yet each writer manages to convey that love is crucial to the way of life that Jesus is bringing.

In Mark chapter 12 verse 28 Jesus is asked which is the most important commandment in God's law. In reply he does not single out any one of the famous Ten Commandments. Instead he chooses two verses from different contexts in the Old Testament law. Both contain the word 'love':

■ **Love God.** From Deuteronomy chapter 6 verse 4 Jesus quotes, 'Love the Lord your God with all your heart and with all your soul and with all your mind and with all your strength.' The Hebrew word used here for 'love', like our English word, has a wide meaning. It can be the powerful force that draws a man and a woman into a passionate relationship. Prophets such as Hosea and Jeremiah were not afraid to compare God's love for his people with the love of a husband fiercely jealous when his bride was unfaithful and broken-hearted when she left home.

The word can also mean the love between parent and child, the one caring and providing, the other receiving and trusting. Or it can be the love between friends such as David and Jonathan who long to be companions and share each other's thoughts and interests. It is also used for the practical goodwill, sympathy and respect which members of a community ought to have towards their neighbours including those who are immigrants.

With all these human kinds of loving in mind, we

The Neighbour

Jesus taught his followers to love God with all their heart, and to love their neighbours as themselves. The commandment to love one's neighbour has its roots in the Old Testament, in the book of Leviticus. Chapter 19 of Leviticus takes up the theme of being a good neighbour.

There should be respect for property and honesty in business relationships; the weak are not to be exploited; local magistrates must be impartial. There is a warning against brooding on hurts and letting hatred grow. If you have been wronged, be frank and

other faiths who are living alongside the people of Israel. They are not to be ill-treated. The love they are to be given is more than cool and careful fairness. It is to include warmth of feeling. Leviticus reminds them of the time Israel herself was in slavery. 'You were aliens in Egypt. Remember what it feels like.'

Who is my neighbour?

In two places in the Gospels Jesus discusses who is to be included as a neighbour.

to stand firm and not befriend those who would undermine the community or lead them away from God. Jewish teachers in Jesus' day tended to limit the command 'Love your neighbour' to fellow Jews and other residents with whom they were at peace.

Jesus startlingly rejected that limit. He went directly to the extreme case. He urged his followers to love enemies, people who actively disliked them and made their lives miserable. Both Jewish people and, later, Christian believers were often victimized, simply for belief in God and

■ **The parable of the good Samaritan.** When asked to define what he meant by 'neighbour', Jesus told a story. Luke records it in chapter 10 of his Gospel. Jesus paints the scene of a man lying mugged by the roadside. Two kinds of religious leaders, a priest and a Levite, pass him without stopping. The audience expects a third person to come by and help the victim. And they expect him to be an ordinary layman, a fellow Jew. But Jesus surprises them. The third man is a Samaritan, a

rebuke your neighbour. Do not seek revenge. Love your neighbour as yourself.

'But,' asked the interpreters of the Law, 'who exactly is my neighbour?' Should this love be extended beyond the immediate community to cover nearby tribes and nations? Or was it limited to fellow Israelites? Leviticus offered at least one extension: the writer mentions resident aliens, people of other races and

■ **The Sermon on the Mount.** Jesus said to his disciples, 'You have heard that it was said, "Love your neighbour and hate your enemy." But I tell you: "Love your enemies and pray for those who persecute you"' (Matthew 5:43). No text in the Old Testament actually says, 'Hate your enemy.' Indeed, a number of verses encourage generosity towards personal enemies. But Israel was often a nation under attack and there are texts which urge the people

loyalty to his standards. In the face of such treatment Jesus urges a love which cares for the welfare of the persecutors, a love which prays for them.

Jesus bases this love for enemies on the example of God. As the creator God, involved with every detail of the universe, he does not discriminate between deserving and undeserving human beings. He sends the essential gifts of sun and rain on all. Those who love him, who are under his rule, must love others with the same unrestricted love.

traditional enemy.

Jesus has shown that loving your neighbour means acting when you meet a person in need, even if it be an enemy, or an inconvenience. 'Don't sit debating who counts as your neighbour,' Jesus is saying. 'Go out and be a good neighbour as need arises.' But Jesus has another point. It is one thing to imagine going out and helping a needy Samaritan. It is harder to admit that the Samaritan might be the person to help us. Jesus' understanding of neighbourly love requires trust and respect as well.

▼ Who is my neighbour? Not just the person who looks like me, but people of all races throughout the world. We are bound together in the human family.

are to love God. It is to be love with heart and soul and mind. These three words sum up all our inner experience of thinking, feeling, imagining and deciding. And we are to love God with all our strength, also, widening the application to the external world, our energy and abilities, our possessions and our power.

■ **Love your neighbour as yourself.** Side by side with the great command to love God, Jesus quotes from Leviticus chapter 19 verse 18, 'Love your neighbour as yourself.' Notice how the words assume that human beings should have a basic warmth and respect towards themselves. With that as a yardstick they are to look outwards and love others.

When these Hebrew commands were translated into Greek, translators were faced with a choice of four words for love. They avoided *eros*, meaning sexual passion. They also turned down a word for family affection and one for love between friends. They chose a much less common word, *agape*, to honour or to welcome someone. This emphasized that this love is not just an emotion that sweeps over us. It is an attitude that can be determined by the will. That is why it can be commanded of us.

Jesus was not alone in highlighting these Old Testament commands to love. Other Jewish teachers were stressing love as the key word to describe our relationship with God. Rabbi Akiba called the command to love one's neighbour a basic principle of the law, embracing all others. It is possible that Jesus was the first to bring the two together like this as a summary of the Law. In Luke chapter 10 verse 27 they are quoted by a lawyer who is questioning Jesus, which may mean either that it was common to link them or that the lawyer knows Jesus taught this. But certainly Jesus was distinctive in the way he applied them and the way he lived them out.

Love interprets the law

Jewish teachers made specific regulations to apply the Old Testament laws to as many situations as possible. Some described this as putting a fence around the Law. If you kept all the rules in the code, they claimed, you would never come near to breaking God's Law.

Jesus was often in conflict with this method. In Mark chapter 7 verse 11 he takes as an example a rule which says that someone who declares a sum of money dedicated to God is free from any obligation to help his parents with the money. Jesus points out that the Law put great emphasis on honouring parents. This 'tradition' was making a nonsense of a command of God. In a very strong speech Jesus said of such teachers that 'they tie up heavy loads and put them on men's shoulders'; they 'shut the kingdom of heaven in men's faces'.

After such strong words it was inevitable that Jesus would be watched very carefully to see if he could be accused of breaking God's Law. There was one area of his life where they began to think they could pin him down. He healed people on the sabbath. One of the Ten Commandments prohibited working on the last day of the week. The people Jesus healed were not just emergency cases; some had been like that for years. Their healing could have waited one more day. But Jesus was unrepentant: 'The sabbath was made for man and not man for the sabbath.'

For Jesus, a day dedicated to God was a particularly appropriate day to bring God's healing love into the lives of men and women. Any interpretation of the Law which did not share that priority was both inhuman and ungodly.

In the second half of Matthew chapter 5, beginning at verse 21, we are given some examples of how Jesus applied well-known sayings of the Old Testament Law. 'Do not murder' is not just about the crime of homicide. It is about something which starts when space is given to selfish or jealous anger. Its next step may be hurtful and destructive words or violent blows. Either way it is the inner attitude which determines whether word and action will be love and therefore good. No human court can judge the heart but God can.

The moment when a partner makes love to a third party appears to be the point of betrayal of a marriage, the act of adultery. But Jesus traces the evil to someone who allows the casual noticing of attractiveness to turn into a long hard look of appraisal and desire. Jesus had no illusions about the strength of the forces involved here. He uses a shocking metaphor from the operating theatre: 'If your right eye causes you to sin, pluck it out.' Urgent and drastic mental action is required if anger is to be controlled and love to remain faithful.

Perhaps the most searching question about love is how it relates to justice. The vivid maxim of the Law— 'an eye for an eye and a tooth for a tooth'—laid down a vital principle of Israel's justice. There were to be no blood feuds, no escalating acts of revenge. A wrong was to receive limited retribution which could be seen as fair.

This, says Jesus, is not a principle to be scaled down into personal relationships. There it becomes meanness and revenge. If someone slaps your cheek, do not slap back. Surprise her with the other

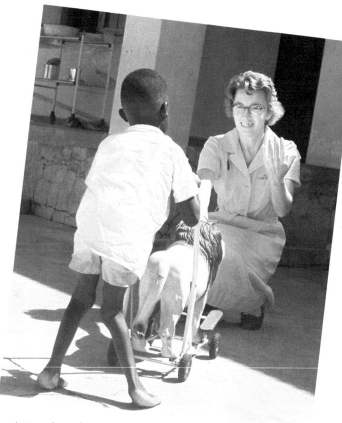

▲ Jesus' way is to serve others. Not as if we are superior, but because he has met our own deep needs.

cheek. Love's aim is to bring violence and need in the world to an end. On the large scale that may require restraining force and accurate calculation. But the love is fundamentally non-violent and overwhelmingly generous. That is how love's followers must be.

Love is response to God

This ethic of love is so far-reaching that many have recoiled from Jesus' teaching. Some see him as a deluded idealist. Others, like the poet Swinburne, fear him as a kill-joy:

Thou hast conquered O pale Galilean.
The world has grown grey from thy breath.

Such views are based on deep misunderstanding. Jesus was not a 'nice' moral teacher telling everyone to be good and love each other. He is a news announcer, whose headline is that the reign of God is breaking into the community. With the arrival of God's kingdom comes new power, new motivation

Law and Love

'Love' is often seen as the opposite of 'law'. When we respond from the heart we have no need of lists of dos and don'ts. So does the teaching of Jesus about love leave a place for moral law in the Christian life? Down the centuries his followers have struggled with this question.

■ **Some see Jesus as a teacher who gave a new moral law which modifies and adds to the laws in the Old Testament.** It has been claimed that Matthew's Gospel understands Jesus this way and presents his 'Sermon on the Mount' in ways that remind the readers of Moses the Old Testament lawgiver.

■ **Others claim that Jesus sets people free from living by laws.** Those who believe in him are changed. They are 'born again' by the Spirit of God and become new people. They do not need laws to follow; they have God's love in their hearts.

The apostle Paul stressed the freedom of love. As a young man he had grown up among rabbis who taught people to work hard to keep God's laws. The aim was to be good enough for God's kingdom. But Paul now knew what an impossible burden this was. And the exciting new message of Jesus was that God was inviting him to enter his kingdom, as he was. From his own experience Paul could teach that once we accept God's generous forgiveness, and start to let his Spirit operate in our lives, then we will begin to be free to live out love. (See, for example, Paul's teaching in Romans 8 and Galatians 5.)

Despite his emphasis on freedom Paul did not believe that Christians simply know in their hearts what is love. He and the other writers of the New Testament go on emphasizing honesty, sexual faithfulness in marriage, control of tongue and temper—all themes prominent in the Old Testament Law and in the teaching of Jesus.

In the 1960s J. Fletcher popularized a new approach which others had begun to suggest. In his book *Situation Ethics* he claimed that the only law which is always good is the command to love. Other rules such as 'do not steal' or 'do not murder' are useful moral guidelines but they should not bind us. We can imagine situations of starvation or suffering where love seems to demand that we steal, or compassion prompts us to kill. Fletcher's 'love' is not a vague sentimental feeling. It includes justice for groups as well as care for individuals.

In medical and sexual morality, situation ethics has had considerable impact. Many now view ending the life of an unwanted child in the womb, or having homosexual intercourse, as actions which may be good because they are the 'loving' thing to do in the situation.

But human beings cannot live with only one absolute moral principle. Asked why we think that our action was the loving thing to do in a situation, we give reasons. And that requires us to have other principles which give content to the word love.

For Jesus, the two great love commandments (love of God, love of neighbour) sum up the moral teaching of the Old Testament. In the Sermon on the Mount he said he had not come to abolish the Law 'but to fulfil it'. What did he mean?

The Law, of course, included ceremonial regulations and civil laws for Israel. It covered matters of diet, of worship, of behaviour. As non-Jews started joining the Christian church, they puzzled whether they should keep all such laws. They remembered Jesus saying that the rules about ritually clean and unclean food were visual aids for the more important matter of moral purity. They concluded that the coming of Jesus had changed certain things. He had 'fulfilled' the ceremonial law by being the perfect example of a life in tune with God. That was what the law pointed to. And by his sacrificial death he had made the sacrifices of the Old Testament Law obsolete. He had fulfilled the moral law by living it out, and by teaching his followers its inward intentions as well as its outward requirements.

There are no short cuts in Christian moral decision-making. Christians have to pray and be responsive to the Spirit of God in the choices they face. They have to work together to apply Jesus' principles and priorities to the dilemmas of the modern world.

and joy. Just as the discovery that the prince loves her brings vitality to Cinderella, so the great secret of God's love for humanity is bringing new life to discouraged and hopeless people as it is revealed.

A great deal of Jesus' teaching is in his parables, vivid stories from everyday life which still come alive for us today. Their central teaching includes that:

■ **God is generous in forgiving,** like a great king who cancels an enormous debt for one of his staff. How terrible that the forgiven man then goes off and threatens a colleague who owes him a pittance.

■ **God is welcoming,** like the father who sees a worthless son returning home, all his money wasted, and hurries out to hug him. How tragic that the older brother is jealous of the welcome the 'prodigal' receives.

■ **God is patient,** like the farmer whose enemy has sown weeds in among his wheat. He waits for harvest time to sort it out, in case the crop should get damaged.

■ **God provides what is healthy and wholesome,** like a parent providing for children. He does not serve up mean or dangerous jokes like stones instead of bread or live snakes instead of fish. And so the golden rule for his children should be, 'Do to others what you would have them do to you.'

Francis of Assisi

Francis of Assisi (1182–1226) did more than anyone else to restore the image of the Jesus of the Gospels to the consciousness of the medieval Church. He did so by reflecting the life and character of Jesus in his own life. Of course, he did this in a way appropriate to his own time and place, but it was in a way that has caught the imagination of Christians and others down to the present day.

Francis' aim was to conform his life to that of Jesus in

and the compassion of Christ. Of course, in his desire to imitate Christ, he knew only too well his sins and failures.

Francis renounced his wealthy background and embraced absolute poverty —not reluctantly but fervently, making it the principle of his whole life and of the order of friars he founded. He did so because poverty identified him with Jesus, who had nowhere to lay his head. He wanted, he said, 'naked to follow the

▲ **Giotto's painting shows Francis preaching to the birds. His love took in the**

every respect. He took the example and the teaching of Jesus in the Gospels straight-forwardly and extremely seriously. As his biographer Bonaventura put it, 'His only desire was to be like Christ and to imitate him perfectly.' In particular, Francis imitated the poverty, the humility

whole of creation, in its loveliest as well as its ugliest forms.

naked Christ.' The final step in his discovery of his vocation came when he heard in church the passage in chapter 10 of Matthew's Gospel, where Jesus, sending out his disciples, orders them to take no money, no bag, no second tunic, no shoes, no staff. 'This is what I long

to do with all my heart,' cried Francis joyfully. Typically he obeyed these words to the letter.

Francis insisted on literal imitation of Christ and the strictest obedience to Jesus' teaching. 'Give to anyone who asks you,' said Jesus, and so Francis did so, however little he had to give. 'Take no thought for the morrow,' said Jesus. and so Francis allowed his friars to earn or beg only enough food for each day at a time.

Yet with this extreme literalism Francis discovered a liberating way of life. He lived with absolute trust in God. Having no material possessions, he enjoyed a kinship with all God's creatures. While he made a principle of never criticizing the rich and the powerful— which would be inconsistent with humility —he was able to live close to the poor and the suffering. It was no accident that he made a special point of caring for and actually living with lepers. As in Jesus' time, these were the most despised and shunned people in society. Francis showed them the Jesus who in humility and compassion comes close to them.

It was especially the crucified Christ that Francis longed to imitate. He never forgot the vision of Jesus on the cross which helped to show him his vocation. He had felt then that the words of Jesus in the Gospels were being spoken to him: 'If you would come my way, renounce yourself, take up your cross and follow me.' He was frequently moved to tears by the thought of Jesus' crucifixion, and treated his own sufferings as inconsiderable by compari-son. Wanting to give himself as totally as Jesus did, he hoped for martyrdom. Instead he received a way of sharing in Christ's sufferings which was then unknown, though many other examples have been recorded since: the *stigmata*. Two years before his death, meditating on the cross, he had a vision

of the crucified Christ which left him with five wounds corresponding to those of Christ. They caused him continuous pain until his death.

A story of a later Franciscan's vision sums up the impression Francis made. Praying in the cathedral of Siena, he saw Jesus enter the cathedral, along with a great crowd of saints. As Jesus walked his footprints remained imprinted on the floor. All the saints tried hard to place their feet in the prints of Jesus' footsteps. Only Francis succeeded perfectly.

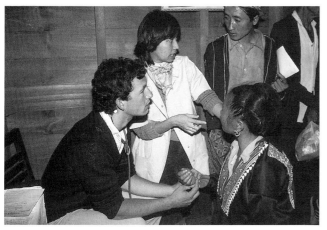

▲ Wherever people live, they need love. Physical pain, the loneliness of city life, are made bearable when people love us and show us we count. This is why Jesus' way of love is so needed, and so revolutionary.

Many other ancient teachers had this rule in negative form: avoid doing things you would not like done to you. It is Jesus, with his good news of the active, generous love of a Father God, who puts it in this challenging, positive form.

So the core of Jesus' message is love as a response. We are to exert ourselves to love others, not just to obey a command, but in response to irresistible love. 'We love,' writes John, 'because he (Jesus) first loved us.'

Jesus the showcase of love

That phrase, 'he first loved us', comes in John's first letter, where it has far more content than just the pictures of a loving God in Jesus' parables. John begins his letter by writing of that 'which we have seen with our eyes, looked at and our hands have touched'. Those who went around with Jesus were not merely hearing words about love. They were seeing it in action. They experienced what it is like to be with someone who is loving to the very centre of his being.

A. Verhey calls his book about the values of Jesus *The Great Reversal*. Love is humble. It does not condescend but comes down to eye level with the ones being loved. Jesus seemed to be the long-awaited 'Christ', God's special, anointed messenger. But he was from an insignificant northern town, and had only an adopted father. He had no higher education but worked through early adulthood at carpentry. When at last he began his life's work, he kept giving time and energy to insignificant people.

He would pause to bless babies.
He spent time with women.
He went to parties given by people on the fringe.
He stopped his whole crowd for a blind beggar.

Not that he was an inverted snob, denying the humanity of the rich or successful. John's Gospel sets a pair of interviews side by side. Nicodemus is a rich, religious, Jewish male, a member of the government. Then in the next chapter Jesus meets a woman who is alone, much divorced, a foreigner of another faith. Jesus treats both with courtesy and seriousness. He meets them where they are.

Love is not only humble; it is costly. Jesus risks infection as he touches lepers. He risks unpopularity as he takes issue with the methods of the lawyers. He risks betrayal as he goes on offering friendship to Judas. He risks desertion by his inner circle as he refuses to exert any control over them except love. He risks his life as he moves step by step towards

The Poverty of Jesus

John Chrysostom, bishop of Constantinople in the fourth century, preached a sermon which would be just as relevant today:

'You eat to excess: Christ eats not even what he needs. You eat a variety of cakes; he eats not even a piece of dried bread. You drink fine wine; but on him you have not bestowed so much as a cup of cold water. You lie on a soft and embroidered bed; but he is perishing in the cold. You live in luxury on things that properly belong to him. Why, were you the guardian of a child and, having taken control of his estate, you neglected him in his extreme need, you would have ten thousand accusers and you would suffer the punishment set by the law. At the moment, you have taken possession of the resources that belong to Christ and you consume them aimlessly. Don't you realize that you are going to be held accountable?'

Jerusalem where the humility and priorities of his love have threatened and humiliated those in power.

Yet the Gospel-writers were convinced that his journey to Jerusalem was more than a gamble that he risked and lost. They claim he knew the outcome and that he went steadily ahead. He moved deliberately towards the great reversal that put all others in the shade. As he hung in agony on a Roman cross he carried all the darkness, hatred, evil and despair that human beings heap up and hurl at God and at each other. They understood his death as the final triumphant demonstration of God's love, the basis on which all his mercy and forgiveness rest: 'This is what love is: it is not that we have loved God, but that he loved us and sent his Son to be the means by which our sins are forgiven.'

That was what was so amazingly new about Jesus' new command to love.

3.10

A VISION OF THE FUTURE

Few people can live without hope. Without something to look forward to, our personalities fall apart. So Jesus' vision of a future world dominated by the loving presence of God is indeed good news.

The promised kingdom of God

Jesus taught that the kingdom of God—the new era promised by God in the Old Testament—had already dawned. His own life and ministry were the first rays of the new day and God's kingdom made its presence felt as Jesus brought to people forgiveness and new life.

Yet the kingdom of God did not fully come all at once. God's total triumph over the powers of evil and his establishing of a world of permanent justice and peace remained an object of hope for the future. So he taught his followers to pray, 'Your kingdom come'. And he spoke of the time when 'people will come from east and west and north and south, and will take their places at the feast in the kingdom of God'.

How will this kingdom come about?

- **Jesus spoke about the growth of God's kingdom.** Several of his parables highlighted the contrast between this kingdom's small and hidden beginnings and its ultimate open success. It is like when a farmer scatters seed which eventually produces a great harvest. Now that the power of God's love is at work in the world, nothing will stop it reaching its triumphant conclusion.
- **Jesus stressed that God's kingdom would come by God's power, as his gift.** It is, after all, the kingdom of God. This stress on God's action does not rule out the call for people to co-operate

▲ The Bible ends with a vision of a city of God. So Christians are called to find ways of living in cities which do not crush our humanity. We are all potential inhabitants of the new Jerusalem.

with God's purpose in trustful obedience. We cannot simply shrug our shoulders and do nothing. But it does rule out the idea that God's kingdom can be spread or built by sheer human effort.

- **Jesus taught that one day he would return to earth.** And at this 'second coming' God would establish his kingdom in its fullness. Jesus' return will mark the end of the present course of history as we know it. It will usher in for ever God's kingdom of peace, justice and love. Then the promises of the Old Testament prophets and the longings of all God's people will be fulfilled.

The nature of the kingdom of God

Jesus offered no detailed description of what this new world will be like. He spoke in the language of

▲ We naturally ask what future are our children likely to inherit. We need to include their spiritual destiny in the answer. What are Jesus' plans for the world's children?

the poet and not with the precision of the scientist. And this was inevitable. Because the world to come remains in the future, and is not simply a continuation of our present earthly life, it can only be described in picture language.

But what pictures! The people of God, said Jesus, will be happy in his presence. There will be laughter and dancing, and the hungry will be filled. People from every corner of the earth will share in the feast along with the fathers of Judaism, Abraham, Isaac and Jacob. There will be no limit beyond which God refuses to give his blessing.

But you cannot have a party on your own! Notice how these pictures stress that life in God's kingdom is life in relationship to others. And it is life in full harmony with others, because all are in true relationship to God.

God himself is the central reality from which his kingdom derives its life and its character. Because God is loving, just and eternal, his kingdom will be characterized by love and justice, and will stand forever. So God's kingdom will be in stark contrast to the self-interest, injustice and instability which often spoils the human use of power.

The future life

Is it possible to trust this vision of the future? Jesus was in no doubt that God would give people eternal life so that they might enjoy his kingdom. He based his confidence on the loving character of God. When opponents tried to ridicule his teaching about life after death, he quoted to them God's words to Moses, words well-known to his contemporaries: 'I am the God of Abraham, the God of Isaac, and the God of Jacob.' And he drew the conclusion, 'He is the God of the living, not of the dead'. Abraham, Isaac and Jacob, the patriarchs of Israel had been dead many years, even in Moses' day. But Jesus was pointing out that, long after their deaths, God could still tell Moses that he was their God. And since it was meaningless to speak of dead people having a God, these words to Moses implied that those whom God loves must also live on after death. Jesus has shown us a God to whom we human beings matter. It is impossible to imagine this God wanting to scrap those who are precious to him.

Jesus gave no more than hints about what people will be like in the future life. 'When the dead rise', he said, 'they will neither marry nor be given in marriage; they will be like the angels in heaven'. This at least suggests that the conditions of our present life do not simply continue without change. But surely Jesus cannot be saying that the future life is just a pale reflection of the joys of marriage? No, he means that the kingdom of God will involve a broadening and deepening of relationships for all.

The resurrection of Jesus himself provides a clue to the nature of the general resurrection. How will the dead rise? The Gospel accounts show that when he appeared to his disciples after his resurrection they did not immediately recognize him. They only did so when he spoke a familiar word or made a familiar movement. This suggests that his risen body was not simply his earthly body restored to its previous life. In some way it was different—a glorious, eternal form. Yet there was enough continuity with his former existence for people to realize that it was really Jesus whom they were seeing. In a similar way, God's people will experience eternal life, but in a new form suitable for his kingdom. Yet they will still be recognizably themselves.

Jesus did not explain what happens to a person in the interval between death and the final resurrection when he would return. Does the believer go immediately to heaven, or is there a stage of unconscious waiting? Questions of timing may be irrelevant, since at death we pass beyond the earthly measurements of time. The next thing that happens after death *is* resurrection. Certainly Jesus assures us at the point of death, as he assured the thief who was crucified beside him, that those who trust themselves to him are secure forever in his love.

The Second Coming

The whole New Testament tingles with excited expectation that Jesus will come again. He who has come in the events of Bethlehem, Galilee and Jerusalem will come in the future to complete God's work on earth. But their hopes were focused not on an event, the end of the world, but on Jesus as the Lord of history.

Jesus himself spoke of his future coming in dramatic picture language. Referring to himself as 'the Son of Man', he foresaw his 'coming in clouds with great power and glory' (clouds were a regular Old Testament symbol for the presence of God).

Three questions are commonly asked about this second coming:

■ **How will he come?** He will come in triumph rather than in the hiddenness and ambiguity of his first coming. But the New Testament does not offer precise descriptions of what this coming will be like. It will not be simply a re-appearance of a man among men. Nor will the nature of earthly existence continue on its more or less familiar course. It will not be another historical event like Jesus' ministry in Galilee. It will introduce a new order, God's eternal kingdom. And that kingdom will be free from the limitations of space and time as we now experience them.

■ **When will he come?** For centuries people have suggested that Christ's coming was near because they believed that 'signs' predicted in the Bible were coming true in their lifetime. But they failed to take seriously Jesus' words when he denounced such date-fixing . He spoke of his future coming as sudden and unexpected. And those promises of Jesus that his coming is 'near' are best understood not as statements of a timetable but as expressions of the certainty that God will complete his work through Christ.

■ **Why is this belief important?** Is it not sufficient to say that Christ has come, to bring men and women into a relationship with God, and that after death they may share life with him? No, for Jesus' life, death, resurrection and coming again are all of a piece. We misunderstand his second coming unless we see it as the completion of what was done in his first coming.

Those events in Galilee and Jerusalem need the triumph of the second coming if they are to be seen in their true light. Otherwise God's action in history is left with a beginning and no end.

We do not know in detail what to expect, or when to expect it. But we know *whom* to expect, and that is what matters.

▼ **Stephan Lochner's sixteenth-century painting of the Last Judgement conveys ideas we now find alien. Yet Jesus taught that we must all give account of our lives.**

Who will go to heaven?

Jesus had a clear vision of God's purpose for his creation and for all people. But he knew too that many resist that purpose. And he nowhere suggested that everyone, irrespective of their attitude towards God, would inevitably enter God's eternal kingdom. He spoke of a process of judgment at his final coming, when the choices we make in this life—to respond to or to resist Christ—are underlined. If we love him now, we shall enter into a fuller experience of his love then. If we have refused his love in the present life, that refusal will be confirmed (look, for example, at Jesus' words in Matthew 10:32,33, or John 3:16–21).

Is it that God is not loving enough to forgive everybody? No, on the contrary, God has done everything necessary to open his kingdom to all who are willing to enter it. But love by its very nature does not force itself on those who are unwilling to receive it. Because God loves us he allows—and respects—our freedom to respond to or refuse that love. Hence the possibility remains that some may choose to separate themselves permanently from Jesus and his love.

We are handling serious issues here, and we cannot speculate on the destiny of particular individuals. Indeed, when people questioned Jesus along the lines, 'Are only a few people going to be saved?' he brushed their question aside and challenged them to be clear about their own response to his message. 'Make every effort to enter through the narrow door. . .'

Living in hope

Jesus' vision of the future is not given to satisfy human curiosity, but to transform human lives. It has very practical implications:

■ **The assurance that God's purpose reaches beyond death brings a new perspective to tragic suffering.**

■ **Christians whose hope is fixed on God's future have challenging and satisfying goals to aim at in this life.** Freed from anxiety about their own death and destiny, they can give themselves in service to others. How different from the man who chose this epitaph: 'Here lies a man who went out of the world without knowing why he came into it'!

■ **The fact of judgment means that God holds each human being responsible for his or her actions.** Choices matter to God. Though we do not always feel it is so, our actions are significant.

■ **God intends his kingdom to be characterized**

The Hope of Life

In his novel *The Brothers Karamazov*, Fyodor Dostoevsky expresses his own feelings:

'It is the great mystery of human life that old grief passes into quiet, tender joy. The mild serenity of age takes the place of riotous blood of youth. I bless the rising sun each day, and as before, my heart sings to meet it, but now I love even more its setting, its long slanting rays and the soft, tender, gentle memories that come with them, the dear images from the whole of my long happy life—and over all the Divine Truth, softening, reconciling, forgiving! My life is ending, I know that well, but every day that is left me I feel how my earthly life is in touch with a new, infinite, unknown, but approaching life, the nearness of which sets my soul quivering with rapture, my mind glowing and my heart weeping with joy.'

▲ A hostage released after a Beirut airport siege greets his child on returning home. Jesus promised a day when he and his people would finally be united.

Christin Our Neighbour

C.S.Lewis had a strong sense of the eternal in every person. In *The Business of Heaven*, he wrote:

'It is a serious thing to live in a society of possible gods and goddesses, to remember that the dullest and most uninteresting person you can talk to may one day be a creature which, if you saw it now, you would be strongly tempted to worship, or else a horror and a corruption such as you would meet only in a nightmare. All day long we are, in some degree, helping each other to one or other of these destinations. There are no ordinary people. You have never talked to a mere mortal. Nations, cultures, arts, civilizations—these are mortal, but it is immortals whom we joke with, work with, marry, snub and exploit—immortal horrors or everlasting splendours.'

by justice, peace and love and Christians are called to show those qualities now.

■ **The characteristics of God's kingdom give guidelines for human society as well as for individual believers.** Human societies will always be imperfect until God's kingdom comes, but the vision of how the human community will *ultimately* live provides goals for nations and communities now. It was Martin Luther King Jr's 'dream', his Christian vision of a nation living as God meant it to live, that drove him to action and kept him going when things got tough.

Is this hope soundly-based?

How can we know that this vision for the future has any solid basis? Might it not be something that developed because people wanted to believe it in order to make life bearable? No. Christians look for the final coming of Christ and his kingdom not because they seek compensation for present sufferings, but because they long for the full experience of what they already know in part—of God's love, the Spirit's power. And since their faith is in Jesus who is risen already, they have confidence in the future resurrection of all his people.

3.11

GOD OUR FATHER

Jesus taught us to think of God as Father.

Some statistics indicate that this is so. The Old Testament is three times the length of the New Testament. The word 'father' occurs about 1,200 times in the Old Testament, and about 400 times in the New—exactly as expected. But while the word 'father' is used to refer to God only about forty times in the Old Testament, it is used in this way 260 times in the New. Why is there this enormous difference?

Part of the answer is that during the three or four hundred years separating Old Testament from New Testament times the Jews began to speak of God more freely as Father. But the main part of the answer lies with Jesus.

Jesus once said: 'No one knows the Son except the Father, and no one knows the Father except the Son and those to whom the Son chooses to reveal him'. This is really a parable, one of the shortest in the Gospels. It is a picture drawn from human life. A father and a son know one another in an exclusive relationship, perhaps as a result of working together on the farm or in the workshop. Today we would use the picture of husband and wife to convey the same point, but in Jewish society the father/son relationship was used to indicate a very close relationship.

Jesus applied this parable to himself in relation to God.

Jesus spoke of God as his Father

Every time that he prayed, he addressed God as 'Father'. The only exception is when he felt himself to be alone and abandoned on the cross.

To address God as Father in prayer may not seem surprising to us, because that is how Christians habitually pray today. But it was remarkable for Jesus to do so for two reasons:

■ **We do not know of any other Jew in Palestine at the time who addressed God as his own Father.** Jews might think of God as the Father of the whole nation, and a group might address God as their Father, but for an individual to address God so was unheard of—a fact all the more remarkable because it did happen in other religions.

■ In one place the actual Aramaic word which Jesus used has been preserved for us. It is *Abba*. This word could be used by a person to address his own earthly father within the family circle. The fact that Jesus (and only Jesus) used this colloquial expression to address God underlines the extraordinary intimacy of the relationship between Jesus and his Father.

Two stories in the Gospels show the basis for this relationship. In Luke chapter 2 verses 41–52 we find Jesus as a young lad staying behind in the temple at Jerusalem after his parents had set off home for Galilee. When they eventually found him there and reproached him for staying behind, he said, 'Didn't you know I had to be in my Father's house?' This brief glimpse into the mind of Jesus shows that he already saw God as his Father and could speak of him as 'my Father'.

Then, when he had reached adulthood, he went to join in the baptism that John was carrying out at the River Jordan. As he climbed out of the water, he had a vision and heard a voice from heaven which said, 'You are my Son, whom I love; with you I am well pleased.'

These passages show that Jesus had a unique relationship to God as his Father.

Who are God's children?

Jesus did not speak about God by this name all the time. He seems to have reserved it for talking to his followers. He did not speak like this to people who rejected his message. For he was referring to a relationship to which he alone could admit people.

This is contrary to what most people think. They believe that God is the Father of all people in that he is their Creator. Although this way of speaking about God can be found in other religions, it is not found in the Bible. This is very obvious in the Old Testament where God is rarely called Father and then only of the people of Israel or of their ruler in particular. In the Bible God is in no sense the Father of all humankind.

Jesus taught that people can *become* children of God, and thus know him as their Father. Having God as our Father and being his children is a new relationship into which we enter. This is the point of the last line of the little parable: 'No one knows the Father except the Son *and those to whom the Son chooses to reveal him.*' We become the children of God and come to know him as our Father not as a result of our creation and physical birth but as a result of being adopted into God's family. This was the great privilege to which Jesus admitted his followers, and to which he alone can admit people.

Christian teachers such as Paul said the same thing. They recognized that it is when we receive the Spirit of God, who makes us children, that we become his children. Only then do we have the right to address him, as Jesus did, as *Abba*.

What are the characteristics of this new relationship?

God treats the members of his family with fatherly care. He is no longer a distant heavenly figure, to be worshipped with awe. He is the Father who cares compassionately for his children. They do not need to worry about the future because he will provide for their needs and protect them from harm.

God's children are to obey their Father. In the Bible a father is a figure of authority who is entitled to obedience from his children. The mark that shows that people know God as their Father is that they gladly obey him, just as Jesus did.

The Lord's Prayer

The disciples asked Jesus how to pray, and in response he gave them this, which has become the Christian family prayer down the centuries.

Our Father in heaven,
hallowed be your name,
your kingdom come,
your will be done
   on earth as it is in heaven.
Give us today our daily bread.
Forgive us our debts,
   as we also have forgiven our debtors.
And lead us not into temptation,
but deliver us from the evil one.

Jesus and the Painters

Every painter has seen Jesus through the eyes of his own culture and beliefs. The paintings shown here span five-and-a-half centuries, and the differences are vast. How did each of us receive our own picture of Jesus?

▲ Gerard David, of the Flemish school, shows the crucified Jesus between the apostle John and Francis of Assisi.

▲ *Top* Jesus the man of sorrows is a recurring theme, as in this seventeenth-century work by Antonio Pereda.

▲ *Above* Jan Breughel (1568–1625) painted Jesus meeting Mary Magdalene on resurrection morning.

▶ Tiepolo's crucifixion is from the eighteenth century.

▶▶ ▼ **This cross on an African hill is by Elimo Njau of Tanzania (1959).**

▼ **William Blake's 'Agony in the Garden' depicts Jesus struggling with the will of God.**

▶ **Fra Angelico, in the early-fifteenth century, shows Jesus telling Mary Magdalene not to touch him in his resurrection body.**

▲ 'Has Christ not appeared to you?' is the title of Karl Schmidt-Rottluf's crucifixion. Made in 1918, this woodcut gives the idea of Jesus tormented by the agony of war.

▶ Francis Bacon's 'Fragment of a Crucifixion' (1950) tries to show the unbearable senselessness of it all.

PART 4

DEATH ... AND THEN

About a third of each Gospel is devoted to the last
week of Jesus' life. The week began with a triumphant welcome
into Jerusalem. It ended with Jesus' crucifixion and burial.
His mission seemed to have finished.

But then something unique happened. And as a result
Jesus' mission did not end in Jerusalem but has continued
and grown ever since.

CONTENTS

SPECIAL FEATURES

Pharisees and Sadducees
Powers of evil
The last week
Were the Jews to blame?
The martyrs
Why did Jesus die?
The shroud
Did Jesus rise from death?
Jesus the living presence
The Jesus of the revivalists
The dawn of new hope
Jesus and Paul

4.1

GROWING OPPOSITION

When Jesus stood before Pontius Pilate, the Roman Governor, those who opposed and accused him were not godless people but the religious leaders of the day. The High Priest together with the chief priests and the whole Sanhedrin, the highest tribunal of the Jews, had declared that Jesus was worthy of death. They brought him to Pilate to endorse their judgment so that Jesus might be executed.

But this was not a sudden development. The trial before Pilate was the climax of opposition to Jesus which had grown through his ministry. Opposition from Satan began before he began openly to preach, when in the desert Jesus was tempted by the devil. Satan lost this battle and left Jesus, but only until an opportune time. The devil would face Jesus again and again until the crucifixion when it seemed Satan had won.

Head-on collision

The most direct opposition Jesus faced, however, came from the religious leaders of the day: the scribes, the teachers of the law, the Pharisees, as well as the Chief Priests and the Sadducees. The large crowds, the common people who followed him, heard him gladly. Why were the leaders so opposed to him?

■ **He claimed to be Messiah**. Soon after his ministry began, Jesus went to Nazareth where he had been brought up. In the synagogue he read the beginning of Isaiah chapter 61 and spoke of that promise of Messiah's coming being then and there fulfilled. First amazed, the congregation soon became hostile. They failed to recognize in Jesus a prophet. He reminded them that when Israel's prophets had met similar unbelief they had worked their wonders among the heathen, implying that the gospel would eventually go to the Gentiles. For

▼ Jesus' teaching was given in the setting of Roman imperial dominance. Many people watched him to see if he would call for active resistance. But violence was an evil which he never countenanced.

4. THE LAST WEEK

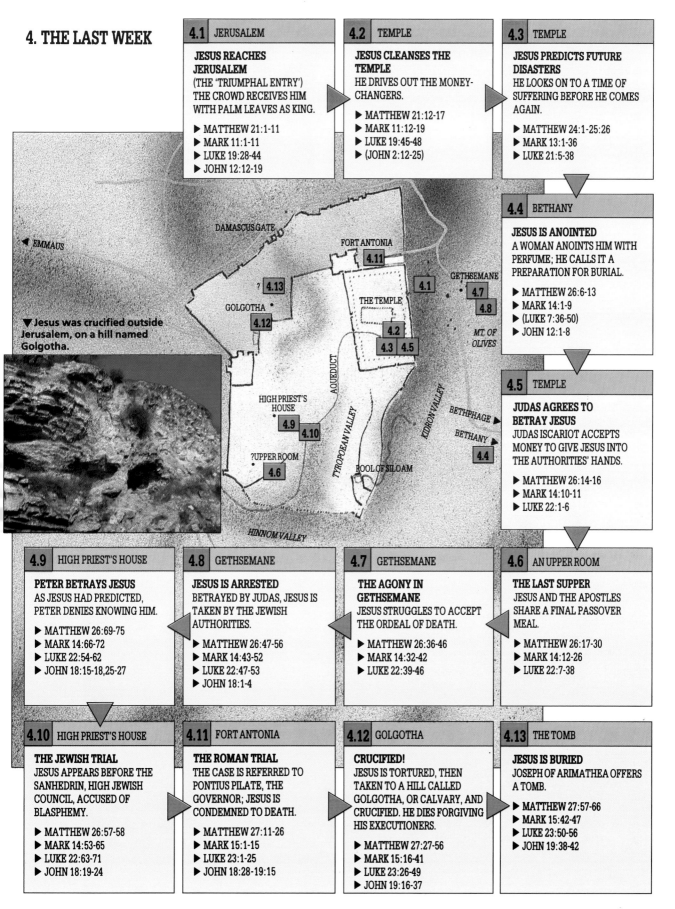

4.1 JERUSALEM

JESUS REACHES JERUSALEM
(THE 'TRIUMPHAL ENTRY')
THE CROWD RECEIVES HIM
WITH PALM LEAVES AS KING.

▶ MATTHEW 21:1-11
▶ MARK 11:1-11
▶ LUKE 19:28-44
▶ JOHN 12:12-19

4.2 TEMPLE

JESUS CLEANSES THE TEMPLE
HE DRIVES OUT THE MONEY-CHANGERS.

▶ MATTHEW 21:12-17
▶ MARK 11:12-19
▶ LUKE 19:45-48
▶ (JOHN 2:12-25)

4.3 TEMPLE

JESUS PREDICTS FUTURE DISASTERS
HE LOOKS ON TO A TIME OF
SUFFERING BEFORE HE COMES
AGAIN.

▶ MATTHEW 24:1-25:26
▶ MARK 13:1-36
▶ LUKE 21:5-38

4.4 BETHANY

JESUS IS ANOINTED
A WOMAN ANOINTS HIM WITH
PERFUME; HE CALLS IT A
PREPARATION FOR BURIAL.

▶ MATTHEW 26:6-13
▶ MARK 14:1-9
▶ (LUKE 7:36-50)
▶ JOHN 12:1-8

4.5 TEMPLE

JUDAS AGREES TO BETRAY JESUS
JUDAS ISCARIOT ACCEPTS
MONEY TO GIVE JESUS INTO
THE AUTHORITIES' HANDS.

▶ MATTHEW 26:14-16
▶ MARK 14:10-11
▶ LUKE 22:1-6

▼Jesus was crucified outside Jerusalem, on a hill named Golgotha.

DAMASCUS GATE

FORT ANTONIA

GETHSEMANE

GOLGOTHA

THE TEMPLE

MT. OF OLIVES

AQUEDUCT

HIGH PRIEST'S HOUSE

TYROPOEAN VALLEY

KIDRON VALLEY

BETHPHAGE

BETHANY

?UPPER ROOM

POOL OF SILOAM

HINNOM VALLEY

EMMAUS

4.9 HIGH PRIEST'S HOUSE

PETER BETRAYS JESUS
AS JESUS HAD PREDICTED,
PETER DENIES KNOWING HIM.

▶ MATTHEW 26:69-75
▶ MARK 14:66-72
▶ LUKE 22:54-62
▶ JOHN 18:15-18,25-27

4.8 GETHSEMANE

JESUS IS ARRESTED
BETRAYED BY JUDAS, JESUS IS
TAKEN BY THE JEWISH
AUTHORITIES.

▶ MATTHEW 26:47-56
▶ MARK 14:43-52
▶ LUKE 22:47-53
▶ JOHN 18:1-4

4.7 GETHSEMANE

THE AGONY IN GETHSEMANE
JESUS STRUGGLES TO ACCEPT
THE ORDEAL OF DEATH.

▶ MATTHEW 26:36-46
▶ MARK 14:32-42
▶ LUKE 22:39-46

4.6 AN UPPER ROOM

THE LAST SUPPER
JESUS AND THE APOSTLES
SHARE A FINAL PASSOVER
MEAL.

▶ MATTHEW 26:17-30
▶ MARK 14:12-26
▶ LUKE 22:7-38

4.10 HIGH PRIEST'S HOUSE

THE JEWISH TRIAL
JESUS APPEARS BEFORE THE
SANHEDRIN, HIGH JEWISH
COUNCIL, ACCUSED OF
BLASPHEMY.

▶ MATTHEW 26:57-58
▶ MARK 14:53-65
▶ LUKE 22:63-71
▶ JOHN 18:19-24

4.11 FORT ANTONIA

THE ROMAN TRIAL
THE CASE IS REFERRED TO
PONTIUS PILATE, THE
GOVERNOR; JESUS IS
CONDEMNED TO DEATH.

▶ MATTHEW 27:11-26
▶ MARK 15:1-15
▶ LUKE 23:1-25
▶ JOHN 18:28-19:15

4.12 GOLGOTHA

CRUCIFIED!
JESUS IS TORTURED, THEN
TAKEN TO A HILL CALLED
GOLGOTHA, OR CALVARY, AND
CRUCIFIED. HE DIES FORGIVING
HIS EXECUTIONERS.

▶ MATTHEW 27:27-56
▶ MARK 15:16-41
▶ LUKE 23:26-49
▶ JOHN 19:16-37

4.13 THE TOMB

JESUS IS BURIED
JOSEPH OF ARIMATHEA OFFERS
A TOMB.

▶ MATTHEW 27:57-66
▶ MARK 15:42-47
▶ LUKE 23:50-56
▶ JOHN 19:38-42

making such a suggestion the furious crowd sought to throw Jesus over a cliff. The religious leaders had taught them God would accept only their own kind.

■ **The company he kept shocked them deeply.** They asked why he ate with tax-collectors and 'sinners'. Surely Jesus would have avoided such people if he were a holy man! When Jesus told his parables of the lost sheep, the lost coin and the lost son, which we can read in Luke chapter 15, it was because the Pharisees and teachers of the law were muttering in disgust that Jesus welcomed sinners and ate with them. Jesus had come to those who knew they needed him. When sinners repented there was rejoicing in heaven even if it displeased the Pharisees. The elder brother in the parable of the lost son represents the Pharisees and the teachers of the law. The parables were an appeal to

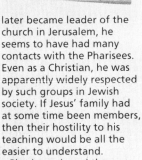

▶ When Jesus preached in the synagogue of his home-town, Nazareth, people were angry. They took him to the top of a cliff – probably this one, known as the Hill of Precipitation – and tried to throw him to his death.

◀ The emperor Nero showed a sadistic streak. Christians proved the perfect scapegoats, and their suffering in the theatres of Rome was appalling. Such persecution has been a recurring theme of Christian history.

Pharisees and Sadducees

The Gospels frequently mention Pharisees and Sadducees together—often in the company of 'scribes' or 'teachers of the Law'—as the opponents of Jesus. As a result, it is easy to get the impression that they were all basically the same. In fact, Pharisees and Sadducees were two quite distinct and separate groups, with very little in common.

Sadducees

In the time of Jesus, they were probably quite a small group. But they were very influential. Many of the priests in the temple at Jerusalem would be Sadducees, along with other well-to-do classes of Jewish society.

They were extreme conservatives. Politically they were happy to collaborate with the Roman forces of occupation. Unlike the Zealots, and others who favoured armed revolt, the Sadducees believed in co-operation as a way of ensuring that the Jewish people preserved at least some influence over their national life.

On matters of religion, their sole authority was the Law given to Moses in the first five books of the Old Testament. This meant that while many Jews believed in life after death, a final judgment and a future resurrection, the Sadducees did not—because such beliefs could not be found in the Torah.

But in everyday affairs, the Sadducees found it necessary to work along with the Pharisees. The supreme Jewish council of seventy members (the Sanhedrin) had members from both groups.

Pharisees

The Pharisees were probably a much larger group than the Sadducees. The Jewish historian Josephus suggests there were as many as 6,000 of them in Jesus' time. They were a national organization, with many local groups in towns and villages throughout Palestine. Their members were not 'professional Pharisees', but were drawn from a wide cross-section of the community. Many ordinary people would belong to them. Indeed, Jesus' own family may well have had a history of close association with this group. When James, Jesus' brother,

later became leader of the church in Jerusalem, he seems to have had many contacts with the Pharisees. Even as a Christian, he was apparently widely respected by such groups in Jewish society. If Jesus' family had at some time been members, then their hostility to his teaching would be all the easier to understand.

Pharisees shared the Sadducees' reverence for the Old Testament—though they accepted all of it as authoritative, not just the first five books. They also realized, however, that their way of life had changed a lot since the first pages of the Old Testament had been penned. To be relevant to new circumstances, the scriptures needed to be given fresh interpretations. Even apparently simple statements such as the Ten Commandments needed to be refined and applied specifically to the sort of challenges faced by ordinary people in everyday situations.

To achieve this laudable aim, and give specific practical guidance on the meaning of their scriptures, they set out many subsidiary rules and regulations. The Pharisees' aim was to 'make a fence for the Law', as one of their writings puts it. That is, explain it in detailed terms so that if people keep

the subsidiary rules there will be no chance of them coming close enough to the Law itself to be in any danger of breaking it.

The Pharisees had distinctive views on other subjects too. Unlike the Sadducees, they had no difficulty in believing that God had a purpose in history, and they could also accept notions of a future life and judgment. They probably shared the general messianic fervour of their day, and though they would not have instigated any form of revolt they probably supported some of those who did.

them to receive the outcasts.

■ **His way of keeping sabbath seemed too lax to them.** Jesus in no way ignored the sabbath: it was his custom to go to the synagogue on the sabbath day. But his attitude was different.

In Mark chapter 3 verses 1 to 6 we see the religious leaders watching whether Jesus would heal a sick person on the sabbath. Jesus brought the matter into the open. He asked the congregation which was lawful on the sabbath: to do good or to do evil, to save life or to kill. And of course he went ahead and healed.

Jesus disagreed with the Pharisees because they made sabbath observance more rigorous than God commanded. But they concluded that Jesus was not from God 'for he does not keep the sabbath'. The opposition to Jesus was growing.

The religious leaders began a smear campaign, calling Jesus names with the aim of discrediting him. They called him 'a glutton and a drunkard, a friend of tax-collectors and sinners'. They said he was a Samaritan, not a pure Jew, even demon-possessed.

But the conflict was not all one-sided. Jesus called his opponents hypocrites. They displayed their piety to be seen by people. Their concern was

Welcome Home To Moscow

In the new situation in the Soviet Union many prisoners of conscience are being released. Among these are Christians who had been, often illegally, interned.

On Friday 20 October 1988, Deacon Vladimir Rusak arrived by train at Yaroslavl railway station in Moscow. He had travelled from Perm, way to the east near the Ural Mountains, where he had been held in a labour camp since 1986.

Relatives had journeyed to Perm to accompany him home, and at the station was a welcoming party of Christians, some of them prominent among those who had stood out for their beliefs and been imprisoned in former years. Zoya

Krakhmalnikova was there, and her husband, Felix Svetov; both of them work to re-establish the link between modern Russian literature and its earlier Christian roots. Gleb Yakunin led the prayers.

Deacon Vladimir prayed fervently, with tears in his eyes. This was the first time in two years that he had been able to pray with friends. He spoke of the hardships at the camp: 'It is easy for the body to survive, less easy for the soul.'

▼ The writer of Revelation received his vision while imprisoned on the island of Patmos. His theme was that

Jesus is sovereign even when state power seems to have the upper hand.

Powers of Evil

The scene is in a synagogue. Jesus is teaching the congregation. Suddenly a man cries out, 'What do you want with us, Jesus of Nazareth? Have you come to destroy us? I know who you are—the Holy One of God.' Jesus commands: 'Come out of him.' The evil spirit in the man shakes him violently and comes out of him with a shriek. The congregation is amazed and ask each other, 'What is this? A new teaching—and with authority! He even gives orders to evil spirits and they obey him.' (You can read the full story in Mark chapter 1 verses 21 to 28.)

In Jesus' ministry we see him in conflict with the powers of evil. Satan, whom Jesus called 'the evil one', is the very essence of evil and wickedness. He has significant power and his opposition to the will of God is real. But Satan is a created being, his power not equal to God's. He can only act within the limits God allows him. Demons or evil spirits are portrayed in the Gospels as agents of Satan, fighting against the advance of the kingdom of God. By driving out evil spirits, Jesus showed that Satan's forces were being defeated.

Before he began his public ministry Jesus went into battle with Satan and defeated him. (We see this in *The Temptations*.) But the conflict was to be resumed later. Throughout his life, Jesus was 'tempted in every way, just as we are', but always he was victorious.

When Jesus sent his disciples out to preach, he also gave them authority to drive out demons. The disciples came back with joy and reported that demons had submitted to them in his name. Jesus saw in this the downfall of Satan. All who follow Christ are called to work for him to complete the overthrow of the powers of evil.

Satan worked through the enemies of Jesus. Those who opposed him were described as belonging to 'your father, the devil', for Satan is continually opposed to the gospel.

The devil also worked through Jesus' followers. When Peter rejected the thought of Jesus dying on the cross, Jesus rebuked him with the words, 'Out of my sight, Satan'. It was Satan who prompted Judas to betray Jesus to his enemies.

When Jesus died on the cross it appeared Satan had struck his victory blow and Jesus had failed. The resurrection showed that, just at the time of apparent defeat, Jesus had overcome Satan and all his forces.

From the Gospel records we see the powers of evil seeking to possess people. But demon-possession is by no means the only way people are affected by spiritual evil. In the Gospels we also find the devil
- Tempting people to sin;
- Snatching away the gospel message from those who hear it;
- **Hardening the hearts of those who do not believe the gospel message;**
- **Diverting people from doing God's will.**

Some people think that Jesus referred to demonic powers, not because they actually exist, but because his contemporaries believed in them and needed to be set free from their fear. But the powers of evil were real then and are just as real today. Any who work for Christ among tribal animists know this. And there is an upsurge of interest in fortune-telling, witchcraft, Satan worship, spiritism, magic and the occult in Western societies, too.

Recently, I have read and heard testimonies of people in Africa who have come to faith in Christ from a background of idolatry, magic, charms and ability to harm others through contact with powers of evil.

Such people acknowledge that the devil has power but they know that Christ's power is greater, for it freed them from their bondage to Satan.

It is a mistake, then, to deny the existence of evil powers. But it is equally dangerous to see them at work wherever things go wrong. This is to lose discernment and the biblical balance.

The powers of evil are real, always hostile to God and God's people. However, 'the reason the Son of God appeared was to destroy the devil's work.' In his life and ministry Jesus demonstrated his victory over the powers of evil by casting out demons. By his death and resurrection he took away evil's ultimate power. When people yield control of their lives to Jesus, he protects them from all evil.

Street Scene

In a European city in 1988, a group of Christians were holding an evangelistic street meeting. They began singing with guitars and tambourines to attract a crowd. They would present a mime, followed by a short testimony and an offer to talk with any interested listeners. What was happening around them demonstrated the powers of evil at work today.

To their left down the street was a group of fortune tellers, palm readers and tarot-card readers. They were drawing people to their tables and encouraging them in their 'spiritual' activities. These may not appear evil but behind them are satanic forces.

To their right was a young man who could walk on a big pile of broken glass without getting cut. Then he would lie down on the glass pieces and have several people stand on top of him, again without getting cut.

Across the street was another group singing 'hard rock' music. Their songs were about Satan worship and black masses. As the Christians were presenting the mime the other group began to shout, 'I hate Christians; I hate Jesus', as part of their music. The two messages were being presented simultaneously, one message about Christ, the other about Satan. Some people turned and began to listen to the Jesus-haters. Others stayed to talk to the Christians. The conflict between Jesus and the powers of evil was all too clear that night.

with externals. The outside of the cup was clean, but not the inside. Matthew records in chapter 23 all the hard words Jesus had to say to the teachers of the law and the Pharisees. Jesus pointed out that they nullified the word of God by their tradition. Such strong words against his opponents served to fuel the growing antagonism.

The climax

As his ministry moved towards its close, Jesus began to teach his disciples that he would be finally rejected by the chief priests and teachers of the law, and about his subsequent betrayal, arrest, trial and death. Jesus knew that the opposition was moving to a climax.

The Mountain Top

Martin Luther King Jr made a prescient speech on 3 April 1968. He spoke like a man preparing for death, a little like Jesus in the upper room and in the Garden of Gethsemane.

'I don't know what will happen now. We've got some difficult days ahead. But it doesn't matter with me now, because I've been to the mountain top. And I don't mind. Like anybody, I would like to live a long life; longevity has its place. But I'm not concerned about that now. I just want to do God's will. And he's allowed me to go up to the mountain. And I've looked over. And I've seen the promised land. I may not get there with you. But I want you to know tonight that we as a people will get to the promised land. And I'm happy tonight, I'm not worried about anything. I'm not fearing any man. Mine eyes have seen the glory of the coming of the Lord.'

The next day he was assassinated.

When Jesus raised Lazarus from the grave after he had been dead for four days, the religious leaders were clear in their minds what they wanted. At a meeting of the Sanhedrin their concern was that if Jesus was not stopped, everyone would believe in him and then the Romans would destroy the Temple and the nation. Their decision was to take Jesus' life.

Matters came close to a head after Jesus had entered Jerusalem in triumph. He cleared the Temple area of the traders and money-changers, charging them with turning this house of prayer into a den of robbers. This scared the chief priests and teachers of the law, and they began looking for a way to kill Jesus. The listening crowd felt differently. They were amazed at Jesus' teaching.

It was while the religious leaders were looking for some sly way to arrest Jesus and kill him that Judas Iscariot, a disciple of Jesus, offered to betray him. Judas it was who led a crowd sent from the religious leaders to arrest Jesus, and identified him with a kiss.

When Jesus was eventually brought to trial, the chief priests and the whole Sanhedrin wanted to put him to death. He was condemned on a charge of blasphemy. In answer to their questioning Jesus had

▲ Archbishop Oscar Romero of El Salvador paid the ultimate price in 1980 when he was assassinated in his cathedral during mass. He had refused to be silenced in any other way from speaking out for social justice and political freedom.

▼ ▶ Adolf Hitler and Josef Stalin were evil leaders. They were twentieth-century examples of the massive suffering which results when evil powers take over the reins of state.

admitted he was the Christ ('Messiah'), the Son of the Blessed One. This charge of blasphemy had been made all through Jesus' ministry. When he forgave the sins of a paralyzed man, the teachers of the law said he was blaspheming. When he called God his own Father, his hearers tried to kill him for making himself equal with God. When Jesus declared, 'Before Abraham was born I am', the Jews again tried to stone him for blaspheming. Among the Jews it was blasphemy for a man to claim to be God.

'If they hate me. . .'

Jesus warned his followers that if people had hated him they would hate them too. And after Jesus' death and resurrection his disciples also faced opposition from the religious leaders of their day. Peter and John were brought before the Sanhedrin and warned not to speak or teach in the name of Jesus. Another time they were flogged, but none of this stopped them from preaching. James the brother of John was put to death by Herod. Paul's sufferings, which he recounts in 2 Corinthians chapter 12, are probably representative of what the other disciples went through.

And people who follow Jesus today can also meet opposition. Some are disowned by their families and friends. In some parts of the world a person who becomes a Christian could be poisoned by his own family. Some Christians even face opposition at government level, when their loyalty to Christ is wrongly interpreted as disloyalty to the state.

But wherever opposition may come from, Christians try to follow Jesus in not letting it deflect them from their mission. If the Master had to go that way, the servants can expect no different.

4.2

THE DEATH OF JESUS

Jesus was executed by crucifixion. It was a form of execution used by the Romans when dealing with slaves or with rebellious subjects such as the Jews. The victim would be flogged or tortured, then either tied or nailed to a cross. By any standards it was a cruel form of execution. Victims could take hours, even days, to die. Eventually, they would lack the strength to breathe.

The Gospels allow us to appreciate the full horror of the crucifixion. They bring home to us how terrified the disciples were when the man they knew and loved was killed. They were devastated, and as we read how the disciples laid the dead Jesus in a tomb, we can feel the full sadness of that first Good Friday.

Yet within days, all this had changed. The first Easter Day dawned, and the disciples were astonished. Something they were never expecting had happened. The tomb was empty, and Jesus came once more to stand among them. He had risen from the dead. The excitement of that moment is captured by the Gospels. They tell us how the disciples were turned from sad and defeated individuals into a band of men and women who went out to win the world for the risen Jesus. The cross became a symbol of God's power to break the power of death.

But what did the death of Jesus achieve? Did he have to die?

The Gospels are emphatic: Jesus did not die by accident. His death on the cross was not an unexpected end to a promising career as a good teacher. That death was somehow part of God's plan to restore the world. Humanity had scorned God's love and needed 'salvation'. We needed to be forgiven and our relationship with God restored.

But how? How could the death of Jesus on the cross have anything to do with salvation? The New Testament gives us some very powerful and helpful ways of making sense of the death of Jesus, and its permanent relevance to all times and places.

You may have seen a jeweller hold a diamond up to the light, and turn it round. Each of its facets sparkles in turn. They are all part of the same diamond, yet each is slightly different. Together they make up that diamond in its entirety. So the New Testament offers many ways of explaining the meaning of Jesus' death. Each is true and relevant; each is part of a greater whole. Just as pieces of a jigsaw puzzle build up to give an overall picture, so each of the New Testament ways of thinking about Jesus' death locks in place to help describe the enormous relevance and significance of the cross. We will look at some of these meanings under three broad categories: liberation, forgiveness and the love of God.

Liberation

One of the great themes of human history is of being held captive. The captivity may be political. Israel was held captive in Egypt, and was liberated, by escaping through the wilderness into the Promised Land. Black slaves in the southern United States knew what it was like to be held captive, and found these great Old Testament stories an inspiration as they dreamed of being liberated from their bondage.

But there are other forms of captivity besides political. Many people are frightened of death, of the fact that one day they will cease to exist. They find this very threatening and it dominates their

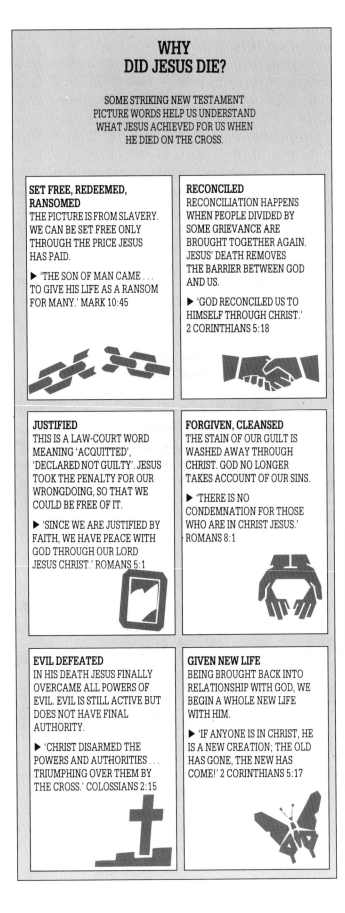

WHY DID JESUS DIE?

SOME STRIKING NEW TESTAMENT PICTURE WORDS HELP US UNDERSTAND WHAT JESUS ACHIEVED FOR US WHEN HE DIED ON THE CROSS.

SET FREE, REDEEMED, RANSOMED
THE PICTURE IS FROM SLAVERY. WE CAN BE SET FREE ONLY THROUGH THE PRICE JESUS HAS PAID.

▶ 'THE SON OF MAN CAME . . . TO GIVE HIS LIFE AS A RANSOM FOR MANY.' MARK 10:45

RECONCILED
RECONCILIATION HAPPENS WHEN PEOPLE DIVIDED BY SOME GRIEVANCE ARE BROUGHT TOGETHER AGAIN. JESUS' DEATH REMOVES THE BARRIER BETWEEN GOD AND US.

▶ 'GOD RECONCILED US TO HIMSELF THROUGH CHRIST.' 2 CORINTHIANS 5:18

JUSTIFIED
THIS IS A LAW-COURT WORD MEANING 'ACQUITTED', 'DECLARED NOT GUILTY'. JESUS TOOK THE PENALTY FOR OUR WRONGDOING, SO THAT WE COULD BE FREE OF IT.

▶ 'SINCE WE ARE JUSTIFIED BY FAITH, WE HAVE PEACE WITH GOD THROUGH OUR LORD JESUS CHRIST.' ROMANS 5:1

FORGIVEN, CLEANSED
THE STAIN OF OUR GUILT IS WASHED AWAY THROUGH CHRIST. GOD NO LONGER TAKES ACCOUNT OF OUR SINS.

▶ 'THERE IS NO CONDEMNATION FOR THOSE WHO ARE IN CHRIST JESUS.' ROMANS 8:1

EVIL DEFEATED
IN HIS DEATH JESUS FINALLY OVERCAME ALL POWERS OF EVIL. EVIL IS STILL ACTIVE BUT DOES NOT HAVE FINAL AUTHORITY.

▶ 'CHRIST DISARMED THE POWERS AND AUTHORITIES . . . TRIUMPHING OVER THEM BY THE CROSS.' COLOSSIANS 2:15

GIVEN NEW LIFE
BEING BROUGHT BACK INTO RELATIONSHIP WITH GOD, WE BEGIN A WHOLE NEW LIFE WITH HIM.

▶ 'IF ANYONE IS IN CHRIST, HE IS A NEW CREATION; THE OLD HAS GONE, THE NEW HAS COME!' 2 CORINTHIANS 5:17

outlook on life. If we are all doomed to die, what is the point in going on living? Others are oppressed by a sense of guilt. They may have done something in the past which they cannot forget, which still troubles them. They need to know that it can be cancelled, forgiven, or somehow neutralized. They want to know that they can put it behind them. They want to be free.

The New Testament uses this idea of liberation to explain the meaning of the death and resurrection of Jesus. Jesus liberates us from the oppression of forces which would otherwise dominate our lives. Two forces which the New Testament identifies as being especially powerful are the fear of death and the grip of sin. And the New Testament says that through the cross and the empty tomb Jesus conquered sin and overcame death. Throughout its pages, the New Testament resounds with the joy of the resurrection. Jesus, the man whom everyone had thought dead and gone, was raised to life by God. The great theme 'He is risen!' echoes in the apostle Paul's letters. But Jesus' resurrection is not seen as being good news for *Jesus*: it is good news for us. Paul makes the point that those who belong to Jesus, those who have faith in him, will be raised to glory, just like Jesus. Fear of death is broken by Jesus' death and resurrection. Those who put their trust in him will share in his victory over the grave.

The Martyrs

The English word 'martyr' comes from a Greek word which originally meant 'witness'. In the New Testament, this is still what it means when Paul, addressing Jesus, calls Stephen 'your witness', and when in the book of Revelation Jesus calls Antipas 'my faithful witness'. But both Stephen and Antipas had been put to death for their faithfulness to Christ, and these passages refer to their deaths. It is because they had been faithful in their witness to Jesus, faithful even to the point of death, that they are preeminently witnesses to Jesus.

So in Christian usage the word came to mean 'martyr' —someone who gave up his or her life rather than deny Christ. It did so because the church saw the martyrs as those who bore witness to Jesus most fully. During the two and half centuries when the early church suffered sporadic persecution and many died for their faith, the martyrs were esteemed and remembered as those who demonstrated most clearly the truth and the meaning of Christian faith.

The martyrs were witnesses to Jesus in several ways.
■ **They witnessed that Christ was the true Lord.** They were put to death because they refused to worship the Roman Emperor or the traditional Roman gods. In other words, they would not take part in the 'political

▶ The Dome of the Rock in Jerusalem covers the summit of ancient Mount Moriah. Ever since Abraham had nearly sacrificed Isaac at that spot, it had been the place of sacrifice, and here the temple was built. But Jesus' sacrifice was made outside the city.

religion' of the Roman Empire. They offered to pray for the Roman Emperor instead of sacrificing to him. But they would not treat the state as divine. They could not give it that unconditional loyalty which belongs only to God. Many of the early Christian accounts of the martyrs end by dating the martyrdom, in the usual way, by the year of the Emperor, but add 'in the reign of our Lord Jesus Christ, who reigns eternally'. The martyrs died for their witness that Jesus is Lord over all human rulers.

■ The martyrs were witnesses that the gospel of Jesus is true. People who are prepared to die for what they believe can make others wonder whether their faith may indeed be something worth dying for. Many people must first have been impressed by Christianity when they saw the courage of the martyrs in the face of brutal torture and death.

■ But above all, the martyrs were witnesses to Jesus because they bore witness *in the same way that he did—* following his path of suffering, condemned to death by the Roman state, dying in public shame. Their death was a witness to *his* death. It was also a witness to his resurrection and living power. They faced death in the confidence that his death had conquered death. The courage and even the joy they showed in suffering were the evidence of his risen presence with them and the hope he gave them that they too would rise again. In their martyrdom they embodied the gospel message of life through death: true life in Jesus through sharing in his death.

The stories of the martyrs make clear that in suffering and dying they felt they came close to Jesus. Bishop Carpus of Pergamum, being burned alive, prayed: 'Blessed are you, Lord Jesus Christ, Son of God, because you considered me, a sinner, worthy of this share in you!' Often the martyr's last words are a brief prayer to Jesus.

The desire of the martyr to be united with Jesus in his suffering and death is nowhere more strongly expressed than by Bishop Ignatius of Antioch in his letter to the Christians at Rome. He was on his way, chained to his Roman guards, to martyrdom in that city. 'Now I am beginning to be a disciple,' he writes. 'It is better for me to die in Christ Jesus than to rule over the whole earth. I am seeking him who died for us. My desire is for him who rose for us. The pangs of birth are upon me.' As he faces death it seems as though his true life in union with Christ is only just beginning. And the key to Ignatius' attitude to his death comes in the words: 'Allow me to imitate the passion (the suffering) of my God.'

Paul exults in this thought: 'Thanks be to God! He gives us the victory through our Lord Jesus Christ.'

Jesus shared our human condition, including death, so that we might no longer be afraid of death. Its power over us is broken. It is like a disarmed enemy, once strong but now defeated. Jesus shared in our humanity 'so that by his death he might destroy him who holds the power of death—that is, the devil—and free those who all their lives were held in slavery by their fear of death.' As long as human beings walk the face of this earth, knowing they must die, the death and resurrection of Jesus will continue to be good news!

Jesus' death also breaks the power of sin. For Paul, sin is like a power which exercises influence over us. It traps us. It is as if we are in some sort of prison, from which we ourselves cannot break free. We need someone to break down the prison walls, and liberate us. We cannot free ourselves. It is like prisoners of war in the closing stages of a conflict. They cannot break free themselves yet they hear rumours of advancing troops—rumours of the imminent arrival of a greater force who can achieve their liberation. So it is with our human situation; we cannot break free from sin's power. But in the death and resurrection of Jesus we see the power of sin confronted and defeated.

This offer of victory over sin is an essential part of the Christian gospel. In his moving discussion of the power of sin, in which he describes himself as

Amazing Grace

A violent storm at sea was the turning-point in John Newton's life.

Motherless at six and sent to sea on his eleventh birthday, he soon became a teenage rebel. He was press-ganged into the navy and flogged for desertion. Newton became involved with the African slave-trade and came close to starvation while living in extreme poverty in Sierra Leone.

But in March 1748, at the age of twenty-three, he was on board a cargo ship which was fighting for its life against heavy seas and rough weather. Worn out with pumping and almost frozen, he called out for God's mercy at the height of the storm, and was amazed to be saved from almost certain death.

Newton's life had many twists and turns. Eventually he renounced his involvement with slave-trading and, at thirty-nine, became a minister in the church. He persuaded the young William Wilberforce to stay in politics, and joined him in the fight to abolish the slave-trade. Above all Newton was a hymn-writer, best known for *Amazing Grace*, which even made the British pop charts.

At his last supper with his disciples, Jesus kept the passover, as Jewish families still do each year. That festival reminds them of deliverance from slavery in Egypt. He changed the words to speak of 'My body given for you ... my blood shed for you'. Ever since, his followers have broken bread and shared wine in memory of his death and to share his life. (They call the service communion, or eucharist, or Lord's supper.) It looks forward, as this catacomb painting does, to a final banquet at the end of the age.

Were the Jews to Blame?

The question is far from academic since the guilt of Jews in the death of Jesus, understood as the guilt of 'deicide' or the 'murder of God', has historically been the cause of an uncalculated amount of 'Christian' hatred and persecution of Jews. Some hold that this misplaced blame lies at the centre of any adequate explanation of the Holocaust, the slaughter of 6 million Jews in Nazi Germany. In light of the perceived importance of this subject it is no surprise that numerous books have been written, especially by Jewish authors, to clear the Jews of blame for any responsibility in the death of Jesus.

Yet it cannot be denied that the Gospels do put the blame for the death of Jesus on Jews. As early as Mark chapter 3 verse 6, the Pharisees and Herodians are plotting to destroy Jesus, and this hostility crops up more than once in the course of his ministry. In the accounts of Jesus' last days, it is the Jewish authorities who arrest Jesus in the garden, who try him in what was apparently a special meeting of the Sanhedrin, who condemn him to death, and who finally deliver him over to Pilate and the Romans apparently on the charge that he was a dangerous revolutionary. Although Pilate himself finds nothing in Jesus warranting execution, he yields to Jewish cries for his crucifixion. Finally the Jewish authorities mock Jesus on the cross. In an infamous verse, Matthew chapter 27 verse 25, we read, 'His blood be on us and on our children'; these words have been tragically and wrongly taken by Christians as justifying the persecution of Jews, even as an apology for the Holocaust.

The Romans actually did the crucifying of Jesus, since it was not a Jewish method of execution and the Jews at that time did not have the legal right of capital punishment. But according to the Gospels the complicity of Jews, primarily the Jewish leadership to be sure, is clear. Jewish writers have attempted to avoid this conclusion by denying the historical reliability of the accounts referred to above and calling attention to the anti-Judaic bias of the Gospels, which reflect the hostility between the church and the synagogue in the latter part of the first century. But the frequent appeal to discrepancies between the Gospels and legal process according to the Mishna and Talmud is not really justified, because these Jewish sources are of relatively late date. And in any event the Jewish trial of Jesus was an evidently exceptional event, which under the circumstances can hardly have conformed to the normal legal procedures of the day. Admittedly there is anti-Jewish bias, not to be confused with anti-semitism, in the New Testament, and this may well have been strengthened by the hostility between Jews and Christians at the time the Gospels were written. This may account for the sharp tone of a few passages and perhaps explains Matthew's Gospel taking up the particular traditional element which lies behind 'his blood be on us. . .' But this cannot explain away as entirely fictitious what has been said above about Jewish culpability, which is so widely placed and thoroughly fixed in the Gospel tradition.

It is true, then, that the New Testament places the blame for the death of Jesus on Jews. But this in no way justifies any form of anti-semitism, and this for several reasons.

To hate, to be prejudiced against, or to persecute the Jews flies in face of Jesus' own commandment. He taught love even of one's enemies, and he forgave those who crucified him.

It was not the Jewish people as a whole who were guilty of Jesus' death in the first century, but only the Jerusalem leadership and their stooges among the people. Still less was it the Jewish people of later centuries or the present.

The cross itself is a sign of God's love for everyone, Jews as well as Gentiles, of every generation.

The blame for the death of Jesus, the true guilt, lies on the shoulders of every sinner, Christians no less than Jews. In the words of an ancient German hymn:

Who was the guilty? Who brought this upon Thee? Alas, my treason, Jesu, hath undone Thee; 'Twas I, Lord Jesu, I it was denied Thee: I crucified Thee.

'sold under sin' and 'a prisoner of the law of sin', Paul concludes: 'What a wretched man I am! Who will rescue me from this body of death? Thanks be to God—through Jesus Christ our Lord!'

Forgiveness

A second facet to the jewel of the meaning of Jesus' death, as the New Testament presents it, is forgiveness. All of us know how important forgiveness is since all of us have been involved in personal relationships which have gone wrong.

Perhaps we have had a disagreement or an argument, or said or done something that has deeply hurt somebody else. And if the relationship means anything to us, we will try to restore it to its former state. And here we find we cannot just ignore what has been said and done, pretending that it never happened. We have to ask for forgiveness. Now asking for forgiveness is difficult because it means admitting we are in the wrong. But if the other person really matters, we will want to restore the relationship, whatever the cost.

The New Testament tells us that our friendship with God has gone wrong. It uses the word 'sin' to refer to this flaw in our relationship with him. That we feel far from God, or guilty before him, or perhaps even that he is not there—these are all part of the same problem. The Bible says that God is able to forgive us our sin 'on account of the death of Jesus Christ'. We can set the past behind us, knowing that our sins have really been forgiven. The cost to God is enormous—yet it is real forgiveness.

The fact that God offers us forgiveness tells us that we matter to him so much that he sent his only Son to die. And the death of Jesus on the cross allows us to set sin behind us. It is no longer a barrier between us and God. The way is clear for us to return to him like an estranged child.

Paul wrote, 'God was reconciling the world to himself in Christ.' We speak of people being reconciled when a broken relationship is restored, and friends come back together again. Jesus is the mediator between us and God, who explains just how much we matter to God and how far from him we are on account of our sin. Paul wrote, 'God was reconciling the world to himself in Christ.' Jesus is the one who makes it possible for us to return to God. He is like a bridge, who spans the gulf between us and God.

Some years ago, a ferry sank off the coast of Belgium, with terrible loss of life. Many accounts of heroism emerged from that tragedy. One story concerned a man who managed to place himself

▶ A Good Friday procession winds its way through the streets of Jerusalem, following the route Jesus is thought to have taken on his way to crucifixion. The cross is the focal point of Christian faith.

A Jesus of Good Causes

British writer Malcolm Muggeridge has often protested against a weakened, sanitized picture of Jesus:

'I was generally uneasy about the whole concept of a Jesus of good causes. I would catch a glimpse of a cross—not necessarily a crucifix, maybe two pieces of wood accidentally nailed together, on a telegraph pole, for instance—and suddenly my heart would stand still. In an instinctive, intuitive way, I understood that something more important, more tumultuous, more passionate was at issue than our good causes, however admirable they might be. Something to do with the deep inner nature of life itself—mine, and all life. Something inescapable, pursuing and pursued, for ever beyond my reach and yet under my hand; part of the air I breathed, and lost in the wide firmament above.'

across a wide gap in the ship's structure, making himself into a human bridge across which others could clamber to safety. Jesus is like that bridge, spanning the gap between death and life, between sin and forgiveness, between us and God.

But how can God forgive sin on account of Jesus' death? Of what relevance is the death of Jesus 2,000 years ago to human failure and greed today?

■ **In the Old Testament animals were sacrificed to secure forgiveness.** They were ritually slaughtered for the sins of the people. The New Testament, especially the letter to the Hebrews, suggests that Jesus is the true sacrifice to which animal sacrifices pointed forward.

■ **A connected Bible approach says that sin is an offence against God's law and requires a penalty.** But Jesus takes our sin and its penalty on himself, so making it possible for God to pardon us.

For the New Testament writers, the important thing was that God had made forgiveness possible through the death and resurrection of Jesus. There is real forgiveness of real sins.

▲ The annual passover meal means much to Jews, as these Sinai settlers demonstrate while they await eviction. Jesus died among all the preparations for that year's passover in Jerusalem. The symbolism was inescapable: his sacrifice was to make redemption available for the whole of humanity.

So, liberation and forgiveness through Jesus' death are central to the New Testament teaching. In accepting that Jesus died for them, people are set free and made clean.

Jesus' death and God's love

The death of Jesus on the cross shows us the full extent of God's love for people. At times, the New Testament writers found themselves overwhelmed by this astonishing truth. Paul could understand why someone would want to die for a really good person. But he was amazed that God should show his love by sending Jesus to die for us while we were still sinners! He found it very difficult to 'grasp how wide and long and high and deep is the love of

Jesus Alone

In his time, Luther reshaped the face of Europe and turned the church upside down. He held fast to the belief that Jesus alone is the sole revealer of God, and only through him can we understand the character of God:

'Christ is the sole redeemer of man from sin and the gates of death. He alone is the hope of any enduring society on earth. Where men do not know him they rave and rage and strive. The angels proclaimed peace on earth and so shall it be to those who know and receive this Babe. For what is it like where Jesus is not? What is the world but a perfect hell with nothing but lying, cheating, gluttony, guzzling, lechery, brawling and murder. That is the very devil himself. There is no kindliness or honour. No one is sure of another. One must be as distrustful of friends as of enemies, and sometimes more. This is the kingdom of the world where the devil reigns and rules. But those who know and accept Jesus not only give honour to God, but treat their fellows as if they were gods. They are free from envy and wrangling, for the Christian way is quiet and friendly in peace and love where each gladly does the best he can for another.'

Luther recognized that having faith in Christ is far from simple. He boldly proclaimed the paradoxes involved in being a disciple of Jesus:

'Christ is an astounding king, who instead of defending his people, deserts them. Whom he would save, he must first make a despairing sinner. Whom he would make wise, he must first turn into a fool. Whom he would make alive, he must first kill. Whom he would bring to honour, he must first bring into dishonour. He is a strange king who is nearest when he is far and farthest when he is near.'

Christ', but he rejoiced in that he lived by faith 'in the Son of God, who loved me and gave himself for me'. (See Romans 5:6–8; Ephesians 3:18, and Galatians 2:20).

In one of the college chapels in Oxford, there is a small memorial to a medical orderly who was killed during the First World War. He was shot while trying to rescue the wounded from no man's land. Beneath the memorial are the words, 'greater love hath no man than this, that he should lay down his life for his friends'—words spoken by Jesus to his disciples shortly before his death. The full extent of the love of God for us is that his Son gave up his life for us. Jesus died to show us how much God loves us, to break the stranglehold of sin, and to open the way back to God.

We have looked at some of the New Testament insights into the meaning of Jesus' death. But there are many others, all of which build up to disclose the full significance of this crucial event. Like an artist's brush-strokes, they combine to give a picture. It is a deeply moving picture, a picture which tells us of a loving God who gave and did everything possible in order to bring us back to him. It tells us of our own greed and failure, our sin, from which we cannot break free unaided. But it shows us God reaching out to us, offering us his hand to lift us up and restore us to relationship with him.

4.3

RAISED FROM DEATH

The resurrection of Jesus was not a meaningless wonder. Rather it is full of significance:

■ **Jesus' resurrection was an act of God**. It was not merely the return of the mortal body to this earthly life, miraculous as that would be. Jesus rose to everlasting life in a radically transformed body. In 1 Corinthians chapter 15 verses 42 to 44 Paul described this body as immortal, glorious, powerful and supernatural. Jesus' resurrection so far exceeds the causal power of nature that nothing we have learned in medical science during the 2,000 years since enables us to explain it naturalistically. The most plausible explanation is that it was in fact a miracle.

■ **Jesus' resurrection confirms his personal claim to divinity**. New Testament scholarship has reached a consensus that Jesus of Nazareth came on the scene with an unparalleled sense of authority to

The Shroud

For years the Shroud of Turin has been an object of reverence. On the fourteen-foot strip of linen can be found no evidence of paint, dye or ink. Yet it bears the faint but vivid likeness of a man's face. How did it get there? Could it have been imprinted as a result of a burst of heat-energy as a man was restored to life after death? Perhaps this was the linen burial shroud which John's Gospel mentions was left rolled by itself when Peter and John found the tomb empty where Jesus' body had been laid.

In 1988, after long controversies, the responsible authorities in Turin submitted the shroud to definitive scientific tests. Three small pieces of cloth were sent to the radio-carbon-dating laboratories of universities in different countries. The result was clear and unanimous: this piece of linen had been woven from flax harvested towards the end of the thirteenth century or the beginning of the fourteenth. Old, but in no way old enough to be Jesus' burial shroud.

Many questions remain about the Shroud of Turin, and how it received its striking image. But it gives no clues as to Jesus' facial appearance nor about how or whether he rose from the grave. The evidence for that is of a quite different kind.

speak in God's place. Taking this claim as blasphemy, the Jewish religious hierarchy had him crucified. But his resurrection stands as the divine vindication and confirmation of Jesus' allegedly blasphemous claim.

■ **Jesus' resurrection completes the work of the cross.** The disciples experienced their Master's crucifixion as castrophic partly because, according to Jewish thinking, anyone executed by hanging on a tree was cursed by God, and this curse was applied to crucifixion as well. But his resurrection reversed the catastrophe of the cross, revealing it in its true light as God's way of saving us. It could now be interpreted in terms of the Old Testament sacrificial system, Jesus himself being the sacrificial Lamb slain for the sins of the world. Thus, the work of the cross is completed by the resurrection, which broke the power of sin, death and hell. Here was the victorious climax to Jesus' life and work.

■ **Jesus' resurrection makes it possible for us to enjoy a personal relationship with him.** The resurrection means that Jesus Christ is not dead. He is alive, and has taken up his full divine glory. Therefore, it is possible to enter into a living relationship with him by placing our trust in him. Indeed, the essence of Christian salvation consists in the union with Jesus wrought by this relationship. As people come to new spiritual life in him, they are brought into a personal relationship and spiritual union with the risen and exalted Christ.

■ **Jesus' resurrection shows that he holds the key to eternal life.** As the one who decisively conquered death, Jesus speaks with authority concerning this most dreaded of humanity's enemies. Jesus believed and taught the doctrine of the end-time resurrection of all mankind to eternal life or punishment. His teaching thus holds out hope to modern people in the face of death. The grave is not the end. And so our present lives and the decisions we make are imbued with an eternal significance.

■ **Jesus' resurrection promises physical and psychological healing for mankind.** His resurrection differed from ours only in being the first. This

DID JESUS RISE FROM DEATH?

THE NEW TESTAMENT MAKES THE STUPENDOUS CLAIM THAT JESUS ROSE FROM DEATH. NO ONE COULD BE EXPECTED TO BELIEVE THAT WITHOUT GOOD REASONS. WHAT REASONS ARE THERE?

DID HIS FOLLOWERS REALLY BELIEVE IT?

THE RESURRECTION WAS THE CENTRE OF EARLY CHRISTIAN PREACHING. AND MANY CHRISTIANS WERE PUT TO DEATH FOR THAT FAITH. WOULD THEY HAVE DIED FOR WHAT THEY DID NOT KNOW TO BE TRUE?

WAS THE TOMB REALLY EMPTY?

IT WAS WIDELY KNOWN WHERE HIS TOMB WAS. THE OPPONENTS OF THE JESUS MOVEMENT HAD ONLY TO PRODUCE HIS BODY AND THE MOVEMENT WOULD HAVE COLLAPSED. BUT PLAINLY THEY NEVER DID.

DID HIS FOLLOWERS REALLY SEE HIM AFTER DEATH?

PAUL LISTS THOSE WHO DID, INCLUDING A 500-STRONG CROWD, 'MANY OF WHOM ARE STILL ALIVE'. THE CLAIM THAT JESUS ROSE COULD BE CHECKED WITH WITNESSES.

implies a picture of the afterlife which may surprise us. The final state of humanity is not a timeless existence as a disembodied soul, but an embodied existence in space and time when, in Paul's words, 'the creation itself will be liberated from its bondage to decay and brought into the glorious freedom of the children of God'. Our bodies will be patterned after Christ's resurrection body. Jesus' resurrection thus promises healing from physical suffering, disease, ageing and death. We shall have supernatural bodies which possess powers our present bodies in no way share. And there will be complete psychological healing as well. All the residual effects of past hurts, complexes, neuroses, self-centredness and so forth will be vanquished, and we shall live as whole, psychologically integrated people—trans-parent, loving individuals utterly free of any defect of body and mind. In short, we will share in Jesus' victory over everything that dehumanizes us. Such is the promise the resurrection holds out.

■ **Jesus' resurrection is the guarantee that he will personally return in glory**. By rising from death he showed that his humanity was not limited to the thirty- year period of his earthly life, but has become a permanent condition of the Son of God. Jesus' second coming marks his personal, bodily return to reign over all creation. And this is not just wishful thinking: the fact of his resurrection makes certain this great promise for the future.

The resurrection of Jesus, then, is not a dead dogma, nor even simply a historical fact. It is an energizing truth full of significance for our lives.

4.4

ASCENSION

Jesus Christ rose from the dead and appeared to his disciples, but these appearances did not continue for very long. Luke records how, after forty days of teaching the disciples, Jesus 'was taken up to heaven as they watched him, and a cloud hid him from their sight'.

The ascension of Jesus Christ is one of the most important themes in the New Testament. The event is rich in meaning and is relevant for Christian living today.

The New Testament records that after his resurrection Jesus of Nazareth was seen alive on many occasions. But it is Luke alone who tells that after forty days Jesus 'ascended to heaven'. After his resurrection, Jesus appeared at intervals to his disciples over a period of forty days. Then came their final physical meeting with him, on the Mount of Olives outside Jerusalem, when he was 'taken up' from them and not seen again. The disciples realized that this was the last appearance of their Master, and that he was returning to the sphere where he rightly belonged. In Old Testament accounts of God meeting with his people a cloud often represented God's presence and glory. And so, at the ascension, when Jesus was taken from his disciples' sight into a cloud, they would have understood the deep symbolic significance of what they saw.

Scientific questions

We now live in a scientific age and questions arise as to how the ascension is to be understood. Clearly some definite indication had to be given to the disciples that the appearances were now over. It would have made no difference geographically whether the ascension had taken place in Galilee, Jerusalem—or anywhere else in this world. It was a symbolic act of upward movement to demonstrate their Master's entry into the spiritual sphere; this was no mere disappearance. Those witnessing the event knew that Jesus had been exalted to the Father's right hand—the place of honour and dignity, having a part in the sovereignty of God over all.

The truths enshrined in the ascension far outweigh questions over the length of the interval between the resurrection and ascension, or the manner of Jesus' departure. The ascension marked Christ's 'coronation', his exaltation. It is the standpoint from which the entire New Testament is written. In particular, the Coronation Psalms (Psalms 24, 47, 68, 110 and 118) which were sung at the festival of the Jewish New Year to celebrate the enthronement of God as universal king were now seen as speaking of Christ enthroned for ever as Lord and King.

Coronation gifts

When Christ first came into our world at Bethlehem he joined himself for ever to the human race. His ascension in his resurrection body, bearing the scars of crucifixion, shows that our humanity has been taken up into heaven. There the ascended Lord represents us (many passages in the letter to the Hebrews speak of this). And this involves more than prayer: it is the means by which he enters fully into every human situation in a way not possible during his days on earth.

Before his death, Jesus plainly stated that it would be necessary for him to leave his disciples in order that the Holy Spirit might come. And when, a few days after his ascension, the Holy Spirit was given to the disciples, Peter explained that the strange phenomena which appeared were the fulfilment of Old Testament prophecy. The wind, fire and 'tongues' were the gift of the ascended Christ.

That day the Christian church came into being, and ever since then believers, individually and corporately, have been able to speak of 'God (who) raised us up with Christ and seated us with him in the heavenly realms in Christ Jesus'.

Christians know that as Jesus ascended to heaven so too will they. And their lives must be based on confidence in this hope and on the challenge to live up to their calling. Christ is our pioneer, going before us to heaven. Because of his total obedience to his Father's will, his body and spirit were taken up through the recreating power of God. This gives believers the assurance of life everlasting.

The ascension points to the ultimate universal reign of Christ as Lord of all. The powers of evil will be finally defeated. The conflict between good and evil will remain until the end of history, but in the words of the Old Testament passage most quoted of any in the New Testament we read that the victory of the ascended Christ is to be finally made complete: 'The Lord says to my lord: Sit at my right hand till I make your enemies your footstool'.

Linking heaven and earth

The ascension marks the separation of the earthly and heavenly life of Christ. But at the same time it unites the two inseparably. The events on earth, the incarnation, crucifixion and resurrection, all demand it, while the gift of the Spirit, our representation in heaven and Christ's final coming in glory are inexplicable apart from it. The ascension holds the Jesus of history and the Christ of faith together.

◀ Graham Sutherland's great tapestry in Coventry Cathedral shows Christ in majesty. The ascension reminds us that Jesus returned to his eternal glory, taking the life of a human being into the life of God.

4.5

THE HOLY SPIRIT

Jesus' disciples did not have to wait until the Day of Pentecost to see signs that the Holy Spirit was powerfully at work. The most obvious thing about Jesus was that he made God's presence and power felt. As Peter was later to claim, it was widely known, 'how God poured out on Jesus of Nazareth the Holy Spirit and power. He went everywhere, doing good and healing all who were under the power of the devil, for God was with him.' Peter's words echo Jesus' own claim, made in Nazareth synagogue, and reported in Luke chapter 4, to fulfil Isaiah's words about one who would be anointed with God's Spirit to bring liberty and the joy of God's rule to Satan's captives.

And it was not just the sick and the demonized who were affected. Those who truly listened to Jesus experienced the Spirit at work through him as a power moulding their own lives and beliefs. They were experiencing at least the beginnings of the great promise of cosmic recreation spoken of in the Old Testament. Israel was to be forgiven, cleansed, transformed. God's people were to be given a new heart obedient to God, one ruled by his Spirit. And all would know God for themselves, as before only the prophets, priests and kings had known him. For God was going to pour the Spirit of prophecy on everyone. This gift was not especially the power to prophesy. It was more fundamentally the means God used to communicate with people, so that they might know his presence and direction.

The writer of the Fourth Gospel saw many of these things beginning to be fulfilled in Jesus' ministry. But in the Upper Room, as he and his disciples shared their last Passover meal, Jesus indicated he was soon to die; he was returning to the Father.

The gift promised

Little wonder John shows us the disciples devastated when Jesus began to speak of returning to the Father. Their whole knowledge of God was bound up with what he did and said. Was all that had begun so gloriously now abruptly to cease? (The vital teaching that followed is described in John chapters 14, 15 and 16, from which much of the information here is drawn.)

In answer to their fears, Jesus promises the Father will give the Holy Spirit to be 'another Advocate of the same kind' as he has been. Far from leaving them 'as orphans', it will actually be to their advantage that Jesus goes, as only then will this Advocate be given them.

How can anything be better than the presence of Jesus? John points to a number of possible answers:
- **The Spirit will bring to the disciples the presence of both the Father and the Son.** In his ministry, Jesus had made the Father's presence real. He was so at one with the Father, that to see him was to see the Father too. So it will be with the arrival of the Spirit as 'another Advocate'. The Spirit will be so united with the Father and the Son that to experience *him* will be to experience *them*.
- **The Spirit will extend and deepen their spiritual grasp of the revelation Jesus embodied.** They found him and his teaching so hard to understand while he was with them.
- **The Spirit, working with and through the disciples, will continue Jesus' witness to the world.** And, like Jesus, the Spirit will convict the world of its sin (chiefly of its unbelief), its tawdry 'righteousness', and its false judgment of the truth Jesus reveals.

◀ The Holy Spirit came on
Jesus at his baptism in the
form of a dove. This has
become a symbol for freedom
– freedom which only God
can give, the true liberty of
the human spirit.

Jesus the Living Presence

In the Gospel of Matthew Jesus makes two promises to his followers:
- 'Where two or three come together in my name, there am I with them,' he assures them, in chapter 18 verse 20. This echoes the way Jewish teachers said that when people come together to study the Law, the *Shekinah* (the glorious presence of God) is with them.
- 'I will be with you always.' So Jesus promised his followers, when he sent them out to make disciples throughout the world (chapter 28 verse 20).

In both these verses we are dealing with something that goes beyond ordinary human experiences. The best that we can say to somebody going off on a dangerous mission is 'I'll be thinking of you' or 'I'll pray for you'. But Jesus speaks as one would speak of God's presence with people.

He also promised his disciples that when they were in dangerous situations before courts of law the Spirit of God would be with them and instruct them in what to say. In John's Gospel he goes further and promises that the Spirit will be with them as what he called the 'Paraclete', somebody who will stand in for him to help them when he is no longer physically present.

Here, then, are two strands of thinking which sometimes come closely together. They recur elsewhere in the New Testament. The first Christians were conscious of the powerful presence of the Holy Spirit with them, and they received his gifts to help them in their witness. But they also spoke of knowing Christ and of his presence within their lives. Paul can speak without distinction of being in Christ, of Christ being in him and of the Spirit living in him. The language seems almost self-contradictory, but it makes sense when we realize that Paul is straining language to express the closeness of the relationship between Christ and his people.

Are these simply two ways of speaking about the same thing? Is the presence of Jesus Christ with us the same as the presence of the Spirit? Does Paul mean that the Spirit in effect replaces Christ and is equivalent to Christ in our experience?

We will stumble here unless we see that we are dealing with the presence of the divine in human experience, and this is something which cannot be explained in human terms. By its very nature human language is inadequate to explain how God can be present with us. We are thinking of a spiritual reality which can and must be expressed in various ways. This is the same in Christian experience today as it was in New Testament days.

On the one hand, we have the element of personal communion with Jesus, who is alive and active. Sometimes he appeared to his followers in dreams and visions and spoke to them.

On the other hand, we have the element of experiencing spiritual power associated with the Spirit. This is a less personal way of speaking (so much so that some people have—mistakenly—doubted whether the Spirit is really personal).

But both ways of speaking are necessary in order to express the varied character of our spiritual experience. Our problem is that we are dealing with a God who is revealed to us in the Bible as one and yet existing in three persons:
- **To him we can pray** (generally to the Father);
- **With him we have** **personal communion** (generally associated with Jesus the Son);
- **From him we receive spiritual power** (generally associated with the Spirit).

The closeness of the relationship between the three persons means that we cannot sharply distinguish between our different spiritual experiences. But equally we must not fuse them into one and fail to do justice to the nature of God as trinity.

Whether we say 'Jesus with me' or 'the Spirit in me', we are speaking of the presence in our lives of the living God.

- **Through the Spirit, the disciples will accomplish 'greater works' even than Jesus himself**—not necessarily more spectacular ones, but with greater power to open people's eyes. What the Spirit will do in the disciples' lives in answer to prayer will now reveal who Jesus is—the exalted Son. And they will show that Jesus and his Father are working together to bring salvation.

In short, the coming of the Spirit will not only continue the work of Jesus, but deepen it and make it more effective. In Jesus' ministry the disciples have felt the Spirit at work in them only through what Jesus has done and taught; beyond the resurrection the Spirit will work in and through all the disciples. And, above all, the Spirit will not come simply to replace Jesus, but as the personal presence of Jesus in the Christian.

The gift received

Then, on the Day of Pentecost, the Spirit was powerfully given. The Book of Acts describes the result. All that Jesus had promised, in John's account, is fulfilled. The Spirit is seen as that which was promised by the prophet Joel: the very means of communication between God and his people. (Peter's sermon tells them this; it can be read in Acts chapter 2.) The apostle assures them that this is what they are experiencing in the flame and the wind and the gift of tongues. All who repent and believe should crystallize that belief in baptism.

Jesus has been exalted to the Father's right hand, and he as well as his Father is now Lord of the Spirit. So Peter can insist that it is Jesus himself who is pouring out these gifts. The Spirit of God has become the Spirit of Jesus too.

Throughout Acts we see Joel's promised gift in action. He gives visions, sometimes of crucial theological importance, as when, in chapter 10, Peter is led to preach to Gentiles. He directs the Christians by word, also, and gives them the right things to say when most needed. Through the Spirit they receive spiritual discernment. In all this the Spirit is seen as the means by which God—the Father and the risen Lord Jesus—dwells with his disciples and makes his presence known among them.

From Pentecost on we see the disciples, who had previously found things so hard to understand, now having a firm grasp of what the gospel is about, and a deep inner conviction of its truth. And they are guided by the Spirit to its implications, as when, in Acts chapter 15, they confer at Jerusalem as to what must be expected when Gentiles turn to God.

The sense of God at work with them brings the disciples a joy that enables them to preach fearlessly even in the face of opposition. They have a new grasp of the significance of Jesus and what he has done, and they have a heavenly wisdom imparted to them by the Spirit as they confront the world. This gives them the power Jesus promised, as they bear witness to him in the world.

Miracles of healing and exorcism also continue, no doubt empowered by the same Spirit. These acts of liberation do more than point to the truth of the gospel; they give it actual substance. The message is of God's redemptive love which liberates from evil. Distorted bodies and crippled spirits are part and parcel of Satan's oppression, from which the risen Jesus continues to free people where his gospel is preached.

Paul's writings give us a similar picture. The Spirit of God is now experienced as 'the Spirit of Jesus Christ' or 'the Spirit of God's Son'. The Spirit makes Christ present to us, and he also moulds us into Christ's likeness. In this sense Paul sees the gift of the Spirit fulfilling the promise made in Jeremiah chapter 31 and Ezekiel chapter 36, the promise of new covenant life in obedience and knowledge of God. (2 Corinthians chapter 3 above all conveys this.) This same Spirit of Christ is experienced in a variety of gifts which simultaneously make the church an integrated body and afford a powerful witness to the outsider.

Jesus the Reconciler

For four days in 1987, 225 people of all races from all over South Africa waged peace in the township of Mamelodi on the outskirts of Pretoria as part of a unique crossing-the-barriers conference known as the Christian Encounter in Mamelodi. To grasp that this was the first time such a group had done such a thing is to comprehend how far-reaching the effects of apartheid are. In spite of the fact that many white Christians have opposed this policy for many years, very few have ever had the opportunity of seeing life as a black person sees it in the segregated townships in which the blacks are forced to live by the Group Areas Act. This exercise was eye-opening, to say the least.

The conference set out to break down the misconceptions and prejudices that people of different races harbour towards each other by putting them to live in each other's homes. One black family filled in their accommodation form as a joke because they were convinced no white person would ever come into the township to stay with them. They were extremely surprised when their guest arrived — and had to shuffle the furniture around to accommodate him. One white delegate, who knocked at a door to ask for directions, found himself drawn inside and begged to stay there, instead of in his allocated home, thereby exploding the myth that whites would receive a hostile reception in the townships.

Dr Nico Smith, a highly-respected academic and professor at Stellenbosch University, the bastion of Afrikaner ideology, gave up his position some years ago and decided to move into a black township to minister to an all-black congregation. This move of his was revolutionary in the history of the Dutch Reformed Church and earned him many death threats which continue to this day. Under his leadership, the Koinonia Fellowship in Mamelodi has flourished and it was they who organized the conference, along with Michael Cassidy, leader of the National Initiative for Reconciliation. Realizing what impact such a stay would have on whites as they stayed in black homes and for blacks as they stayed in white homes, they knew that those who took part in the encounter would come back completely changed. And so it was.

The Spirit today

Christians would hold that the same basic experience is available today. When people receive the Holy Spirit at conversion, they begin to sense God alongside them and Jesus lovingly moulding and directing their lives in a quite new way.

Sometimes the Spirit 'speaks' by convicting the reader of truths read in the Bible. At other times, the Spirit is felt to speak through a preacher, teacher, or some other fellow Christian, as though

The Jesus of the Revivalists

Eighteenth-century preachers John Wesley (1703–91) and George Whitefield (1714–70) came to have a revolutionary impact on their generation. Passionately loved or passionately loathed, these men could not be ignored; both friends and foes agreed their sermons were powerful and spell-binding. Many considered Whitefield the greatest orator of his age.

In the English-speaking world, the eighteenth century was a remarkably immoral time; we would even find it so today. Life was nasty, brutish and short, and many alleviated its distresses by drowning themselves in gin, or amused themselves with brutal, cruel sports. Revivalists such as Wesley and Whitefield sought to awaken people from their spiritual stupor, to bring them to realize their sinfulness, and to show them the fearful state of their souls without Christ.

Their impassioned preaching was a far cry from the dry, moralizing lectures normally read by ministers to sleepy congregations. Jonathan Swift, famous author and Dean of Dublin, once instructed a young clergyman that he was to inform people of their duty and then convince them to do it. A respectable minister was not to speak of sin and salvation; he certainly would not mention 'Hell to ears polite'. Given such expectations, the revivalists were not 'respectable'. They spoke of Jesus in intensely personal terms, and when they prayed and preached they seemed immediately aware of his presence. This they were able to communicate to their listeners.

Friend of the poor

While most ministers commended Christian morality in a refined and cultured manner to 'polite' audiences, the revivalists confronted common people with Jesus himself. John Wesley insisted that the poor were the focus of Jesus' ministry on earth. Two New Testament phrases recur in his sermons and in the hymns of his brother, Charles: 'The poor have the gospel preached to them' and 'The poor heard him gladly.' Jesus was familiar with the poor, he had fraternized with them; Jesus understood the poor, he knew their needs and problems; Jesus had been rich, but had chosen poverty to befriend the poor. His friendship was their greatest treasure, the most important thing that anyone could desire. The poor were reassured that this approachable friend was the image of his Father; he was just like God. Thus Jesus' love for the poor was the same as God's love for the poor. What is more, Jesus was not just the friend of the poor but especially the friend of 'poor sinners' who stood in need of his forgiveness; he had suffered rejection and crucifixion to be able to offer forgiveness to them.

The aim of these preachers was neither to explain a religious tradition nor to argue intellectual concepts, but to confront people with a choice. They wanted people to make up their minds about this man. Jesus offered friendship to those whose sin had caused his suffering. The decision facing them was put in the starkest terms: would they repudiate sin and openly identify with Christ?

Often Jesus was vividly portrayed as being present, waiting for them to make their decision. Sometimes, like the Roman Catholic writers of the sixteenth century, they would describe his suffering on behalf of the sinner, suffering to cleanse their sin:

'See where our blessed Lord stands and weeps, and stretches out his arms towards you. . . See the print

◀▲ **John and Charles Wesley were heroes of eighteenth-century England, and their influence also swept America. Their message was of the need to be born again through the Holy Spirit of Jesus.**

of the nails on his dear hands and feet. It is your sins that made them! Ah! how pale and worn he looks!. . . They spat upon him and buffeted him, they scourged him, they mocked him, they laid the heavy cross on his bruised shoulders. Then they nailed him up. Ah! what pain!'

Such creative use of the imagination was perhaps employed most effectively by George Whitefield, who could keep upwards of 30,000 people hanging on his every word. Benjamin Franklin was one of his great admirers. Lord Chesterfield, a notorious British noble-man, once heard Whitefield picture a blind man approaching the edge of a cliff un-awares, and was so caught up in the description that he is reputed to have cried out 'For heaven's sake, Whitefield, save him!'

In one of the best representations in nineteenth-century literature of Wesley's style of preaching, we get a sense of how direct the preacher could be in confronting individuals. A Methodist evangelist is addressing a young woman:

'Poor child! poor child! He is beseeching you, and you don't listen to him. You think of ear-rings and fine gowns and caps, and you never think of the Saviour who died to save your precious soul. Your cheeks will be shrivelled one day, your hair will be grey, your poor body will be thin and tottering! Then you will begin to feel that your soul is not saved; then you will have to stand before God dressed in your sins, in your evil tempers and vain thoughts. And Jesus, who stands ready to help you now, won't help you then: because you won't have him to be your Saviour, he will be your Judge.'

Such a bold presentation of the matter was as offensive to many of their listeners as it is to many modern readers. The revivalists did not apologize for this, as they felt that they were being true to the Bible's message.

American revivalism

Although Wesley and Whitefield were both English, the revivalists' portrayal of Jesus had its greatest impact in North America. Whitefield made some seven trips to America and was a key figure in what is known in American colonial history as the 'Great Awakening', which was at its peak in the years 1839–42. In the long run, however, it was the followers of John Wesley's brand of Method-ism that were to be most successful in America, adapting the revivalists' message and approach to the urban setting as well as to America's frontier. The revivalist tradition became so well-established in America that historians consider it a major factor in the high level of religious observance in the United States today.

In the nineteenth century Americans dominated revivalism and revivalism dominated the American religious scene. Two Americans: Charles G. Finney (1792–1875) and Dwight L. Moody (1837–99), were the most successful revival preachers. Finney, a lawyer by training, was fiery and flamboyant, focusing on people's ability to turn away from their sins toward God. Moody was less of an orator but more of an organizer than Finney; he worked closely with local churches and used mass publicity for the first time. His preaching emphasized the love of God shown in Jesus, but he did also preach on hell and less 'polite' subjects.

It came as a surprise to many when Moody was well received in Britain in the mid-1870s. He was the first major revivalist since Whitefield to develop a significant international ministry. After Moody, however, revivalism went into decline, due in part to the reputation of some of its more unusual preachers. It was only to be rescued from oblivion in the 1940s

by the efforts of a remark-ably effective and widely-respected American evangelist.

This century's best-known revivalist has also been called the twentieth-century's 'best-known religious figure'. He is, of course, Billy Graham (born 1918). Graham's message has been centred on presenting Jesus as the Gospels describe him; he has called people to make a decision about the person of Christ. In this he stands in a well-defined revivalist tradition now known throughout the English-speaking world. Graham, however, has adapted the tradition to the twentieth century, employing all the mass media available to him. He has also developed a carefully-planned strategy for following-up those who make 'decisions for Christ' during his meetings, so that they receive Christian teaching and are linked to churches. He has emphasized the love of Jesus in his preaching, but again, like his predecessors, he has not shrunk from warning people that they will face God's judgement in the future. Billy Graham has preached about Jesus throughout the world, often using his influence to ensure that his meetings have been racially integrated. His appeal was ascribed by a noted British newspaper columnist in the 1950s to 'the power of simplicity'.

▲ **Billy Graham has probably preached to more people than anyone else in history. He has combined a traditional message of repentance and faith with a careful policy of nurturing those who respond in Christian discipleship.**

God had given that person some special wisdom or gift, and made Jesus' own presence felt in it. At other times still, Christians claim to have received special wisdom and power from Christ, as they themselves have spoken or acted on his behalf. Or they have been conscious of particular direction from him, perhaps in a time of worship or. prayer, that they just *know* (usually with great joy) that Jesus has spoken to them.

Some (mainly Pentecostals and Charismatics) claim Jesus still occasionally gives them visions or special dreams, and the gift of tongues and special words of prophecy about the church or about individual needs. Strangely enough, those who make this claim have often held that an experience of the Spirit distinct from conversion is necessary before such gifts are possible. (They often call this 'baptism in the Spirit' or 'being filled with the Spirit'.) Luke would have been puzzled by such a claim. Why does a person who can already experience the Spirit giving him, say, a strong sense of Christ's direct guidance, still need some further distinct 'baptism in Spirit' in order to receive from God the essential content of a prophecy or a word of knowledge? Rather *both* the ability to 'know' Jesus and receive his guidance, *and* the ability to receive a prophetic word belong together as outworkings of the one gift of the Spirit. They share exactly the same spiritual dynamic. For Luke, after Pentecost, the one gift of the Spirit promised by Joel provides virtually *all* the means by which we continue to know the risen Jesus.

By the same token, Luke might also have been puzzled by those who oppose the Charismatics and

Set Free

Evangelist Jackie Pullinger tells this story from Hongkong:

'Ah Ming was a heroin addict. His encounter with Jesus transformed his ruined life, much to the amazement of his mates. One day whilst he was leading a Jesus procession, accompanied by singing and dancing in the streets, he stopped at one of the largest heroin dens and began to preach. Inside the den, a tall young Chinese called Ah Mo had just injected himself. Immediately he had to think about how he was going to get money for the next fix. Just as he was planning his next robbery, he heard the singing and dancing outside. He was amazed to see his old friend Ah Ming, telling the street how Jesus had changed his life. It was obvious to him that something very wonderful had taken place, for only three weeks ago he and Ah Ming had been squatting together taking heroin side by side in that very same den. Forgetting his projected robbery he joined the end of the procession, followed it until it wound up some thirty minutes later back at the club, and came in to listen with wonder as other boys he had known told him how his life could also be transformed by Jesus.'

claim that tongues, prophecy, visions and the like are not for today. Had Peter not promised Joel's gift to everyone—then and later? And are not prophecies, dreams and visions as characteristic of that promise as the ability to know Jesus and receive his guidance?

No, when the Holy Spirit reveals Jesus to people, he also brings to life in them the capacity to experience all the aspects of Christian living of which we read in the Acts of the Apostles.

4.6

THE CHURCH BEGINS

In his ministry, Jesus did not attempt to set up churches in Israel. He did not call people out of Israel into the church. And he did not call Gentiles at all. Instead, he called all Israel to have a part in God's dawning reign, and to share in the fulfilment of the ancient promises God had given the nation of new covenant life. It was highly symbolic that he chose an inner circle of twelve; around these disciples God was beginning to restore the twelve tribes of Israel.

Jesus called all Israel, yet he knew his message would divide Israel. And the issues of division were sharpened by the events of Easter and Pentecost. As Peter declared in his sermon at Pentecost (see Acts chapter 2), God had confirmed by raising Jesus from death that he was Messiah. All Israel were therefore summoned to give their allegiance to their anointed king, and to enter the community of his people through baptism in his name. Those who refused him their allegiance were warned they were cutting themselves off from the people of Israel. The divide was now clear. The issue had become 'Where is the true Israel?' And the church's answer was 'At the feet of her true king, of course'—an answer not calculated to please the Jerusalem leaders.

Israel fulfilled

This tension, between those Jews who rejected Jesus and those who received him, comes out repeatedly in the first eight chapters of Acts. Within a short time after Pentecost, according to Luke, the numbers of those who heard the message and became followers had risen to five thousand. And

for every one of those there must have been several others who were impressed by the message, by the boldness and lifestyle of these followers of Jesus, by the joy of the community, and by the power of God apparently displayed in it. For various reasons, however, they shrank from commitment to the new party; partly this was natural conservatism, partly respect for, even fear of, their leaders, partly unbelief. It is a story repeated throughout Christian history.

Others, including most of the religious leaders, simply could not accept the claims. The offence of Jesus' ministry was too great, and his death on a cross could only be a sign he was under God's curse. For them, whether the tomb was empty or not, the claim that God had resurrected such a man, and exalted him in heaven, verged on blasphemy. So they tried to silence Peter and John, and a collision course seemed set. But the nerve of the church did not falter. They brought the impending threat before God in prayer, and received fresh filling by the Holy Spirit and further boldness to preach. Their 'defences' before religious courts became spirited presentations of the gospel, seasoned with attacks on the unbelief of the very Jewish leaders accusing them, and they learned to count floggings for the sake of Jesus a joy and privilege.

But the divide could only deepen. His followers were even claiming that Jesus was Lord of the Spirit, and that he was thus 'the Lord' on whose name men should call for salvation—indeed that 'there is no other name. . .by which we must be saved'. In other words, the experience of the presence of Jesus by and through the Spirit naturally led them to believe that Jesus was truly God. Who other than

5. THE DAWN OF NEW HOPE

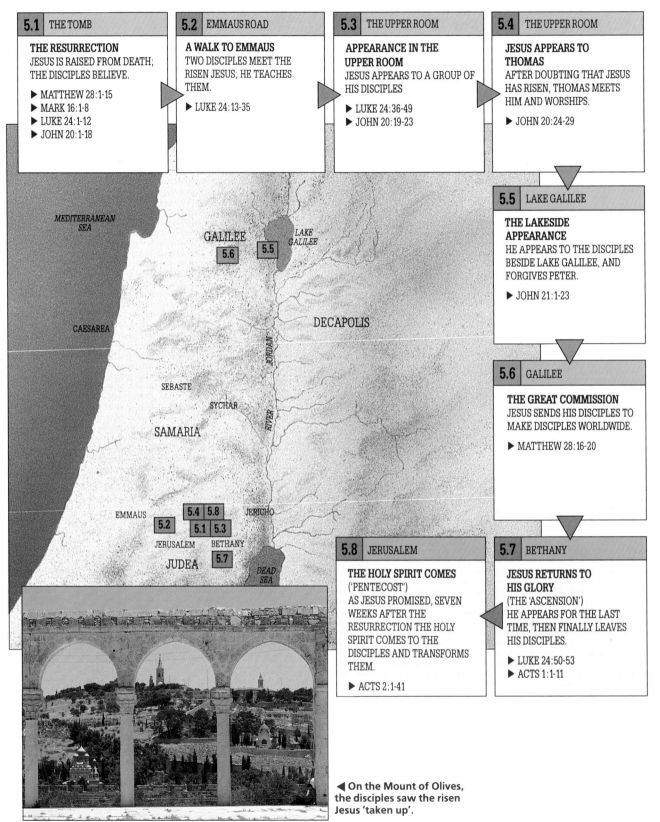

5.1 THE TOMB

THE RESURRECTION
JESUS IS RAISED FROM DEATH; THE DISCIPLES BELIEVE.

▶ MATTHEW 28:1-15
▶ MARK 16:1-8
▶ LUKE 24:1-12
▶ JOHN 20:1-18

5.2 EMMAUS ROAD

A WALK TO EMMAUS
TWO DISCIPLES MEET THE RISEN JESUS; HE TEACHES THEM.

▶ LUKE 24:13-35

5.3 THE UPPER ROOM

APPEARANCE IN THE UPPER ROOM
JESUS APPEARS TO A GROUP OF HIS DISCIPLES

▶ LUKE 24:36-49
▶ JOHN 20:19-23

5.4 THE UPPER ROOM

JESUS APPEARS TO THOMAS
AFTER DOUBTING THAT JESUS HAS RISEN, THOMAS MEETS HIM AND WORSHIPS.

▶ JOHN 20:24-29

5.5 LAKE GALILEE

THE LAKESIDE APPEARANCE
HE APPEARS TO THE DISCIPLES BESIDE LAKE GALILEE, AND FORGIVES PETER.

▶ JOHN 21:1-23

5.6 GALILEE

THE GREAT COMMISSION
JESUS SENDS HIS DISCIPLES TO MAKE DISCIPLES WORLDWIDE.

▶ MATTHEW 28:16-20

5.8 JERUSALEM

THE HOLY SPIRIT COMES
('PENTECOST')
AS JESUS PROMISED, SEVEN WEEKS AFTER THE RESURRECTION THE HOLY SPIRIT COMES TO THE DISCIPLES AND TRANSFORMS THEM.

▶ ACTS 2:1-41

5.7 BETHANY

JESUS RETURNS TO HIS GLORY
(THE 'ASCENSION')
HE APPEARS FOR THE LAST TIME, THEN FINALLY LEAVES HIS DISCIPLES.

▶ LUKE 24:50-53
▶ ACTS 1:1-11

◀ On the Mount of Olives, the disciples saw the risen Jesus 'taken up'.

God could direct 'the Spirit of the Lord'? With this step it was inevitable that the church would begin to worship Jesus, with the Father, as God, and pray to him. The dying martyr Stephen, although he had just received a vision of Father and Son together, committed his spirit specifically into Jesus' hands.

Judaism, for all its tolerance, could not accom-

▶ When Emperor Constantine became a Christian in the fourth century, the whole position of the church changed. Constantine adapted the form of the basilica to fit Christian worship, and so gave a shape to church buildings which lasted more than a thousand years. This is the Constantine Basilica in Rome.

▶ The Acropolis is here seen from the hill known as Areopagus, where Paul made his first attempt to spread the Christian faith to exponents of Greek philosophy. This attempt eventually came to dominate Christian thinking.

▼ The city of Antioch, in present-day Syria, was the first place where Jesus' followers were called Christians. It was also the first truly multiracial church.

modate a movement that offered any man (far less one crucified) the worship and prayer due to God alone. A considerable persecution was unleashed on the church and its scattered members fled, carrying their message far and wide.

Bursting the wineskins of Judaism

Divided as it was from mainline Judaism, still the church saw itself as a Jewish movement. With rare exceptions, the church only preached to Jews, proselytes, or those thinking of becoming proselyte Jews.

But then things began to change dramatically, as we see from Acts chapter 8 onwards. At first God led Peter to preach to a single Gentile household. Then, later, Paul's mission yielded churches with big majorities of Gentiles. Jewish Christians in Jerusalem argued against this innovation. How could these Gentile believers continue as Jesus' followers without being circumcised and keeping the

No Pit Too Deep

As Nazi madness swept across Europe, the Ten Boom family saw the lights go out on a free Holland. With the growth of discrimination and hatred, they were motivated by their love for Christ to provide food, strength and a place for Jews to hide from the terrors of Hitler's forces. For Corrie and her sister Betsie, this meant facing the stark brutality of life in Ravensbruck concentration camp. Here, with hundreds of other women prisoners, they were forced to work in the most appalling conditions, often in poor health and with minimal food and clothing. Even there, the two sisters found that their faith in Jesus was sufficient to sustain them. 'We must go everywhere and tell people that there is no pit that is so deep that God's love is not deeper still,' said Corrie. 'They will believe us because we have been here.'

▲ The early Christian gatherings took place in people's houses, and today this is beginning to happen again. Followers of Jesus meet informally to worship, to pray, to study and to encourage one another in faith.

covenant? Jesus was Israel's Messiah, so his people should keep Israel's Law. Otherwise they would cut themselves off from grace. This was the argument Paul countered in his letter to the Galatians, and at the Jerusalem Council reported in Acts chapter 15.

For Paul, this requirement that Gentiles should keep the Jewish Law constituted an impossible attempt to keep the new wine of Jesus in the old wineskins of Judaism. Jesus was not merely the beginning of a new Israel. Paul's encounter with the risen Jesus convinced him Christ was the beginning of a whole new humanity. Those united with Jesus, whether Jew or Gentile, became one new humanity in him. Jesus was the answer to God's ancient promise to Abraham, that in his seed all nations would be blessed.

With the eventual acceptance of Paul's vision, the church emerged from Judaism to become what it is today: neither a Jewish religion nor a Gentile one, but one that claims to transcend both. Against opposition from its Jewish roots and from the pluralistic world in which it flourished, the early church was adamant that its gospel was unique— the only way to experience God's dawning salvation. They had the temerity to make this claim, because they became convinced it was uniquely justified—by the life, death, resurrection and exaltation of their founder, Jesus. The question was only whether the church of later years would be as faithful.

4.7

JESUS WORSHIPPED AS LORD

To worship somebody means that we honour them and express this honour in appropriate ways. But, while we may honour ordinary people, we reserve the word 'worship' for the honour we give to God.

The Bible insists that worship is to be given only to the one God, the God of Israel who is the same God as is worshipped by Christians. This point had to be stressed in a world where numerous gods were worshipped, for although exclusive claims were made on behalf of some of them, in practice people could worship several simultaneously. It was of course natural in the ancient world to give worship to such supernatural agents of God as angels. But this is dismissed as being inappropriate in the New Testament.

This worship of only one God, this monotheism, makes it all the more remarkable that Christian worship in a Jewish environment extended to include a second figure alongside God, Jesus Christ. We can understand Paul the Jew writing to his friends in a pagan city where there were 'many "gods" and many "lords"': 'For us there is but one God, the Father, from whom all things came and for whom we live.' What is astounding is that he goes on to say: 'and there is but one Lord, Jesus Christ, through whom all things came and through whom we live'. How did this way of understanding Jesus develop?

The Lord

How did it happen that Jesus came to be regarded as a figure worthy of worship? The beginnings of the process are lost to us. It was appropriate to give respect to the agents through whom God was seen

to work and so it is not surprising that already in his lifetime people 'worshipped' Jesus when he performed mighty acts of healing or otherwise displayed divine powers. At the same time we notice that people also worshipped God for what Jesus did and 'praised God, who had given such authority to men'. But any worship of Jesus during his lifetime was spasmodic and confined to a few individuals. It did not necessarily indicate that he was regarded as divine.

After his resurrection the situation changed. Matthew tells us that when the risen Jesus appeared to his disciples they worshipped him. This would not be surprising for a person seen to be possessed of unusual spiritual powers.

By the time Paul wrote his earliest letters a much more fundamental change had taken place. It had become natural to place God the Father and Jesus Christ side by side as the source of the spiritual blessings which Christians receive. This is done in the most natural manner, without any reflection or explicit justification, and it demonstrates that within some twenty years of his death Jesus was placed alongside God in a way that must have shocked strictly monotheistic Jews.

At the same time Jesus was referred to as 'Lord'. There is no doubt as to the force that could be put into the word 'Lord'. In the Hebrew Scriptures the name of God was written as *YHWH*. Hebrew was originally written without any vowels, and people automatically supplied them in pronunciation; at a later time vowel marks were added to the text. In the case of *YHWH* the vowels which were written were those of the word *Adonai*, which means 'Lord', and the intention was that, since the name of *YHWH* was so sacred that people must not utter it for fear of blasphemy, they should substitute *Adonai* instead. The same thing happened in the Greek translation of the Scriptures used by early Christians. The Greek word for 'Lord', *Kyrios*, was used for the name of God. So when Christians used *Kyrios* to refer to Jesus, they could have been using the title associated with God.

But the 'could' is important. For the word *Kyrios* was also a perfectly ordinary Greek word used every day in ordinary ways. It was used for an owner of property or slaves, and you would address a teacher or other senior person by it as a mark of respect. (We may compare the varied uses of 'Sir' in Britain; it can be a title of honour bestowed by the sovereign, or it can be simply a mark of courtesy when used by a shop assistant.) The word is respectful but ambiguous. When is it applied to Jesus as more than just a sign of respect?

There are times when it seems clear that it is

being used to stress that Jesus is superior even to the Roman emperor. The emperor too was known as 'Lord', and Christians who called Jesus 'Lord' recognized that they were demoting the emperor from his supreme position. In the Book of Revelation the worship of the emperor is particularly in mind, and it is here that Jesus is designated 'King of kings and Lord of lords'. But this is to take us to the end of the New Testament period. Our concern is with how this understanding of the supreme position of Jesus grew up.

Other titles

The question cannot be settled on its own. We must observe some parallel processes going on in the way people spoke of Jesus. (We will see more of this under *Titles of Jesus*.)

■ **Jesus the Son of man.** Jesus used this phrase to refer to himself. It was understood by his followers in the light of a passage in Daniel's vision (chapter 7 verse 13) where a figure like a (son of) man is

The Lord is my Probation Officer

As chaplain in Erie County Jail, New York, Carl Burke was faced with how to communicate to New York's toughest and most hostile youths. Instead of trying to preach at them, he encouraged them to retell stories from the Bible in their own language. This is one interpretation of Psalm 23, the Shepherd Psalm.

The Lord is like my Probation Officer,
He will help me,
He tries to help me make it every day.
He makes me play it cool
And feel good inside of me.
He shows me the right path
So I'll have a good record,
And he'll have one too.

Because I trust him,
And that ain't easy,
I don't worry too much about
What's going to happen.
Just knowing he cares about me
Helps me.

He makes sure I have my food
And that Mum fixes it.
He helps me stay sober
And that makes me feel good all over.
He's a good man I think
And he is kind;
And these things will stay with me.

And when I'm kind and good
Then I know the Lord
Is with me like the Probation Officer.

▲▶ Mount Tabor (top) and Mount Hermon have both been suggested as the site of Jesus' transfiguration. He climbed a mountain, with Peter, James and John. While they watched, his whole appearance altered and they understood his true glory.

brought before God and given the highest honour and sovereignty. It is plausible to think of this figure as divine, and this will be how the early Christians thought of Jesus: he was an agent of God very closely associated with him. However, this term soon dropped out of Christian use, though not before it had helped to indicate the high status of Jesus.

■ **Jesus the Messiah**. In Jewish thought the future king who would restore the kingdom of David and bring about peace, righteousness and prosperity was a human figure, a descendant of David. He would possess the Spirit of God in exceptional measure. But it seems likely that Christians thought of the Messiah more and more as a divine figure. Already in his lifetime Jesus was recognized as the Messiah, and the effect of his resurrection was to confirm that this was his status.

Jesus and Paul

Anybody who compares the Gospels with the letters of Paul will see a very great difference between them in style and content. Even when we recognize that stories about a wandering preacher in Galilee will be different from letters written to young churches facing all the problems of Christian life in a pagan society, and that there are bound to be differences between the teaching of the founder of a religious group and of one of his followers over twenty years after his death, we may still find the contrast puzzling.

Indeed, some people would argue that the simple religion of Jesus, centred on the fatherhood of God and the need for people to love both their neighbours and their enemies, has been radically transformed by Paul and other Christians. The work and teaching of Jesus are ignored, say such people, and Paul concentrates instead on Jesus' death and resurrection, his spiritual presence and his future coming. He introduces a complicated set of doctrines including reconciliation with God by the sacrificial death of Jesus, and an elaborate system of church life has developed. Is this the same thing as the religion of Jesus?

In one very obvious sense it is not and was never meant to be. People who want to bypass Paul and go back to the so-called religion of Jesus forget that the foundation of Christianity is not just the teaching of Jesus but also Jesus' own death and resurrection and the coming of the Spirit. There were some things that the followers of Jesus could not fully understand until after his death. Jesus' teaching, of course, included hints that pointed to these future developments. But he could hardly teach people about the significance of his death when they could not accept the fact that he actually had to die.

In fact there are very many lines of continuity between the teaching of Jesus and that of Paul:

- **Both teach that God is the Father of his people.**
- **Jesus taught about the kingdom; Paul about the King.** Jesus' message was about the coming of the kingdom of God. Implicitly his role in its coming was that of God's agent, the figure known in Judaism as the Messiah. It is not surprising that his followers shifted the emphasis in their message from the kingdom to the King.
- **Both stressed forgiveness.** Jesus' teaching recognized people's weakness and sinfulness. He offered forgiveness and the possibility of a new life to those for whom there was little human comfort and hope, especially to outcasts from the Jewish religion. Paul likewise taught—but more explicitly—that everybody has sinned and that God offers forgiveness to all. He extended the scope of God's concern (hinted at by Jesus) to include the non-Jews (the 'Gentiles') who were conspicuously outside God's covenant with the Jews.
- **Both spoke of the significance of Jesus' death.** Jesus spoke to his disciples of his coming death both as a kind of ransom for sinners and as a sacrifice which initiates a new relationship with God. These ideas are at the heart of Paul's thinking and he powerfully develops them.
- **Both taught about the Spirit of God.** Jesus sometimes spoke about the future coming of the Holy Spirit. This new experience of the powerful presence of God, which in a sense replaces the earthly presence of Jesus, becomes much more prominent in the thought and experience of Paul.
- **Both saw implications for the place of Law.** Jesus recognized that the Jewish Law was no longer literally binding in all its parts, although he stressed its permanent value and validity. Similarly, Paul claimed that he upheld the Law, that is, the moral principles contained within it, but he saw that much of it had come to a conclusion with the coming of Jesus and the establishment of the new covenant.
- **Both Jesus and Paul saw that the Law is summed up in the great commandment to love our fellow human beings as ourselves.**
- **Both Jesus and Paul looked forward to the future coming of Christ.** This would be the triumphant completion of God's purpose in the One who is both Son of man and Lord.

We see that the essential structure of the messages of Jesus and Paul is the same, despite the differences in the manner of presentation and the inevitable development of Christian thinking.

- **Jesus the Son of God**. Jesus' own consciousness that he was the Son of God led his followers to see that he had a relationship to God of unique closeness. This was acknowledged at least as early as Paul's first letters, Galatians and 1 Thessalonians, and probably earlier.

The development of these ways of recognizing Jesus' status encourages us to see the use of 'Lord' as more than just a mark of human respect. The term came to carry the conviction that Jesus shared the functions and the status of God the Father.

Jesus' lordship confirmed

We can see this right at the beginning of the church's life. In Acts chapter 2 verse 36 we read that on the Day of Pentecost Peter explained what God had done by raising Jesus from the dead: 'He has made him both Lord and Christ (Messiah).' Peter was alluding to Psalm 110:1, in which God confers the title of Lord on the Messiah, and he saw the resurrection of Jesus as the act by which God confirmed that this was indeed who he was.

A very important use of the title 'Lord' is to be seen in 1 Corinthians chapter 16 verse 22. Here Paul cites the phrase *Maranatha*. This comes from the Aramaic language and represents a prayer or statement made by Christians in their meetings. It was in use before the letter was written, and its language shows that it was used in an Aramaic-speaking church, and must therefore be an early development. The phrase means 'Our Lord, come' or 'Our Lord will come'. It refers to Jesus and looks forward to his future coming. This links up with Jesus' promise that the Son of man would one day return, but in fact the language here reflects Old Testament expectations of the future coming of God to execute judgment. Already at this stage the future judgment is being transferred from God to Christ, and with the transfer of function goes the transfer of the title.

A third significant passage is in Paul's letter to the Philippians chapter 2 verses 5 to 11. In this very early hymn, Paul describes the 'career' of Christ who moves from being equal with God before his incarnation, through the humiliation of earthly life and death, to being exalted by God, receiving the name that is above all names. 'At the name of Jesus every knee should bow. . .and every tongue confess that Jesus Christ is Lord.' The 'name that is above every name' is undoubtedly that of 'Lord'. It is the name of God which is being transferred to Jesus, and it is accompanied by the worship given to God—although God the Father continues to occupy the supreme place. The same Old Testament verse, Isaiah chapter 45 verse 25, which lies behind the wording of this hymn is also used by Paul with

reference to God the Father (Romans 14:11). Paul had no difficulty in applying the same Old Testament Scripture about Yahweh to both God the Father and to Jesus.

The Father and the Son

Some New Testament passages indicate that the actual title of 'God' was given to Jesus. But these are few in number, and the interpretation is not always absolutely certain. There was evidently a reluctance to adopt what could be a confusing mode of speech which might suggest that God the Father was not being given his appropriate status over against his Son. It was automatic for Jews to think of a son as being inferior in status to a father.

The problem was solved by taking over the divine title of 'Lord' for Jesus. Early Christians used it to indicate a more than human respect for Jesus; the title was increasingly filled with the content attached to 'Lord' as the name of God in the Old Testament, and as they came increasingly to use the title so they began to worship the Son of God alongside his Father. Paul said that Christians could be identified as those who 'call on the name of our Lord Jesus Christ'.

It is not surprising that 'Jesus (Christ) is Lord' became the characteristic distinguishing mark of early Christians. This succinct but revolutionary phrase appears to have been used as the confession Christians made as they were baptized. It incorporated and summed up the distinctively Christian belief about Jesus, that he was worthy to be worshipped and held in divine honour.

PART

5

WHO WAS JESUS?

So far this book has investigated the evidence about Jesus,
his life, his death and what happened after.

Now the question must be asked, where does all this evidence lead?
Can we know who he really was?

CONTENTS

SPECIAL FEATURES

Jesus, God's servant
The human Jesus
The Son of Man
Understanding who Jesus is
The titles of Jesus
The Trinity

5.1

THE AUTHORITY OF HIS TEACHING

We have grown so used to thinking of Jesus as a great teacher that we forget how breathtaking that fact is. The teachings of a comparatively obscure man from Palestine nearly two thousand years ago are still the inspiration and guide of millions of Christians today. Why do they have such impact?

Our search for the answer must start with the actual teachings of Jesus in the Gospels, and two features are most impressive about them.

Strange authority

Jesus taught with a strange authority. First-century teachers were, of course, plentiful. Many Rabbis went about proclaiming the Law and interpreting its commandments. There were two main traditions of teaching: Shammai, a leading traditionalist, and Hillel, who was more modern and outward-looking. Followers of both schools were careful to pick their way through the minefield of interpretation by weighing the authority of bygone scholars: 'Rabbi Hillel said this but. . . on the other hand Rabbi Shammai taught that. . .' The greatest of authorities appealed to was, of course, Moses who received God's Law in the first place. It was heretical to go beyond this fountain of truth—and whoever did was in trouble. But Jesus came with teaching that was startling in its simplicity and truth. 'You have heard that it was said (Moses said it) "Do not commit adultery". But I tell you that anyone who looks at a woman lustfully has already committed adultery with her in her heart.' Or, 'You have heard that it was said (again the hearers would have picked up the implied reference to Moses) "Do not break your oath. . ." But I tell you, do not swear at all.'

The content of Jesus' teaching is the subject of part three of this book. But in summary we can say that the teaching of Jesus falls into three clear divisions:

- **The call to the kingdom** A great deal of the earlier teaching seems to concentrate on setting out what God's kingdom is like and how we enter it. We must become like little children and learn to trust God as Father.

- **The standards of the kingdom** He revealed the way of living required of those who had entered the kingdom, in both personal and social forms. In this way the Law was interpreted in his day. For Jesus the ethic of love dominated law.

- **The coming of the kingdom** Here we find a tension between what has already come and what is yet to be. The kingdom has arrived because Jesus himself has come. All who follow him belong already to the kingdom. But this kingdom is only partially fulfilled now; it awaits its consummation when Jesus, the Son of man, comes again.

Jesus' teaching showed a quiet assurance. 'I tell you' speaks of a direct authority, rather than the derivative authority which the scribes and religious lawyers had. His hearers would have been in no doubt. This man was claiming an authority superior to that of Moses. Indeed, he was claiming to speak for God.

Together with this we must draw attention to what he said about his Father. He spoke of God as his 'Abba'. This was an extraordinary way of talking about God in his time because for Jesus' contemporaries God was a deity, wonderful and awesome and separated from the life of human beings. If it was characteristic for Jews of Jesus' time to think of

God as 'Father in Heaven', still it can be said with confidence that no one before Jesus made it his practice to address God simply as 'Abba'. This term 'Abba' spoke of intimacy; our word 'daddy' comes closest to it. And it is obvious that the relationship with his Father was at the basis of his assurance, in his teaching and in his behaviour.

Although Jesus' miracles are part and parcel of the Christian story, they are really secondary to his teaching. Thus, when a paralyzed man was carried to Jesus by four of his friends, before talking at all about this man's health Jesus says to him: 'My son, your sins are forgiven.' Some of the Rabbis present at once noted the apparent heresy: 'Only God can forgive sins; who does this man think he is?' The miracle that follows serves to drive home the point that they were quite right in making this deduction, 'So that you may know that the Son of man has authority to forgive sins. . . I say to you, get up, pack up your bed and go home.'

Great attractiveness

Jesus taught also with a wonderful attractiveness. What an amazing teacher he must have been! Not for him the technique of spinning webs of theological intricacy, the tedious homilies which obscured

▲ A rabbi has authority over his student, the authority of an interpreter of the law. But

Jesus' teaching was different. His own words carried the authority of God.

truth from the ignorant and illiterate. It would seem that most of his teaching was spontaneous, arising from personal encounters with people, responding to their questions, challenges and needs. He was clearly master of the thought-provoking epigram or arresting picture story. When he said something like 'It is impossible for a rich man to go into heaven just as it is for a camel to go through the eye of a needle', we need to imagine him saying this with laughter, everyone joining in the joke of a camel with a hump going through a tiny needle. But the joke conveyed a profound truth that things in real life get in the way of what really matters.

Jesus taught in parables and picture stories, drawing on nature, human life and practical experience. No wonder people hung on every word, crowding the houses where he visited, the places where he taught, the roads he passed along. The technique of teaching through parables and picture language was not new; most good teachers employed this tool. But in Jesus' hands this became the major vehicle for communicating the message of the kingdom.

Picture stories

Why did he choose this indirect method of speaking in parables? Much ink has been spilt by scholars on this question. It may partly have been because it enables attention to be caught. There is nothing like a good story to arouse interest, and Jesus exploited the fun and the irony provided by parables. There is something extremely paradoxical about a good shepherd abandoning a whole flock because one sheep has got lost. Again, people do not normally sell up everything to buy one pearl; guests do not normally refuse an invitation to a good feast, especially in poverty-stricken Palestine; servants do not normally owe ten thousand talents; people who work for one hour do not usually get the same amount as those who work all day. And in Jesus' parable of the Good Samaritan, none of his hearers could have imagined that a Samaritan could possibly be the hero of a story. Picture a prejudiced Ulsterman telling a story in which the hero is a Catholic priest.

But there is probably another reason why Jesus spoke in parables. Central to most of the parables is a challenge to people to decide for or against him. The direct method—'I am the Son of God and you had better take it or leave it'—would have infuriated half the population and stopped them exploring the question of Jesus for themselves. Because the message of Jesus was primarily about the kingdom of God— how to enter it, its values and its relationship with himself—the method of the parable allowed people to make decisions, even to the point of becoming followers of the mysterious teacher from Nazareth, without tradition getting in the way.

Yet a point was reached where parables served less well. It is clear from the Gospels that at some stage in Jesus' ministry his teaching changed. At Caesarea Philippi, when Jesus was alone with his disciple he asked them: 'Who do people say that I am?' The disciples reported the common gossip about their Master: 'Some say you are one of the prophets; some people are also saying that you are Elijah returned to earth.' Then Jesus asked them the direct question, 'Who do you think I am?' And to this penetrating challenge Peter gave his historic answer: 'You are the Christ, the Son of the Living God.' This significant answer was the key that opened the disciples' understanding into the mystery of Jesus. From that point in the story of Jesus he turned away from parables and from talking to great crowds; from then on he spent time with the disciples teaching them about his destiny and preparing them for his death.

The time has come to return to the question with which we started this study. Why has this man of Nazareth had such impact on millions of people? The reason is not that he was such a splendid teacher—though he was; nor that he was such a fine man—which he also undoubtedly was. The reason lies in who he really was: in his identity with God the Father. We find him making assertions which do not come to us as exaggerated, unreal or absurd. They have about them the quiet certainty of divine authority. He declared that he was God's Son and God was his Father. There are important passages where Jesus makes astounding claims which begin with the phrase 'I Am'. This phrase has a backward glance to the Old Testament where God identified himself as 'I Am.' Throughout his ministry Jesus gave glimpses of his real nature which make the conclusion inescapable that he can only be understood by bringing in the idea of God. He forgave sins; he challenged the authority of the entire Jewish interpretation of the Law, claiming to be superior to Moses; he went about healing people; he presented himself not first as a prophet but as the subject of all prophecy.

In studying Jesus as teacher, therefore, we are led beyond Jesus the man, to the Father he was so often talking about. Jesus demonstrated God; illustrated God. He gave God his right name 'Abba' and Christian experience subsequently discovers Jesus as the right place to meet God. Not simply as a doctrine to be discovered and learned, but as the very life and power of God himself. The challenge of Christianity is that we find God in Christ, not outside him.

5.2

'ARE YOU THE COMING ONE?'

John the Baptist was unsure. In his own teaching he had spoken of the coming of 'one more powerful than I', for whom he was merely the forerunner. He had offered repentant Israelites a symbolic baptism with water, but preached that the coming one would baptize with Holy Spirit and fire.

Now, from his prison, he had heard of Jesus at work, of his teaching and healing and the crowds who followed him. But where was the baptism of Spirit and fire? Was this the great climactic work of God to which he had looked forward?

John had expected Jesus to take on the role of the Messiah. The problem was that that word could mean very different things to those who used it. We, who are brought up to think of Jesus as *Christ* (the Greek word for Messiah), can read into the word all that we see in Jesus. With hindsight, we may think it is obvious what the Messiah should have been like. But for John and his contemporaries it was not so easy. And so he sent messengers to Jesus to ask if he really was the coming one, or whether he should expect another.

Jewish expectations

The Hebrew word *Messiah* means 'the anointed one' and is normally used in the Old Testament to refer to either the king or the high priest. Both were anointed as a mark of the special role for which they were set apart, to lead God's people in their communal life and worship.

It was only after Old Testament times that the title came to be used not for any actual figure in Israel, but for a future leader whom God would send to deliver his people. His role would be to bring in the promised time of restoration and blessing. The Old Testament writers usually spoke of what God himself would do for his people in the last days, but sometimes there was the vision of another person involved as God's agent, even though the term Messiah was not yet used to refer to him.

Different prophets and psalmists offered their own individual portraits of this future deliverer; there was no single expectation. The most frequently expressed hope was that God would give them a new king, like David, to lead his people to victory (and when the word Messiah came into use as a term for a future figure it was most often applied to this 'Son of David'). But others hoped for a great prophet to continue the noble line of those who from the time of Moses had acted as God's spokesmen to his people. Still others looked for a priest of the line of Levi, who would lead them back to the true worship of God. And there were other more individualistic visions.

Each of these main lines could be developed in different ways. Often the hopes expressed reflected the dissatisfaction which people felt with their existing leaders, or their frustration that the royal line of Judah no longer occupied the throne in Jerusalem. Other hopes developed alongside these, or combined with them.

For the Jews of Jesus' day, the concept of the Messiah was not at all clear or agreed. So it is hard to know just what John the Baptist had hoped to see. But at least he is likely to have had in mind something rather more spectacular than Jesus' ministry of teaching and caring among the ordinary people of Galilee. Perhaps John expected a more

political angle to the Messiah's mission with a focus on the national fortunes of Israel. Certainly that is what talk of a Messiah would be likely to conjure up in many Jewish minds at the time.

Keeping it in the dark

This ambiguity in the title 'Messiah' goes a long way towards explaining the puzzling fact that Jesus was not keen for people to use it of him. The only place in all the Gospels where he volunteers the information that he is the Messiah is, significantly, when he is talking not to a Jew but to a Samaritan. (See John chapter 4.)

▲ Giotto's painting represents Jesus' triumphant entry into Jerusalem, when he was recognized as the coming king. But it was a strange triumph, experienced in a deeply humble way, riding an ass.

The issue came to a head near Caesarea Philippi when Jesus asked his disciples what people were saying about him. 'You are a prophet' was the gist of their answer. 'Then who do *you* say I am?' asked Jesus, and for the first time Peter declared that he believed Jesus was the Messiah. We would expect Jesus to have been delighted (and indeed Matthew chapter 16 verse 17 suggests that he was), but his

Jesus, God's Servant

The early Christian preachers sometimes referred to Jesus as 'God's servant'. This may seem a very undistinguished title for one they loved to call Lord and Son of God. But behind it lies an important theme in their understanding of Jesus, one to which he himself had pointed the way.

In the latter part of the book of Isaiah is a series of passages in which the Old Testament prophet speaks of 'God's servant'. Sometimes it is clear that he is talking about Israel, outlining the experiences which the nation must expect to undergo as it faithfully follows the way God has marked out. But sometimes, especially in the great poem of the suffering servant in Isaiah 52:13 – 53:12, this 'servant' is described in such strongly individual terms that it seems that the prophet must be thinking of a particular person rather than of the nation as a whole. This

person's role is spelled out in terms of suffering and even death—a death which in some mysterious way is *on behalf of* God's people. It is they who speak of the servant's sufferings and of what he has thus achieved for them: 'He took up our infirmities and carried our sorrows. . . He was pierced for our transgressions. . . By his wounds we are healed. . . The Lord has laid on him the iniquity of us all.'

Christians have found in this passage one of the clearest statements in the Bible of the meaning of Jesus' death, even though it was written so long before his time. It was this belief that led the early Christian preachers to speak of him as 'God's servant'. And Jesus himself found in Isaiah's vision the basis for his conviction that it was his mission to be rejected and to suffer for the sake of others.

When Jesus was baptized by John in the Jordan, he

heard a voice from heaven which addressed him in words echoing the first introduction of God's servant in Isaiah: 'You are my Son, whom I love; with you I am well pleased' (Mark 1:11, compare with Isaiah 42:1). At his transfiguration, just after he had explained to his disciples what his mission must involve, a similar declaration came again, as if to confirm him in this course (Mark 9:7). His repeated teaching that he *must* suffer was based on 'what is written', and it is hard to see where he could have found such a message more clearly than in these passages of Isaiah.

The words of the poem in Isaiah 53 sometimes come to the surface as Jesus talks about his coming death. He came, he said, 'not to be served but to serve, and to give his life as a ransom for many'. His blood was to be 'poured out for many for the forgiveness of sins'. He was to be 'numbered with the transgressors' (Luke 22:37, quoting Isaiah 53:12).

During Jesus' ministry Peter strongly opposed Jesus' notion of going to

Jerusalem to die. But when in later years he reflected on the meaning of Jesus' death, it was in the light of Isaiah 53 that he understood it. In his first letter there is an extended meditation on phrases from Isaiah. Here Peter interprets Jesus' suffering and death as that of the sinless servant of God who suffers for the sins of others: 'By his wounds you have been healed.'

Far from being an undignified title, 'God's Servant' takes us to the heart of what Jesus came to do.

next words were, 'Do not tell anyone'. He went on to speak of himself not as the Messiah, but as the Son of man, which was the term he always preferred to use.

From this moment on Jesus began to teach the disciples that his mission was not one of glory and conquest. He was to be rejected by the leaders of Israel, and to suffer and die in Jerusalem. It is hard to imagine a more complete contrast to what the Messiah would have meant to most people. Peter objected to this apparently defeatist language—and was in his turn sharply rebuked by Jesus for thinking men's thoughts and not God's.

If Peter, with his special relationship with Jesus, could be so badly mistaken, is it any wonder that Jesus was cautious about letting people talk about him as the Messiah? It is not that Jesus had any doubts that he was 'the coming one', and that it was his mission to fulfil what the prophets had said about a coming deliverer of God's people. But his understanding of what that deliverance was to be, and how it was to be accomplished, was not one

The Song of Christ's Glory

A very early Christian hymn, which Paul included in his letter to the Philippians, chapter 2.

Christ Jesus was in the form of God,
but he did not cling to equality with God.
He emptied himself taking the form of a servant
and was born in the likeness of men.
Being found in human form he humbled himself
and became obedient unto death, even death on a cross.
Therefore God has highly exalted him,
and bestowed on him the name above every name,
that at the name of Jesus every knee should bow,
in heaven and on earth and under the earth,
and every tongue confess that Jesus Christ is Lord,
to the glory of God the Father.

The Human Jesus

For many Christians of the early middle ages, Jesus seemed more divine than human. He was Christ in majesty, the King and the Judge. But in the later middle ages—from the twelfth to the fifteenth centuries—the church rediscovered the human Jesus of the gospel story.

In their worship and devotion Christians of this period focused on the Jesus who lived and suffered on earth, while in their lives they tried to follow the model of his earthly life. Naturally, they did not forget that Jesus is God. But they believed that it was through the human life of Jesus that they could find and know God. One fourteenth-century friar spoke for all the religious writers of this period when he said, 'The humanity of Christ is the road that leads to his divinity.'

What especially appealed to them in the human Jesus was his humility, his poverty and his sufferings. Poverty, sickness and death were never far from the experience of many people of this period. In the fourteenth century Europe was devastated by the Black Death. In the human Jesus people found a God who had come close to them, who lived a human life like theirs, in poverty and suffering, and who had conquered death. In his company they found help to bear their sufferings. And out of love for him they even embraced poverty and suffering for his sake.

It was also a period in which people were experiencing themselves more as individuals. Intimate personal relationships—love and friendship—were valued. Jesus became the Beloved and the Friend. In Jesus they saw God's love for them in human form, reaching them and drawing out their love for him. 'There is nothing so sweet as loving Christ,' said the English mystic Richard Rolle, summing up the kind of personal affection for Jesus which is so characteristic of the period.

Theologians laid the basis for this medieval devotion to the humanity of Jesus—especially Anselm of Canterbury, Bernard of Clairvaux, and the great Franciscan theologian Bonaventura. A very special role was played by Francis of Assisi. The way that Francis reflected Jesus in his own life and character captured the imagination of the whole of Christendom, and made the human Jesus vivid and real to people as never before. Devotion to the humanity of Jesus was popularized by the preachers, especially the friars, and intensified by the great mystics of the period. Also worth noticing is the prominence of women in the religious life of this period —as mystics, visionaries and spiritual writers. Something of their influence can be seen in the emphasis on affection and compassion for Jesus.

Meditation on the life of Christ

One way in which Jesus could be known and loved was through meditating on the events of his life, from his birth to his death and his resurrection. Of course, the Gospels themselves were read for this purpose, but there were also several works which retold the Gospel story. Most popular were *The Meditations on the Life of Christ*, written by an unknown Franciscan around 1300, and *The Life of Christ*, about fifty years later, by the Carthusian Ludolph of Saxony. In these the events of the life of Jesus were recounted in such a way as to help the reader to imagine them happening and to see their significance for him. The aim of meditation was to engage the imagination and the emotions. The person meditating would imagine himself present with Jesus in the events of his life and so would react to them in a very direct way. Meditating on the past events of Jesus' history became a way of living with Jesus in the present.

Meditation through reading was not possible for the mass of the people, who could not read. But there were other ways in which the same aim could be achieved. The liturgy, and especially the 'eucharist' (see *Last Supper*), was a means of participating in the events of the human history of Jesus. This was aided by special devotional practices, such as the 'stations of the cross', in which people paused to reflect on each stage of Jesus' way to the cross. The mystery plays dramatized the story of Jesus in a way which appealed to the ordinary people. Popular preachers brought the Gospel story alive, and painting and sculpture made the scenes of Jesus' life vivid in the imagination. Pilgrimages to the holy land were made for the sake of contact with the places where Jesus had lived his human life. In all these ways people were encouraged to know Jesus through the imagination and the senses. By reliving his story they came to love him and found him present with them in their own life stories.

Childhood and Passion

Devotion to the infant Jesus and devotion to the crucified Jesus were particularly popular. In Jesus' childhood and his suffering, God's love for us seemed especially clear and powerful. Here God could be seen sharing our weakness and suffering.

Francis of Assisi helped to make Christmas a popular festival. He called it 'the feast of feasts', because it shows us the poverty and the weakness which God embraced when he became human. The story of how Francis celebrated Christmas at Greccio is well-known. He recreated the scene at Bethlehem—with a manger and live animals—in order to make it vivid for the people. It is typical of Francis that remembering the poverty of Jesus also meant remembering the poor of his own time. He wanted the rich to give food to the hungry at Christmas.

The late-medieval Christ was above all the Jesus who bore all the pains and griefs of humanity, as well as their sins. Theologians wrote of his 'passion', his suffering. This, they insisted, was the cruellest and most shameful suffering anyone has ever endured. And the artists portrayed it: in the sorrowful Christ of thirteenth-and fourteenth-century crucifixes and the bloodstained Christ of the fifteenth century. In

▼ The Messiah was expected to be a majestic king. But when he was born it was to quite ordinary parents in a crowded town. God had entered the most everyday of human lives.

▲ Medieval paintings often focus on Jesus as the Man of Sorrows. Even as late as this seventeenth-century work by Carlo Dolci, they emphasize his suffering and weakness, identified with men and women in the hardness of their lives.

the art, literature and sermons of the time the events of the passion were depicted with the utmost realism—in all their violence and cruelty. Jesus had to be seen to suffer the pains and death of all people. In this way he brought God close to people in their own suffering.

Devotion to the passion led also to special devotions to the wounds of Christ and to the blood of Christ. Devotion to the sacred heart of Jesus also grew up in this period, as a way of contemplating the suffering love of Jesus for us. Jesus' heart, pierced by the lance-wound in his side, represented the fullness of his love.

In much of the piety of the period the figure of the crucified Jesus moves the Christian not only to gratitude, but also to compassion. And in the mystics—such as Elizabeth of Schonau and Angela of Foligno—this becomes an actual experience of participation in Christ's sufferings.

Mystical contemplation

Some theologians of the time taught the practice of mystical union with God. In their writings devotion to the humanity of Christ leads on to contemplating his divinity and to union with God. The aim is to move on from the human Jesus who can be pictured in the imagination to the divinity hidden in his humanity and so to God the Trinity. Love for the human Jesus is a lower stage of love because it involves the senses. Its purpose is to lead us on to a purely spiritual love for the invisible God. Like Mary Magdalene, who was forbidden to touch the risen Jesus, we have to leave behind the tangible Christ and know him as he is in his eternal deity.

Again it is the suffering of Christ which seems especially to take us beyond the human Jesus into union with God. 'The soul enters into God through union with the passion of Christ,' writes the German mystic Henry Suso. Catherine of Sienna writes frequently of the crucified Jesus as the bridge or the ladder that connects us with God, or as the door which opens for us into the Trinity.

Sometimes it sounds as though devotion to the human Jesus is therefore just a temporary stage of the Christian life. In fact most of the mystics see it as a stage we can never do without. We need continually to find God in the humanity of Jesus, where he has humbled himself and come down to our level. And continually we are led beyond the human to the divine.

Imitation of Christ

Devotion to Christ and union with Christ lead to imitation of Christ. This theme pervades late medieval Christianity. It does not reduce Jesus to a moral example. The Jesus we imitate is first known as Saviour and Friend, and as we follow in his footsteps he accompanies us on our way.

Again it is the humility, the poverty and the sufferings of Jesus which dominate the picture. It had long been the aim of monks to imitate the humility, the poverty and the chastity of Jesus. Francis of Assisi founded a new kind of religious order, the Friars Minor (or Franciscans). He called the friars to take the poverty of Jesus even more seriously. The monks could own property in common. But Francis wanted his friars to live altogether without property, living from hand to mouth as Jesus did. And whereas the monks sought to imitate Jesus in withdrawal from the world, Francis made the following of Jesus a way of active service in the world. In their poverty the friars could identify with the poor and serve them.

Francis took the poverty of Jesus as seriously as it was possible to take it. But the ideal of 'evangelical poverty' —meaning the poverty which Jesus practised and enjoined on his followers— was taken up very widely in Francis' time. It inspired many new religious movements. Some of these, like the Franciscans, remained within the Catholic Church, but others found themselves disowned as heretical. Peter Waldo, for example, leader of the 'Poor Men of Lyons' —later known as the Waldensians—preached the love of poverty and the imitation of Jesus. Groups like his criticized the church hierarchy for not living according to the gospel, and taught that priests could not properly administer the sacraments unless they lived holy lives. The poverty and simplicity of Jesus was the basis for much of the criticism of the wealth and decadence of the late-medieval church.

The life of Jesus became the model, not only for those who joined religious orders, but more widely for lay people in the world. The Franciscan 'third order' provided for people, living in their own homes but supporting each other in associations, to live a life of relative poverty and loving service of others. Many other such lay groups sprang up spontaneously. Sometimes their orthodoxy became suspect, but their motivation was frequently that of imitating the poverty and the love of Jesus.

The Son of Man

The title 'the Son of man' is as odd in Greek as it is in English. From an early period interpreters of the New Testament thought Jesus used it to draw attention to his humanity—it was in contrast to 'Son of God'. But that was not why Jesus chose it.

It is a phrase which occurs so often in the sayings of Jesus in the Gospels, and so seldom elsewhere, that we are justified in describing it as his favourite way of referring to himself, even as his own coinage. But why did he choose such an odd expression?

In Hebrew and Aramaic 'a son of man' just means a human being, one belonging to the category 'man'. It is used in this way many times in the book of Ezekiel as God's way of addressing the prophet, emphasizing that he is just a man. But Jesus seems to have drawn his title not from Ezekiel, but from a passage to which he referred repeatedly in describing his own mission, the seventh chapter of

Daniel. And there it has a very different meaning.

Daniel's vision of the future is of a series of terrible beasts which represent the pagan empires ruling on earth. After these will come 'one like a son of man': a human figure who comes in the clouds to the judgment throne of God. There he will be given everlasting authority and dominion over all nations. This human figure represents 'the saints of the Most High' who are thus made supreme over the nations which had oppressed them.

It is a vision of the vindication of Israel and its future glory. But Jewish interpreters of the text saw in the human figure not just a symbol of Israel, but an individual. They believed the 'son of man' would be a messianic figure who would lead his people to their promised glory. It was in this figure that Jesus found much of the inspiration for his mission; several times he spoke of himself as the Son of man coming in the clouds

to the throne of God and reigning in glory. So his phrase *the* Son of man was a deliberate reference back to Daniel's vision. It was as that Son of man, not just any son of man, that he had come.

The phrase, once coined, could of course be used more broadly than simply in direct reference to Daniel's vision. Jesus used it not only of his future glory and authority, but also of his life on earth. He had in mind his authority and yet his human weakness, which was to be especially focused in the fate awaiting him in Jerusalem. It was the Son of man who must be rejected and suffer and die, because it was written of him.

In statements which looked towards the cross, Jesus may have used his favourite title to refer to himself, but what he said about his mission was drawn not from Daniel but rather from Isaiah's visions of the suffering servant of God. His goal was the glory of Daniel's Son of man, but the road to that glory was to be through the suffering of Isaiah's Servant.

Daniel's vision was well known, but the phrase 'the Son of man' was not commonly used to refer to

its central figure. Jewish teachers used titles such as 'the one who came in the clouds'. So Jesus' personal use of this phrase had an air of mystery, especially since its basic meaning was so general. Who was this special man? his hearers must have wondered.

And surely this was what Jesus intended. Instead of titles such as 'Messiah' or 'Son of David' (which had ready-made, but potentially misleading, meanings—see *Are You the Coming One?*) here was a phrase into which Jesus could pour his own content. He need not fear misunderstanding.

◀ John the Baptist called Jesus 'the Lamb of God', meaning the sacrificial lamb of Old Testament ritual. The triumphant lamb features strongly in the symbolism of Revelation, and became important in medieval art.

which most of his hearers could have been expected to understand.

After arresting Jesus the high priest at last had the opportunity to put the question directly to Jesus: 'Are you the Messiah, the Son of the Blessed One?' Mark tells us that Jesus responded with a clear yes. But Matthew and Luke indicate that his words were perhaps more guarded, though no less affirmative: 'That is how you put it'. But Jesus went on to substitute his own preferred title, calling himself the Son of man and talking not of earthly conquest but of heavenly glory. With crucifixion and the apparent end to any hopes of leading God's people to deliverance only hours away, Jesus could see his mission as the Son of man on the verge of

▲ The medieval mystery plays featured ordinary people acting out Gospel stories. They are currently enjoying a revival, and this crucifixion scene has all the drama of ordinary life transformed into the life of Jesus.

Jesus. His contemporaries who tried to match him with their own preconceived ideas of the Messiah found that he did not fit. And the same has been true ever since. People have tried to make Jesus fit in with their political or theological schemes, using him as a figurehead for programmes which they themselves have devised. But he simply does not fit. He is the eternal paradox. He is too big for any human measurement.

He *was* the Messiah but not at the level of their formulas. And it is a question whether most of his modern interpreters, even after centuries of theological reflection, have done justice to the enigma which is Jesus.

Jesus himself once publicly questioned the traditional understanding of the Messiah. Speaking in the temple in Jerusalem, he asked how the experts could call the Messiah the Son of David. 'Son of David' was a conventional title for the Messiah, and one which many had already used of Jesus during his public activity as they saw his unique authority expressed particularly in healing. But Jesus queried it. The Messiah, he argued from Psalm 110, is David's Lord, not his son. Jesus did not go on to relate the title to his own role, but in the light of the language people were by now using about him the point was obvious: Jesus was not just another David, another king to rule a national Israel. His authority and his rule were on a higher level altogether. He was David's Lord, seated at the right hand of God.

By this time John the Baptist was dead. Perhaps if he had lived he would have come to recognize, as some of his disciples did, that Jesus was indeed the 'greater one'. Indeed, he was so much greater that the messianic categories of Jewish religion would prove quite inadequate to do justice to him. He had come not merely to deliver Israel, but to gather together God's people of all nations under his universal rule as the Son of man enthroned at God's right hand.

fulfilment. And Jesus believed that it was in, and not in spite of, his rejection and death that the messianic mission would be accomplished.

The man who fits no formula

This phrase, from the writing of Swiss theologian Eduard Schweizer, aptly sums up the impact of

5.3

JESUS AND GOD

Jesus, like all other Jews, accepted that there is only one God. His God was the God of Abraham, Isaac and Jacob, and the God who brought their descendants out of Egypt and made them his own people at Sinai. Throughout their history the Jewish people had had to struggle against the religion of surrounding peoples who often believed in many gods. At the heart of their religion was the declaration, 'Hear, O Israel: The Lord our God, the Lord is one.' To be a Jew was to be committed to maintaining this faith.

Yet within a generation of Jesus' death his followers were speaking of him not just as the Son of God, but in terms appropriate only for God himself. They prayed to Jesus, and worshipped him. They took Old Testament statements about God and simply transferred them to Jesus, apparently without feeling the need to defend such an outrageous practice. And they were Jews!

How did such a remarkable development take place? Did Jesus himself start it, or did his followers misunderstand him and invent a new Jesus-religion which he himself would have repudiated with horror?

Father and Son

Jesus often spoke of God as Father. There was nothing new in this, though certainly Jesus used this sort of language a lot more freely than other Jewish teachers and writers seem to have done. The thought of God as Father of his people, or even of individuals who trusted him for guidance and support, was one which had come naturally to other Jews.

What was different about Jesus was the way he used such language. While he taught his disciples to think of God as their 'Father in heaven', it is remarkable that he never associated himself with them in this by speaking of 'our Father' (except, of course, when he was telling them how *they* should pray). It was always 'your Father' or 'my Father'. And the things he said about his relationship with his Father were on a different level from theirs.

At one point Jesus said, 'All things have been committed to me by my Father. No one knows the Son except the Father, and no one knows the Father except the Son and those to whom the Son chooses to reveal him'. Jesus indicated that he stood in a unique, intimate relationship with God, and that the access of others to their heavenly Father depended on their relationship with him. Other sayings pointed the same way, including one in which Jesus spoke of 'the Son' being closer to God than even the angels.

Behind such language lay Jesus' experience when he was baptized by John: a voice from heaven declared, 'You are my Son, whom I love'. The same declaration was repeated at the transfiguration, but this time it was for the benefit of his disciples. The heavenly voice underlined his unique authority, urging the disciples to listen to him. When Jesus talked about himself as 'the Son' and about God as his Father, it was this special relationship which was in view.

John's Gospel uses this language of special relationship more freely than the other Gospels. According to John, Jesus frequently spoke of himself as 'the Son of God' or just 'the Son', and made statements such as 'I and the Father are one', or

TITLES OF JESUS

THESE ELEVEN TITLES ARE AMONG THE MOST IMPORTANT GIVEN TO JESUS IN THE NEW TESTAMENT. TOGETHER THEY GIVE A GOOD IDEA OF WHO HE WAS AND WHAT HE CAME TO DO.

JESUS ▶
HIS PERSONAL NAME, SO COMMON THAT HE WAS CALLED JESUS 'OF NAZARETH'. HEBREW EQUIVALENT, **JOSHUA**, MEANS 'THE LORD SAVES'.

CHRIST ▶
GREEK FORM OF HEBREW **MESSIAH**, MEANS 'ANOINTED ONE', THE DELIVERER GOD WAS EXPECTED TO SEND. JESUS RELUCTANT TO USE IT, PERHAPS BECAUSE OF POLITICAL MEANING; HE WAS TO BE SUFFERING MESSIAH.

SON OF GOD
USED IT OF HIMSELF; VERY IMPORTANT NEW TESTAMENT TITLE. REFERS TO HIS ESSENTIAL NATURE, SHARING GOD'S BEING.

SON OF MAN
ONLY USED BY JESUS HIMSELF. BASED ON FIGURE IN DANIEL 7 GIVEN AUTHORITY BY GOD.

THE LORD
MAINLY USED AFTER RESURRECTION TO SHOW JESUS' UNIQUE AUTHORITY. 'JESUS IS LORD' WAS GREAT CONFESSION OF FAITH. SAME GREEK WORK USED FOR NAME OF GOD IN OLD TESTAMENT.

SERVANT OF GOD
OCCASIONALLY USED, SOMETIMES BY IMPLICATION, TO CONNECT JESUS WITH 'SUFFERING SERVANT' OF ISAIAH 53, WHO BORE PEOPLE'S SINS.

SON OF DAVID
MESSIAH WAS TO BE DESCENDANT OF KING DAVID, AS JESUS WAS. USED MOST BY MATTHEW.

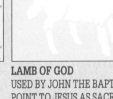

THE WORD
(GREEK 'LOGOS'). USED ONLY BY JOHN, LATER BECAME VERY IMPORTANT. LINKS OLD TESTAMENT WORD OF CREATION WITH GREEK PRINCIPLE CONTROLLING UNIVERSE. THIS WORD 'BECAME FLESH'.

LAMB OF GOD
USED BY JOHN THE BAPTIST TO POINT TO JESUS AS SACRIFICE FOR PEOPLE'S SIN. IMPORTANT SYMBOL IN REVELATION AND IN CHRISTIAN ART.

SECOND ADAM
TAKES UP IDEA IN PAUL THAT ADAM'S SIN SPOILED GOD'S IMAGE IN HUMANITY, BUT JESUS' OBEDIENCE RESTORES THAT IMAGE.

ALPHA AND OMEGA
FIRST AND LAST LETTERS IN GREEK ALPHABET. USED IN REVELATION TO SHOW JESUS AS BEGINNING AND END OF EVERYTHING.

Understanding Who Jesus Is

In the first few centuries after the death of the apostles there were many controversies in the young Christian church about the question who Jesus really was.

In a way this is quite understandable. On the basis of the apostolic teaching the Christian church believed that Jesus came from God. In many different ways this is attested in the New Testament. Jesus clearly had a unique relationship with God. In particular after his resurrection his disciples began to realize increasingly that he was not just one of the prophets, but a very special emissary of God: not just 'a' son of God but 'the' Son of God. They even believed that he existed with God before he was born of the virgin Mary. He was pre-existent. The Gospel of John starts with a statement about the Word (Greek: *logos*) that was already with God when the word was created, and then goes on to say that 'this Word became flesh' and was none other than Jesus. In some places in the New Testament Jesus himself is even called 'God'.

At the same time the New Testament also tells us in many different ways that he was a true man who knew all the experiences that ordinary men and women have, such as hunger, tiredness and sorrow. At the end of his life he had to pass through deep suffering — in the garden of Gethsemane he was so vexed by anxiety that his sweat became like great drops of blood. Finally he died as a criminal on the cross. How could he have suffered all this, if he had not been a true man? Yet his life did not end in death, but after three days God raised him from the dead. And forty days later he ascended into heaven.

Is it any wonder that the Christian church, which firmly believed that he was the long-promised Saviour of Israel and of the whole world, could not help asking itself: Who is this Jesus? What is his relationship to God? What is his relationship to us? How does he really fit into all our accepted patterns of thought and knowledge?

Both man and God

Because of this twofold picture of Jesus in the New Testament itself, we are not surprised to discern a twofold movement in the following centuries. There were Christians who put all the stress on Jesus' true humanity and from that perspective tried to determine his relationship with God. There were other Christians who put him fully on the side of God, and from that perspective tried to determine his place within humanity.

In the first period of the Christian church there were certain Jewish Christians, known as the **Ebionites**, who as true sons of Israel firmly adhered to Jewish monotheism, the belief that there is only one God. For this reason they were unable to see Jesus 'on the side' of God. For them Christ was the new Moses, on the same level as the prophets of the Old Testament. He was the natural son of Joseph and Mary, who at the time of his baptism received the Holy Spirit. Thus he was chosen as the Messiah and became the adopted Son of God.

There were other Christians, however, who tried to bring together Greek thinking, with its strong separation of spirit and matter, and the gospel of Jesus Christ. For them it was impossible to believe that the pre-existent Son of God had really lived in a real human body. They therefore held that during his stay on earth the eternal Son of God had only a phantom body. This kind of thinking is usually called **docetism** (from the Greek word 'to seem'). Later on these ideas were very popular in the various Gnostic sects and systems.

The majority of Christians rejected both these views, because they felt that neither did justice to the witness of the New Testament. But around the turn of the second century elements of both views returned in two new forms. Both new groups were called Monarchians, because both stressed the unity and the sole monarchy of God and were strongly opposed to the rising idea of a plurality within God. But they developed the idea of God's unity in opposite ways.

One group, whose major representative was Paul of Samosata, Bishop of Antioch, regarded Jesus as a mere man, who at his baptism was endowed with divine powers and adopted as the Son of God. This kind of position is often called **adoptionist**.

The other group, also taking its starting-point in the unity of God, went in the opposite direction and regarded Jesus as a mode of manifestation of the one God. The one God is not Father, Son and Spirit at the same time, but at a certain moment in history the Father appears on the scene of history as Son and afterwards as Spirit. This kind of position became known as **modalist** christology.

The majority of leading theologians rejected these two views. The adoptionists were wrong because the Son eternally shares the 'substance' of the divine being with the Father. The modalists because the Son and the Spirit are not just temporary 'modes of manifestation' of the Father, but eternally there are three 'persons', Father, Son and Spirit, within the one Godhead.

The Arian controversy

A major controversy arose around 310 when Arius, a presbyter in Alexandria, began to teach that Christ could not be the Son of God in the true sense of the word, because God is one and indivisible. Everything that exists besides God must have been created, and this also applies to Jesus Christ. Arius was prepared to give much honour to Christ, even being willing to say that Christ was created before all other creatures, perhaps even before time. But still Christ is a creature, and 'there was a time that he was not'.

Because Arius came from Alexandria, an important centre of theological learning, his views attracted the attention of many people. At first his own bishop, Alexander, a peace-loving man, did nothing, but soon he began to realize that Arius' teaching struck at the very heart of the Christian faith. If Christ is only a creature, his coming into the world can never be God's perfect revelation and redemption. Around the year 320 Alexander excommunicated Arius on the ground of heresy.

But the controversy was by no means finished. Arius had many ardent and influential supporters in all parts of the Eastern church and the possibility of a schism in the church was by no means imaginary. Such a schism would also endanger the unity of the Roman empire and therefore Emperor Constantine called a general council, in the year 325 at Nicaea in modern Turkey. Between 250 and 300 bishops attended the council.

After some heated debates the Arian position was condemned. As its own starting-point the council adopted a local creed that confessed Jesus as 'the Son of God, begotten from the Father, God from God, Light from Light, true God from true God'. The emperor himself managed to introduce into this creed a term which literally means, 'of the same substance' (with the Father). Although it was meant as a formula of compromise, open to many different interpretations, this term afterwards became the catchword of orthodoxy, especially in the hands of Athanasius, the great defender of orthodoxy.

After the council the Arians and semi-Arians vigorously opposed the decision. It took almost fifty years before the next ecumenical council (held at **Constantinople**, in 381) could settle the matter. It was this council that adopted the considerably longer credal formula, which today is known as the **Nicene Creed** but which actually contains elements from both councils. It is the most universal of all Christian creeds, since it is accepted by nearly all churches, both in the (Greek-speaking) East and in the (Latin-speaking) West.

The two natures of Christ

Nicea confessed: Jesus, the son of Mary, is God-in-the-flesh. But how are the divine and the human in Christ related? Fairly soon after Nicea, Apollinaris, bishop of Laodicea and a staunch defender of the Nicene position, tried to give an answer. He argued that in the incarnation the *logos* took the place of the human spirit, the 'I', in the man Jesus. His opponents charged him with detracting from Jesus' full humanity.

Around AD400 a controversy started between the two major theological schools of that time: Alexandria and Antioch (in Syria). The school of Alexandria, in some ways, continued Apollinaris' line of thought. Although they rejected his idea of an incomplete humanity, they shared his emphasis on the unity of the God-man. They

did believe that in the incarnation the *logos* had adopted a complete human nature, but they so strongly emphasized the unity of divine and human that at times their view seemed to imply a merging of both natures. Antioch, on the other hand, emphasized the distinction between the two natures and insisted that each retained its own unique qualities. But this could easily lead to a duality of two persons in Jesus Christ.

It is impossible here to give a full description of the ensuing controversies. Nestorius, who in 428 became patriarch of Constantinople, argued that the rather ancient designation of Mary as the 'mother of God', or 'God-bearer', was misleading. His own view was that Mary gave birth to the man in whom the Word had taken residence. The eternal Word and the person of Jesus remained two different entities. Some acts of Christ (such as his miracles) must be attributed to the Word, others to the man Jesus (such as his suffering and death). The danger inherent in this view was that it could eventually lead to the idea of two persons in Christ.

Nestorius' view was strongly opposed by Cyril, the patriarch of Alexandria. He put all emphasis on the unity of the two natures, even going so far as to describe it as a substantial unity, a view which could easily lead to a conception of Christ as a mixed divine-human nature. At the Council of **Ephesus**, in 431, Cyril's point of view emerged victorious and Nestorius was condemned and deposed. But a few years later a supporter of Cyril, Eutyches, a monk in Constantinople, went far beyond what Cyril had ever advocated and intended. He taught that after the Word became man, there was only one nature in Christ, a divine-human nature in which the human was so

permeated by the divine that it actually ceased to be truly human.

In the meantime Pope Leo I had been involved too. He published a letter outlining the thinking of the Western church. At the general council that convened near Constantinople at **Chalcedon**, in 451, consisting of 600 or so bishops and some papal delegates, Leo's letter played a decisive role. The final decision of the council is known as the Creed of Chalcedon. It brought together the justified concerns of both Alexandria and Antioch, and has been the benchmark of orthodoxy since then.

This creed begins with the clear affirmation that Jesus Christ is perfect in Godhead and in manhood. He shares both the Father's divine substance and our human substance. He is one person in two distinct natures. The creed formulates the relationship between the two natures in negative rather than positive terms: 'without confusion or change, without division or separation'. So Chalcedon set out four boundaries that may not be crossed.

Somewhere within these four borderlines lies the mystery of Jesus Christ. The mystery itself cannot be defined; the inexpressible cannot be forced into conceptual forms.

Since the nineteenth century this decision has often been criticized as being far removed from the 'simplicity' of the New Testament. To some extent this is true. The language used in this creed is more abstract and more philosophical than that of the New Testament. But then, of course, we should remember that much had happened since New Testament days. The church living in the Hellenistic world could express its understanding of the mystery of Christ only in the patterns of thought and language that were available, and perhaps no other language was more suitable

for answering the many questions involved in the church's belief that in the man Jesus of Nazareth we have to do with God himself.

Chalcedon certainly did not mean the victory of Greek speculation over Christian faith. In fact, the creed of Chalcedon clearly affirmed something utterly foreign to all Greek thinking — that the eternal Word of God became human flesh.

▲ Jesus, so John the
evangelist tells us, is the
Word of God through whom
the world was created.

The Earth is the Lord's

If Jesus is Lord of creation, then physical as well as living things can express his presence. Humanity was made from the dust of the earth, and Jesus used even the mud to restore a blind man's sight. In the light of this, Teilhard de Chardin has written:

'God is not far away from us, altogether apart from the world we see, touch, hear, smell and taste about us. Rather he awaits us in every instant of our action, in the work of the moment. There is a sense in which he is at the tip of my pen, my spade, my brush, my needle — of my heart and of my thought. . . . Nothing here below is profane for those who know how to see. Everything is sacred.'

even 'Anyone who has seen me has seen the Father'. But there is enough similar language in the other Gospels to make it clear that this was not just John's extravagant theology. Jesus really did present himself as so uniquely close to God that he could be described as *the* Son of God.

Jesus in the place of God?

Jesus sometimes said and did things which seemed calculated to shock orthodox Jews.

■ **People were amazed at the authority with which he taught.** Unlike their teachers, who carefully quoted other authorities, Jesus boldly declared '*I* say to you. . .' He even said that though heaven and earth might be destroyed, his words would never be lost. And this is what the Old Testament had said about the word of God!

■ **Jesus once pronounced a man's sins forgiven.** When religious leaders objected that only God

could forgive sins, Jesus did not apologize but healed the man physically as well. He told his critics he acted so 'that you may know that the Son of Man has authority on earth to forgive sins.'

■ **He also spoke of people coming on the day of judgment to him as their Judge.** He himself would pronounce on their fate. And the basis of that decision would be whether or not *he* knew them! Indeed in his great vision of the final judgment, it is 'the Son of man' who is the king, sitting on the throne and dividing the nations before him, and this is not the only place where he presented himself as the future king in the kingdom of God. He even spoke of being able to give people life, because he 'has life in himself', just like the Father.

■ **Sometimes Jesus quoted Old Testament passages about God as if they referred to him,** as when he defended some children who sang his praises by quoting a psalm about children praising God. He described his mission as 'to seek and save the lost', when those words had been used by the prophet Ezekiel to describe what *God* would do for his people.

It would be wrong to see all this (and there is more like it in the Gospel records) as like a deliberate campaign by Jesus to get people to treat him as divine; the implications of what he says and does are not usually argued or even made explicit. It rather shows Jesus 'naturally' assuming a level of authority and a role in human affairs which is in fact appropriate only to God. It is this sort of evidence which eventually led his followers to realize that there was more to Jesus than simply a man of God. Ultimately such claims led them to worship him.

The worship of Jesus

To talk about 'worshipping' a historical human being sounds preposterous, at least in the setting of Jewish monotheistic religion. When an officer in the Roman army fell at Peter's feet he was shocked: 'Stand up; I am only a man myself.'

So on most of the occasions when the Gospels tell us that people fell down before Jesus, they were probably not strictly 'worshipping him'. These were rather acts of oriental politeness or homage, especially when (as was often the case) the person concerned was asking a special favour. Sometimes, however, more may be involved, as when the disciples on the lake, overcome by what they had seen of Jesus' power, 'worshipped him, saying, "Truly you are the Son of God"'.

But the remarkable thing is that people did not stop appealing to Jesus even after he was dead! From the very beginnings of the church people prayed to Jesus: Stephen at his martyrdom, Saul at his conversion, Ananias when 'the Lord' sent him to welcome the newly-converted Saul (and as the story unfolds it becomes clear that 'the Lord' here is Jesus, who appeared to Saul on the Damascus road, in Acts chapter 9.)

Once Paul quotes an ancient Aramaic prayer, *Marana tha*, which means 'Our Lord, come'. This shows that, long before the mid-fifties AD when Paul was writing, Aramaic-speaking Christians must

have been in the habit of calling on Jesus as Lord. Indeed, it soon becomes clear that the adherents of the new religion can be defined as 'those who call on the name of the Lord Jesus'. And in the Old Testament to 'call on the name of the Lord' was a formula for the worship of the one true God.

The phrase 'the Lord' soon became quite ambiguous. In the Greek version of the Old Testament it was the standard translation for 'Yahweh', the name of the God of Israel. But it was this term which Christians quickly began to use to refer to Jesus after his resurrection, and so it became even easier to apply to Jesus Old Testament passages which were originally about God. In the letters of Paul it is often impossible to say whether he is referring to God or to Jesus when he speaks of 'the Lord'. It rather looks as if, for him, it does not much matter, since what he can say of the one he can say also of the other.

Yet this is less than a generation after the carpenter of Nazareth was executed on a Roman gibbet. It is hard to explain such a striking development, unless it was in fact working out more explicitly what was already implied in the words and deeds of Jesus himself: 'I and the Father are one.'

The Apostles' Creed

This ancient statement of faith dates back at least to the third century. Called 'the Apostles' Creed' probably because it encapsulates the faith taught by the apostles, it has been a central creed of the churches for many centuries.

I believe in God, the Father almighty,
    creator of heaven and earth.

I believe in Jesus Christ, his only Son, our Lord.
He was conceived by the power of the Holy Spirit
and born of the Virgin Mary.
He suffered under Pontius Pilate,
was crucified, died, and was buried.
He descended to the dead.
On the third day he rose again.
He ascended into heaven,
and is seated at the right hand of the Father.
He will come again to judge the living and the dead.

I believe in the Holy Spirit,
the holy catholic Church,
the communion of saints,
the forgiveness of sins,
the resurrection of the body,
and the life everlasting.

5.4

GOD IN A HUMAN LIFE

It took some time for the full truth about Jesus to dawn on the first Christians: that this man was God's own human presence in the world. In one sense they did know it from the beginning. They knew it intuitively in experience. They expressed it naturally in worship. This man who made God real to them in a remarkable new way was no mere prophet. All their experience of God came through him. All their relation to God centred on him. They could not help associating him with God in the closest possible ways, which to other Jews must have seemed blasphemous. They prayed to him, they worshipped him, they treated him as God.

So we can see the early Christians in the New Testament searching for adequate ways of saying what they knew intuitively: that this man Jesus was uniquely identified with God and God uniquely identified with him. But it was not easy for them to say this. They had no ready-made doctrine of the Trinity to help them understand it. They could not, of course, say simply that Jesus was the God of Israel, the God whom Jesus himself obeyed and worshipped and called his Father. They did not wish to reduce God to Jesus. Nor did it enter their minds that Jesus could be a second god, some kind of lesser divine being alongside God his Father. The God whom Jesus revealed was the one and only God, the God of Israel, and his disciples never swerved from Jewish monotheism. And, finally, they did not wish, by calling Jesus divine, to deny or to reduce his humanity. Yet they found it essential to their faith to find ways of saying that Jesus was God's own human reality, that in Jesus' human life God was present with them.

One simple way of saying this was Matthew's.

Right at the beginning of his Gospel he applied to Jesus Isaiah's prophecy of the child called Immanuel, which means 'God with us'. The God who had been present with his people Israel in their history in various ways had now, at the climax of their history, come among them in a new way, by living the human life of Jesus.

The Image of God

Other New Testament writers, especially Paul and the writer to the Hebrews, took up the language Jewish writers had used about the Wisdom of God and applied it to Jesus. In Jewish thought, Wisdom was spoken of as a person distinct from God—God's agent in the world's creation and in God's revelation of himself in that world. It was by his Wisdom that God made himself known to his people and was present with them. Yet this Wisdom was God's own Wisdom, belonging to his very being. The presence of the divine Wisdom was God's own presence. Sometimes Wisdom was called 'the image of God'—a perfect reflection of the divine nature, as though in a mirror.

By using of Jesus the language Jews had used of Wisdom, Christians could think of Jesus as one with God yet distinct from God. He 'is the radiance of God's glory and the exact representation of his being' (Hebrews 1:3). It was as though God's Wisdom had become a human being. All the divine activity of creation and revelation reached its climax here. Jesus is God's own divine presence in a human life. He is a reflection of the divine nature in human form, the visible image of the invisible God. So Paul can write that the God who created light

214

▼ Matthew gave Jesus the title 'Immanuel', meaning 'God with us'. The most everyday human experience can be transcended, and lifted up into the life of God.

The Trinity

The Jewish faith was always monotheistic, teaching of only one God. Worshippers reminded themselves of this every morning and evening in the words of the *Shema*: 'The Lord our God is one Lord. . .' Jesus endorsed this prayer by quoting it to a lawyer who asked him about the relative importance of the commandments. Having more than one god was also strictly forbidden in the Ten Commandments: 'You shall have no other gods but me.'

The earliest Christians clearly shared this belief in only one God. Yet they also believed that Jesus himself was more than just a messenger from God, and as they looked at what was happening through him in their own lives they felt that God's presence was with them in a personal and dynamic way. Out of all this, belief in God as Trinity eventually emerged in the fourth century, when it began to be expressed in statements of belief now known as 'creeds'. But the roots of this belief go back much further than that. Back to the New Testament itself.

Jesus the Lord

One of the paradoxes of the New Testament is that, though its writers were happy to believe in only one God, they were also insistent that Jesus himself was a divine person. For example, they had no hesitation in applying to him the title 'Lord'. In some contexts this is used in a way quite similar to our modern English 'sir', merely as a term of respect. But in a Jewish context, the

word was best known as one of the titles of God himself. When pious Jews came in their reading of the Old Testament to the personal name of God ('Yahweh'), they would usually replace it by the term *Adonai*, meaning 'my lord'. And so when Jesus was addressed as 'Lord', he was being

identified with God himself.

The way Jesus is portrayed in the Gospels conveys the same message. When he claimed to be able to forgive the sins of a paralyzed man, those standing around could see well enough that Jesus was claiming for himself a power that belonged only to God. For them, that made him a blasphemer, but for the Gospel-writers it was evidence of Jesus' own special authority—an authority that was then

validated when he healed the man's paralysis. There are several other stories that indicate Jesus had power over the forces of nature ('Even the winds and waves obey him'), and again this kind of creativity was something that, in Jewish thinking, was the sole prerogative of God himself. Other writers in the New Testament drew the obvious conclusions from such incidents and wrote of Jesus existing before time began,

▶ In Jusepe Ribera's painting, it is God the Father who helps Jesus down from the cross. The dove of the Holy Spirit is there too, showing the whole Trinity involved in this central act of redemption.

a claim that also seems to be implicit in Jesus' own statements about the nature of his authority. There are other places where Jesus appears to claim near-identity with God himself, as for instance in Matthew chapter 11 verse 27.

The Holy Spirit

In addition to these claims about who he himself was, Jesus taught about the Holy Spirit in such a way as to suggest that Father (God), Son (Jesus) and Spirit together form the one divine entity that we call 'God'. (A reading of John chapter 14 verses 16 to 26 shows this clearly.) The Spirit is to be the practical means whereby both God and Jesus are made relevant to the lives of Christians. It was not long before these three together were being used as a formula to sum up the Christian belief about God, and new converts were baptized 'in the name of Father, Son and Holy Spirit.'

There can be no reasonable doubt that the earliest Christians thought of God, though one, as having these three clearly identifiable expressions of his nature. But we must admit that none of the New Testament writers had what we might call a 'doctrine' of the Trinity—not if by that we mean a carefully worked-out theoretical concept of the nature of God. To some, this may seem a disadvantage. But we need to remember that few beliefs are worked out in the Bible as carefully worded doctrines. The New Testament writers believed that Christ had died for their sins, but they set out only a very sketchy doctrine of 'the atonement'.

Further elaboration of New Testament beliefs only became necessary in succeeding generations, as Christian thinkers were faced with new questions and challenges from the philosophical trend-setters of their age. As a result,

Christian theology came to be defined by reference to the assumptions of the prevailing Greek philosophical mind-set, where previously believers had been content with the less pedantic approach of oriental thinking.

In this intellectual climate, church leaders often came up with definitions that today seem complex and mind-boggling, and there can be no doubt that the creeds they formulated would benefit from some rewriting if their usefulness is to continue. Yet whatever their deficiencies, there can be no doubt that their statements about the Trinity reflect, in the broadest sense, what we find in the Bible itself, that the one God whom believers trust is known as Father, Son and Holy Spirit.

out of darkness has now 'shone in our hearts to give the light of the knowledge of the glory of God in the face of Christ'.

The Word made flesh

The fullest and finest statement comes in the prologue which opens John's Gospel. Here it is God's 'Word' which is distinct from God and yet one with him. God's Word is his self-expression. In his Word God expresses *himself* and so his Word belongs to his own being. Before Jesus, God expressed himself in creation and in revelation. But in Jesus God expresses himself *as a human being*: 'the Word became flesh and lived among us'.

This is the way God's very nature—his glory—can be perceived by human beings. God in himself is the unknowable mystery which none can penetrate: 'no one has ever seen God', writes John. He can be known by us only as he makes himself known to us. We can know him only as he expresses himself in our world. We can know him most fully when he expresses himself as a human being, as Jesus of Nazareth. In Jesus God's nature is reflected and expressed in the way people most readily understand, in the life of a person.

Thus John's prologue calls Jesus God's human self-expression. But it also calls him the unique Son of the Father. God can be human because he has a Son. The Son expresses the Father's nature, he reflects the Father's glory, and does so in a human life. So it is *as the divine Son of his Father* that Jesus makes God known. To quote John once again: 'No one has ever seen God, but God the only Son, who is in the bosom of the Father, he has made him known.'

So John's Gospel portrays Jesus living a human life of dependence on God and obedience to God's will, the dependence of a son on his father and the obedience of a son to his father. In dependence on and obedience to his Father, Jesus teaches, performs miracles, suffers humiliation and death. This is how the Son expresses the Father's nature in a human life: 'He who has seen me has seen the Father,' said Jesus. We recognize God in Jesus when we see the Father expressed and reflected in the Son.

God's humanity

In these ways the early Christians were able to see Jesus as the 'incarnation' of God. 'Incarnation' literally means 'taking flesh': Jesus is God become human. This certainly does not mean that Christians lost sight of Jesus' thoroughly real humanity.

The Ancient Hymn of the Trinity

This hymn, originally written in Latin in the fifth century AD, has beeen a regular part of Christian worship for centuries. It is known as the Te Deum, from the first words of the hymn (the first section is here omitted).

You, Christ, are the King of glory,
   the eternal Son of the Father.
When you became man to set us free,
   you did not abhor the Virgin's womb.
You overcame the sting of death,
   and opened the kingdom of heaven to all
   believers.
You are seated at God's right hand in glory;
   we believe that you will come and be our judge.
Come then Lord and help your people,
   bought with the price of your own blood;
and bring us with your saints
   to glory everlasting.
Save your people, Lord, and bless your inheritance;
   govern and uphold them now and always.
Day by day we bless you,
   we praise your name for ever.
Keep us today, Lord, from all sin;
   have mercy on us, Lord, have mercy.
Lord, show us your love and mercy,
   for we put our trust in you.
In you, Lord, is our hope;
   let us not be confounded at the last.

The whole point was that God became *human*. Had they seen Jesus as less than fully human, the point would have been lost.

This distinguishes the early Christian view of Jesus very sharply from pagan ideas about appearances of the gods in human form. In the old Greek myths the gods were thought sometimes to appear on earth in human or animal forms in order to play some part in human affairs. But these were just transient appearances, like an actor's costume put on and off at will. The Greek gods did not really become human. They did not live a properly human life from birth to death.

Such views about divine appearances in human form may have influenced some early Christians, known as 'Docetists', who thought of Jesus' humanity as just an appearance. Jesus, they thought, could

not have been subject to real human weakness or have suffered physical pain or death. But such teaching is strongly condemned in the first letter of John. John there makes the statement 'Jesus Christ has come in the flesh' the test of genuine Christian teaching. Jesus' humanity was not a pretence, not a bit of divine play-acting, but absolutely real.

When the prologue to John's Gospel declares that the Word became flesh, it does not mean just a human body. Jesus was human through and through, as human in his mind, in his thinking and emotions, as in his body. God would not have become one of us otherwise. But 'flesh' describes human nature in its weakness and frailty, in all that distinguishes it from divine nature. The incarnation means that God in his love identified with us in all our creatureliness and weakness. In Jesus' humanity he suffered, both physically and mentally, and died a real human death.

Jesus fully shared our humanity. The early Christians allowed only one qualification of that: that he did not commit sin. He was 'tempted in every way, just as we are—yet was without sin', proclaims the writer to the Hebrews. But sin does not belong to the essence of being human. To meet temptation without yielding to it is not really to be less human than the rest of us but to be more human than we sinners are. Jesus lived without sin, not through some divine immunity, but through his utter devotion to his Father's will and his absolute dependence on his Father's grace.

Not only did the early Christians maintain that Jesus was fully human. They also insisted that he was a particular historical person. That particular human individual, Jesus of Nazareth, was God's human self-expression. God became not just human in general terms, but that particular man. So they told Jesus' story. They told all the stories about Jesus that we find in the Gospels. They told the stories Jesus told—his parables. They remembered the way he lived and what he had taught and what had finally happened to him—his cruel, criminal death on a Roman cross. And the risen Christ they worshipped was none other than Jesus of Nazareth, crucified and risen. Jesus never became, for the early Christians, a mere symbol or abstraction. He kept the concrete, particular features of the human Jesus the first Christians had known in the flesh. Only in that way could they find God in Jesus.

The meaning of incarnation

It is important for us to remember that the first Christians knew Jesus as a human being before they

The Word Became Flesh

John opens his Gospel with this great declaration of who Jesus is. He describes him as 'the Word', logos in Greek, God's unique way of making himself known and understood.

In the beginning was the Word, and the Word was with God, and the Word was God. He was with God in the beginning.

Through him all things were made; without him nothing was made that has been made. In him was life, and that life was the light of men. The light shines in the darkness, but the darkness has not understood it.

There came a man who was sent from God; his name was John. He came as a witness to testify concerning that light, so that through him all men might believe. He himself was not the light; he came only as a witness to the light. The true light that gives light to every man was coming into the world.

He was in the world, and though the world was made through him, the world did not recognise him. He came to that which was his own, but his own did not receive him. Yet to all who received him, to those who believed in his name, he gave the right to become children of God—children born not of natural descent, nor of human decision or a husband's will, but born of God.

The Word became flesh and made his dwelling among us. We have seen his glory, the glory of the One and Only, who came from the Father, full of grace and truth.

recognized him as God. The church has sometimes forgotten this and lost sight of Jesus' real and particular humanity. We shall not understand what God's incarnation in Jesus means if we lose sight of Jesus' humanity. Only when we are sure that we are thinking of Jesus as thoroughly human, no less human than ourselves, can we see what it really means for Jesus to be God. Only when we remember who Jesus actually was, the life he actually lived, can we see what it means to say that his life was God's own human life.

Sometimes the idea of God's incarnation in Jesus has seemed to lift Jesus out of real human history into the realm of pure myth. But this was not its effect for the early Christians and it should not be its effect for us. The point of incarnation is not to lift Jesus out of real history, but quite the opposite: to involve God in human history. Jesus' thoroughly human story is the story of God's presence with us in our human world.

The importance of this for us is twofold:

- **Jesus is God's human identity for us.** If we are to be able to relate to God in a personal way, we need to be able to identify him. We need to know who he is and to form a concrete image of him. This is why religion so easily tends to idolatry. Because we need to know who God is, we imagine a fantasy God, God as we would like him to be or God as we fear he might be. But Jesus is the remedy for idolatry, because he is the identity God has given himself. In Jesus God has come out of his mystery and given himself a human identity so that we can know him. Of course, he still remains a mystery. He is not reduced to Jesus. But in Jesus he has expressed himself in human form. Jesus is the visible image of the invisible God.

- **In Jesus God identifies with us.** He shows himself to be the kind of love which identifies with those whom it loves. God does not wish us well while holding aloof from us. His love for us impels him to come among us, to become one of us, to identify with us. Through Jesus' human life of loving identification with men and women, God's love reaches us. As Jesus heals lepers, forgives sinners, associates with tax-collectors, goes fishing with his disciples, lifts children onto his knee, dines with Pharisees—God's love reaches people of all kinds in the concrete reality of their lives. It did so then, and through the story of Jesus it does so still.

Finally, God's identification with us in Jesus is such that Jesus' life ended on the cross. There he identifies with us in our victimization and our failure, in the worst that human cruelty can do to us and in the worst that we can make of ourselves. The cross lays bare the human condition as it really is—in suffering, failure and condemnation. The cross is where any of us might end up. Jesus dies abandoned by his Father, as suffering people feel God has left them to suffer, and as guilty sinners feel God has left them condemned. But even in that fate Jesus is God with us. He is God identified with us in that extremity. And so God's love can reach us even there. When it does so, God's absence becomes his presence, condemnation becomes forgiveness, death becomes resurrection.

PART

6

JESUS TODAY

This final part brings the enquiry right up to date,
by looking at three contemporary themes. As belief in Jesus has
mushroomed round the world in the twentieth century,
how has people's
idea of him translated into new cultures? How do his followers
worship him today? What does it mean to say Jesus is for all the world?

Part five asked who Jesus was. This part considers
who Jesus is today.

CONTENTS

6.1

INTO ALL THE WORLD

The impulse to share the message of and about Jesus Christ is intrinsic to Christianity as a religion. It is such an extension of Christian witness that has made the religion founded by Jesus truly a world faith in our time.

Christianity is a world faith in at least two senses:

■ In a **geographical** sense, the message about Jesus has reached every corner of the globe. This is not to say that everywhere the Christian religion is found to the same extent or with the same intensity; but it is present nonetheless.

■ Christianity is a world faith also in a **cultural** sense, in that it has been the most culturally adaptable of all religious movements in the world. Having no one permanent earthly centre, but instead able to be at home in every cultural context, faith in Jesus has acquired many centres and every culture where it is accepted becomes a potential centre.

Missionaries from the West

This worldwide presence of Jesus in the twentieth century cannot be conceived historically apart from the modern missionary movement from the West, starting in the late eighteenth century and continuing into the early decades of this one.

The modern missionary movement was the most massive organized extension of the message about Jesus in Christian history. The missionary enterprise arose from a deepening conviction in large sections of the Christian communities of Western Europe that the message about Jesus was meant to be communicated to the rest of the world. Christians began to sense a call out of their own country to others who also needed to know about Jesus and to believe in

▲ Many of today's third-world Christians once practised another religion, such as animism. To worship Jesus is a quite new experience, bringing deep peace and a fresh grasp of our humanity.

him. The message about Jesus was perceived to have not only spiritual but also physical benefits, and so missionary work early acquired the character of educational, medical, agricultural and other technical services, alongside evangelism. It is important to recognize the extent to which this modern worldwide spread of the message about Jesus meant also what we today would call a technology transfer to the non-Western world!

The missionary enterprise shared the confidence

in European cultural values and outlook common to that period. Not surprisingly, therefore, it reflected Western expectations and models of church government, Christian life and discipline, as well as styles of worship. The images of Jesus that were conveyed seemed to suggest that Jesus was a white man and that the way to him lay through the channels by which white people conceived of reality and the world.

The actual results of the impact of the message about Jesus often turned out to be quite different. In specifically religious terms, the single most significant feature of this coming of a worldwide faith in Jesus was that the Bible became quite early available in the mother-tongues of the people who were then learning about Jesus. In areas where the acceptance of the message has been most widespread, as in tropical Africa, having the Bible in African languages enabled African converts to discover parallels between the biblical world (not just in the Old Testament, but also in the New Testament) of miracles, exorcisms, healings and prophecy, and their own cultural and religious world of spirit-beings and supernatural forces.

The Bible in the mother-tongues of Africa became a time-bomb which exploded into the numerous and diverse 'independent' churches proliferating on the African continent. But the Independents only exemplify in the extreme what is now true also of many of the mission-established churches of Africa. Far from being the work of 'foreign agents' promoting an imperialist religion, this mushrooming of churches in fact indicates how at home Africans are in the message about Jesus. In African Christianity, it is not a Western Jesus who reigns, but the Jesus who is powerful to save in the African world.

Except for the times when Latin dominated in the 'European' phase of Christianity, the Christian faith has in the course of its expansion developed generally as a 'vernacular' (mother-tongue) religion. This refusal of an imposed 'sacred' language has meant that the Bible in whatever language always remains the Word of God. Here is the clue to what has been called the 'infinite cultural translatability' of the Christian faith.

A Latin American equivalent to this African scene is the emergence of 'base communities'—an explosion of the discovery of Jesus by ordinary people, mostly poor, reading the Bible for themselves in their situation of poverty and oppression, often to the discomfiture of the official church. The 'Jesus of the poor' thus reverses the 'Jesus of the conquistadors'.

All this goes to show that the association of the Christian religion with the colonial expansion of

▲ A grassroots community join in worship in Latin America. Known as 'base communities', hundreds of thousands of groups have sprung up among poor people, mainly in Latin America but also in Africa and Asia. They study the Bible from the standpoint of their own experience of oppression, and find it comes to life.

Western European nations ought not to be regarded as more than what it was: a historical convergence of two movements with quite different motivations. The association may have been convenient in places, but it was not essential for the progress of the faith. Africa, perhaps, provides the most illuminating indicator of the more general trend. For Christian expansion in Africa in the post-colonial era has far outstripped its growth in the colonial period. All along, in fact, local African initiative and agency were much more significant than foreign missionary intervention. Yet this fact was previously obscured by the dominance of the missionary factor, since Christian expansion was then viewed as an aspect of European imperial and political history.

With the demise of the empires, we can gain a better perspective and see what was really happening: people were responding to Jesus for himself rather than for the gifts of the foreign missionary.

A world of many faiths

This modern phenomenon of a worldwide faith in Jesus fulfils what the earliest communicators of the message about Jesus expected to happen—that through this message God's plan would be realized to bring an alienated and fragmented world into unity and harmony again. In the end, people drawn from 'every race, tribe, nation and language' (the Revelation vision) will be united by their common faith in Jesus. Each will bring their peculiar gifts of praise and worship to the one God of the whole earth and the one Saviour of all humankind.

That end is clearly not yet. The massive religious cultures of Islam, Hinduism and Buddhism in the Middle East and Asia remain largely resistant to faith in Jesus. Large portions of the world's population—in China and Eastern Europe—live under political regimes which, until very recently, have denied any place to God and religion in the national conscious-ness. And the former heartlands of Christian faith in Western Europe have experienced rapid erosion of the faith under the impact of an increasing secularization of outlook. At the same time Islam and the ancient religions of Asia have become aggres-sively missionary, producing an unprecedented religious ferment in the world.

The notion of a territorial Christianity is now past. From now on the message about Jesus must compete for a hearing in the open forum where alternative ways of salvation jostle for attention. Modern com-municators of the message about Jesus now find themselves in a situation not dissimilar to that of their earliest predecessors in the New Testament.

In a sense it is possible to see the present pluralism in the world also as the result of the impact of the message about Jesus. Christianity calls not merely for adhesion to inherited custom, but also for conversion and religious change. And so it is bound to encourage and deepen the notion of personal freedom in the human consciousness. The impact of the teaching and example of Jesus himself can also be traced in reform and humanitarian movements which have not become overtly 'Christian'. Many leaders of liberation movements for African self-determination and independence owed part of their inspiration to the impact of Jesus' teaching on the infinite value of the human person, which they received in Christian schools.

▼ Christians from the Pacific lead a service at the Vancouver assembly of the World Council of Churches in 1983. The churches of the developing world are beginning to take the lead in worldwide Christianity.

▲ In Africa the Independent churches are seeing rapid growth. They represent an attempt to adapt the way of Jesus to African culture.

Yet the message about Jesus cannot be reduced to any or all of its social and political benefits. It remains essentially a religious message, centering on God's relationship with the universe and his costly initiative to redeem the world from its alienation and futility through Jesus' incarnation and sacrificial death on a cross. The resurrection of Jesus then vindicates the promise that both the world and human life can become different, and that human beings have a destiny to triumph over death.

As the Christian religion soon enters its third millennium as a distinct faith in the world, it is clear that its fortunes will not be tied to any particular political regime or ideology or economic system or culture. Rather it will be shaped by the sense of the contemporary relevance of Jesus discovered by all those millions of groups, all over the world, to whom the message about Jesus has been communicated.

Is this quest for a culturally relevant Christianity something new? Not at all. I end with a story from my home town, of an event which took place in 1835.

In the kingdom of Akuapem in the Eastern Region of Ghana, soon after the Basel Mission pioneer, Andreas Riis, arrived from Denmark, there was some serious discussion in the king's court as to whether the message about Jesus might not destroy the local culture. They wished to see a Christian community arise, but a community of authentic African Christians in the local setting. The Mission found the answer by inviting several Christian families of African descent from the West Indies to settle in the kingdom's capital, Akropong. Apparently the king and his court accepted the Mission's solution. The descendants of the West Indians continue to this day to live in Akropong as citizens of Akuapem. Nobody doubts that Jesus can be just as real to Africans as to Danes.

6.2

WORSHIPPING JESUS TODAY

At the centre of Christian life and believing is worship. Jesus worshipped—in the open air as well as in sacred buildings—and he expects his followers to worship, too.

But Jesus never offered a handbook on how, when and where worship should be offered. So naturally the worship of God's people varies from denomination to denomination, from country to country, and from age to age. What we now call worship—in a Gothic cathedral or a suburban house-group—is a far cry from what the apostles did in first-century Jerusalem. But the intention is still the same.

Worship is giving God his worth in praise, love, wonder and—if we take the psalms seriously—sometimes also in anger, frustration or uncertainty.

But ask many people what they think of worship today and they will polarize between those who find it 'dull and boring' and those who find it 'spirit-filled and lively'. The former critics are often referring to regular parish worship, the latter to 'charismatic' gatherings (bubbling with the gifts, *charismata*, of the Holy Spirit).

Yet it would be wrong to imply that all traditional worship is dull and that all 'renewal' worship is inspired and inspiring. Worship is one of the more conservative human activities, and it is as easy to become stuck in a charismatic rut as in any other.

Why is worship so conservative? Why will people readily welcome changes in medical treatment or in education yet be stubbornly resistant to innovation in their devotional life? It may be because we make a false association between God and the church. We learn that God is changeless. And so we presume that everything to do with God should reflect that changelessness.

If that is so, why did the psalmist call us to 'sing a *new* song to the Lord'? Or why did Jesus say to the writer of Revelation, 'Behold, I make all things *new*'?

In recent years, and across the denominations, there have been significant movements to make the church's worship more relevant and meaningful to twentieth-century Christians. After all, emptying churches are not a good advertisement for the gospel and, as Jesus put it, new skins are required to hold new wine. Christians in different places have re-discovered pictures of Jesus, absent or ignored in the traditional worship of the church, which compel them to do new things for God.

Four pictures of Jesus have been instrumental in reshaping the worship of Christians. Because God made us all different, some of these trends will be more appealing to one individual and less so to another.

Jesus, God among us

In October 1962, Pope John XXIII convened an assembly of Roman Catholic bishops and theologians which was to have a ricochet effect throughout the Christian church. The Second Vatican Council (Vatican II as it was called) made a major reassessment, among other things, of what the church is and how it should worship.

Up until then, this church had distanced Jesus from his people by cloaking him in ritual and the Latin language and requiring priests to be the principal or sole participants in worship. Now it was to undergo a major transformation: Jesus was to be celebrated as God among us rather than God distant from us.

◀ A child in Ecuador typifies many who lack life's essentials. Worship which ignores the poor has little to do with the life of Jesus.

Significant changes were quickly made to give effect to this new emphasis. Jesus had been addressed in formal Latin; now he was prayed to and spoken of in the language or dialect most accessible to the local congregation. Jesus had become bread and wine in the mass out of sight of the congregation; now he was central to the celebration as altars were moved nearer to the people. Jesus had been depicted in stained glass and statue images which fixed him in the middle ages; now he was portrayed as a twentieth-century saviour.

Alongside these structural changes, the role of the laity became more significant. Jesus was no longer to be addressed mainly by ordained ministers. The priesthood of all believers (a protestant concept) was to be made real in the worship. Thus it is possible to attend a Roman Catholic mass today and find very ordinary people leading the prayers, leading the singing, reading the scriptures and assisting the priest in administering the sacrament.

The lead which Vatican II gave to the renewal of worship was quickly followed by other denominations. The Anglican church, whose liturgy bears a close resemblance to that of the Roman church, began similarly to change the style of its celebrations and to increase lay participation. A relaxation of the rigid formality of the eucharist has enabled worship to take in expressions of mime, dance or other visual media. For example, in 1986 the Anglican Cathedral of St John the Divine in New York held a eucharist in honour of the memory of Francis of Assisi and portrayed the effect of the gospel on the saint's life by use of contemporary dance, a light show and a procession of circus animals.

In reformed churches, where a set liturgy has played a less important role in the worshipping life of the congregations, there have also been signs of moves to bring Jesus nearer to his people. Contemporary translations of the Bible and the 'hymn explosion' of the sixties and seventies have been incentives to worship Jesus as a living Saviour rather than a historical one. It is difficult, after all, to read the words of Jesus in crisp twentieth-century language and then to pray to him in Elizabethan English!

Jesus, the victor

Like the previous emphasis, this has deep biblical roots. Many of the New Testament letters refer to Christ's triumph over sin and death, and Revelation, written at a time when the young church was being persecuted, affirms Jesus as Lord over all the powers of light and darkness.

This stress on Jesus as victor is not shallow triumphalism. Christians, largely in the charismatic and house-group movements, have felt challenged in the face of seeming apathy in the traditional churches to focus attention on the power of Christ. Their belief is that on the cross Jesus ultimately triumphed over sin and disorder, and it is the obligation of Christians to claim that triumph in the world today.

Thus the songs of these Christians are very much 'praise songs', ascribing glory, honour and power to Jesus. In prayer and testimony there is an emphasis on what Christ has done and will do. Doubt or negative feelings are held in suspicion, and music is melodically and rhythmically simple, sung with gusto.

In some gatherings, these phenomena will be reinforced by speaking, prophesying or singing in tongues, symbolizing the worshippers' surrender to the will of God and the leading of the Spirit. Hands may be raised in the air, and there may be spontaneous clapping or shouting.

In other worship assemblies, the triumph of Christ may lead to a more confrontational style of worship. Individuals who have been sinful in the past or have fallen from commitment may be confronted with their need to repent and, by word or touch of the worship leader, may be 'slain in the spirit'. Those who are afflicted by illness or by obsession may, in a

▼ A group of British Christians march down London's Whitehall singing. At the main centres of government they stop and pray. Many Christians now believe in the need to pray against the evil which can come to dominate state power.

◀ Dance is one example of
the use of the arts in worship.
It is a way of using our bodies,
as well as our minds and our
tongues, to offer to God.

dramatic fashion, have hands laid on them while the power of Jesus is invoked to triumph over their disease or to exorcize the evil within them. Or it may be that in open-air witness, a march through a town or city stops at significant public buildings where, in word and song, Christians claim the triumph of Christ over whatever social malaise is brought to mind.

As stated above, this worship of Jesus as victor is not the preserve of one denomination or sect. Enthusiastic and powerful charismatic worship is as likely to happen in a small house-church as it is in a Pentecostal Gospel Hall. Many of the black churches in Europe and America excel in the dynamism of their music for such worship, yet enthusiasm for the triumphant praise of Jesus can be just as fervent in white middle-class congregations.

Jesus, the loved one

The meditative or contemplative worship of Jesus is an old tradition in the Christian church. Monks and mystics from earliest times have, in different ways, encouraged the followers of Jesus to worship him in the silence of their hearts. With their eyes and ears focused on his love, his passion, death and resurrection, Jesus was revered beyond the ritual liturgies of the church.

Most of us, at some time in our lives, have sensed this more passive and awesome kind of worship.

Perhaps it was as children, gazing wide-mouthed at the Christmas nativity scene, or perhaps as adults we have watched a candle burn and found ourselves pondering Jesus' title as light of the world.

It is largely to the credit of the Taizé Community, an ecumenical foundation based in France, that contemplation and meditation have become accessible today, not just to monks and ministers, but to people of all types and ages across the social and denominational boundaries.

Taizé draws mainly young people from many countries, and its worship encourages them to share in singing meditative songs and chants in which the words may be repeated over and over again, almost like an Indian mantra. This is not intended to induce a state of hypnosis, but rather to let the worshipper focus on one line of the Bible, one saying of Jesus, or one statement of faith, enabling it to be rooted deeper and deeper inside. The kind of phrase sung might simply be *O adoramus te, domine* ('How we love you, Lord') or *Bleibet hier und wachet mit mir* ('Stay here and watch with me').

By using biblical and religious phrases in different languages, worship becomes very quickly an international and ecumenical experience. Such repeated chants may be interspersed with long periods of silence, or with reading passages from the Bible, broken up into short sections so that the response may be sung. Simple yet very meaningful actions are also included in the acts of worship. These may range from lighting candles held by all worshippers from one solo flame, to having worshippers come forward to a large cross and touch it with their heads in token of their repentance and devotion.

The central worship area at Taizé may allow for thousands to participate in singing meditative chants and in silence, but this same devotional style may be equally effective and meaningful when employed by a few people in the intimacy of their own home. The focus of attention is not the mechanics of liturgy or the promptings of inspired individuals, but quiet, positive concentration on Jesus as the one who deserves our attention, devotion and love.

Jesus, the liberator

The interchange in Central and South America of the experience of poor peasants and the knowledge of skilled academics gave rise in the 1970s to the term 'Liberation Theology'. At its core, this understanding of the Christian gospel for today sees in the death and resurrection of Jesus a pattern which has to be encouraged and celebrated all through life. Thus, where a political system oppresses people or where a pattern of church life inhibits genuine participation, Christians are encouraged to let the oppressive scheme of things die, believing that God will bring new life.

In Nicaragua, forms of worship and biblical reflection have resulted which claim to involve the people far more, to be more rooted in their daily experience, and to liberate them more fully than previous patterns of church life. The use of folk tunes and folk instruments in the music of worship is a further indication that Jesus is liberating the ordinary, poor people to praise him.

In Europe, the worship of Jesus as liberator rarely develops in the kind of grassroots or 'base' communities which have sprung up in the Third World. Yet those who struggle with the issues of justice and peace have been encouraged to look again at Christ and see in who he is and what he did God's challenge to the status quo.

Thus women, who have traditionally been assigned a subordinate place in worship and who for ages have heard praise and prayer expressed in exclusively male language, have identified Jesus as the one who calls

for an end to discrimination. They see that he accepted women in a way at odds with contemporary Jewish practice. Translating this into present-day terms, they require that the conduct of worship be no longer an all-male preserve and that the language of worship be 'inclusive'—'humankind' instead of 'mankind', 'children of God' rather than simply 'sons'.

Christians who have a passionate concern for peace and the reduction of nuclear arsenals have identified Jesus not only as the one who liberates from bondage of war, but also as the liberator from stifling church traditions. Thus priests and laity have celebrated holy communion or shared prayer while trespassing on land reserved solely for military use or, as in London on Ash Wednesday in 1988, a gathering of concerned Christians, including monks, smeared pleas for peace with charcoal on the walls of the Ministry of Defence.

In yet other, less public places, the image of Jesus as the liberator, the upsetter of the status quo, has encouraged clergy to dispense with their traditional

▼ A large congregation, led here by an orchestra, can convey a powerful sense of the strength of Christianity, despite its many aspects of weakness. The followers of Jesus worldwide include about a third of the human race.

▲ The worship of a West Indian Pentecostal church is full of exuberance. This strand of Christianity has grown faster than any other this century.

dress, Roman Catholic priests to share the consecrated bread and wine with those not of their own denomination, and young people to shape services of worship which provoke questions rather than conform to expectations.

Authentic worship

All these styles of worship have their limits and these must be recognized. Those who try to adapt traditional liturgies to emphasize the centrality of Christ, run the risk of becoming more concerned with words and form than with the Spirit. Those who favour emotionally-charged charismatic worship are often in danger of encouraging highly subjective experiences with no room for a proper concern for the world for which Jesus died.

The devotees of the contemplative style of worship can often miss out on the prophetic edge which preaching offers or may view their devotions as an alternative to the rest of life rather than an offering and preparation for it. And those who try to enshrine the liberating power of Jesus in their worship inevitably run the risk of being caught up in worthy causes rather than worthy worship.

Yet it is right and proper that such different notes should exist side by side. After all, in the New Testament church we find evidence of quite varied worship practices. Divergence is not a new thing; it is part of God's pattern.

In the end, whatever the style of worship, how is authentic Christian worship to be recognized?

■ **Worship must always be rooted in the Bible.** The Psalms constituted Jesus' hymnbook and the prophets supplied many of his texts and illustrations. God's word must always be central to our celebrations.

■ **Worship must always rely on the inspiration of the Holy Spirit**, whether it be a formal liturgy, expository sermon or pentecostal prayer meeting. We who worship must come expecting God to inspire us, and leaders must be aware that they walk a tightrope between the bliss of the Holy Spirit and the blasphemy of spiritual manipulation.

■ **Worship should allow the whole of the person to face the wholeness of God.** It is wrong to sing Hallelujah when we need to ask 'How long, O Lord?'

■ **Public worship must always be a shared event rather than a performance.** The worship of the Bible is a co-operative venture, and gifted preachers or skilled guitarists must never make their contribution the central feature.

■ **Worship must be contemporary.** God is not caught in a time warp and neither should we be. The ultimate test of worship is not whether it is aesthetically pleasing or good to take part in, but whether it enables men and women to encounter and respond to Jesus who promises to meet us in the world of today.

▶ Candles, stained-glass windows, favourite hymns – an unchanging piety links us to centuries of traditional worship. This continuity over centuries of Christian life lends a deep security to our faith.

6.3

THE FINALITY OF JESUS

The first Christians made remarkable claims about Jesus. For example, in 'The Song of Christ's Glory', that God 'had bestowed on him the name which is above every name, that at the name of Jesus every knee should bow, in heaven and on earth and under the earth, and every tongue confess that Jesus Christ is Lord'. In Jesus, they believed, God had made himself known as fully as he could within human history—not just through a messenger, but through the presence of his own Son, the reflection of his own being in a human life. In Jesus, God had acted decisively for the salvation of all human beings—so that, to quote one of Peter's early sermons, 'there is salvation in no one else'.

One summary of early Christian belief was that 'there is one God, and there is one mediator between God and men, the man Christ Jesus, who gave himself as a ransom for all'. Not that human history had ground to a halt with the death and resurrection of Jesus. God's decisive action in Jesus had still to achieve its goal in the completion of his purposes for the world in the future. But when that day came, so the first Christians were convinced, Jesus would prove to be the key to it. At the end of history it is Jesus who will be revealed in glory as the judge of all people and the goal of all creation.

This conviction that Jesus is of decisive significance for the life and destiny of all human beings was meant entirely seriously. They did not just mean: Jesus has decisive significance *for us*. They really meant: he has decisive significance *for everyone*. This is why they set about telling everyone about Jesus. The same conviction has inspired the missionary task of the church ever since. Christians have never believed that Jesus was just one prophet among others, one mediator among others, or one saviour among others. In many different ways they have always testified to his finality—his unique and decisive significance for all humanity. And for this reason they have been confident in telling others about him. If this had not been so, no one who is a Christian today would be a Christian.

In the early Christian centuries—when Christians were an insignificant group of followers of an insignificant figure from a backwater of the Roman Empire—it took great conviction to maintain that Jesus was God's decisive word for all people. Now it is a fact of history that Jesus has continually proved his relevance to men and women in every period of history and every part of the globe. Though some cultures have felt his impact more than others, he has found at least some followers in almost all. To identify his worldwide influence with the imperialism and expansionism of the modern West is a travesty of the truth. He was known in Ethiopia, Iran, India and China many centuries before Western political and cultural expansion.

Jesus' image has been distorted and misused for alien purposes, but people have always been able to rediscover him. Even when oppressors have tried to make him a sanction for their oppression, the oppressed have not rejected him but have seen through the distortion. Even when one culture may seem to have made him entirely their own, this has not prevented people in utterly different cultures from also finding him relevant and making him their own in quite different ways. He has always had a special appeal for the poor, the sick, the marginalized and the excluded. But he has also inspired great writers and artists, political leaders and social reformers, scientists, philosophers and visionaries. It is a fact of history that no other religious figure has proved relevant to so many very different human lives in such a wide variety of cultures and societies.

Is Jesus for everyone?

However, the uniqueness and finality of Jesus are a problem for some people today. They seem inconsistent with the pluralism of the modern world: the fact that the human race has many religions and other philosophies of life, and that this plurality shows no sign of disappearing. This pluralism is of course nothing new for Christians in many parts of the world, where the Christian church has been a minority alongside people of other religions. But Western Christians have recently become more genuinely aware of it than they used to be. In view of the stubborn pluralism of our world, must we not admit that Christianity is after all just one religious tradition among others? The question is connected with the relativistic habit of thought so common today. Surely no religious tradition can claim absolute truth, only a relative and limited insight? Jesus may be the final revelation of God for Christians, but it would be arrogant, surely, to claim that he must be that for people of the other great religious traditions too?

This is a big question, and a number of different issues are bound up with it.

■ **Is it arrogant** for Christians to claim that Jesus is the decisive revelation of God? This question must be taken seriously, because it is sadly true that Christians often have been arrogant in their attitude to others. They have sometimes persecuted people of other faiths, and often been superior and condescending. But the finality of Jesus is no real excuse for Christian arrogance. It is not our Christianity which is the decisive revelation of God, but Jesus. He is always more than we have yet discovered, and our faithfulness even to what we do know of him leaves much to be desired. Christian lives are often put to shame by those of other faiths and none. And if Jesus is the standard by which all human religions are found wanting, that includes our Christianity. Jesus is not a badge of Christian superiority. He can be shared with others only in a humble awareness of grace.

■ **Is it unfair** that one historical man, a first-century Jew, should be God's fullest revelation of himself? It means that many people could never have the opportunity to know God in this full revelation. There was never any chance that the gospel could reach Australasia or the Americas until fairly recent times. Even today people's opportunities for learning about Jesus are extremely unequal.

The answer has to be that we live in history. Our knowledge and understanding of everything is conditioned by historical circumstances. If God's revelation of himself was to be relevant to us as historical beings, it could be no exception to this rule. It had to take history seriously and be committed to the processes of history.

Of course, we must trust that in the end there will be no unfairness. All have some access to knowledge of God. Salvation will not finally depend on the accidents of history. But these difficult issues need not throw doubt on the finality of Jesus.

■ **Is it unhistorical?** Is finality possible within history? Surely all history is relative? Jesus was as limited by his place in history as any other human being is. He cannot embody absolute truth, according to this objection, for this is not to be found within history.

It will help to meet this problem if we realize that for the first Christians it was Jesus' resurrection which gave finality to him. Resurrection was an event of the end of history; it belonged to the completion of God's purposes for humanity, when all people would be raised from death. If one man, Jesus, had already risen from the dead, ahead of all others, then he stands in a unique relation to the end of history. In him God has already disclosed his final purpose for human life—not in the fullness of revelation which must be reserved for the end of history itself, but as clearly as is possible within history.

Also, the significance of Jesus is continually coming to light in different ways and in different circumstances and is never exhausted. His finality does not mean that we have ever finally grasped his entire meaning for all of us. It means rather that his full meaning always exceeds our grasp. Only at the end of history shall we see him as he is. Meantime, Christians in various times and places are always forming fresh images of Jesus. Sometimes these more or less distort his reality. But they also claim those aspects of his reality which come to light and are relevant at that time and place. This is the way in which Jesus proves able to meet the particular concerns and needs of specific cultures and groups of people. It is the way his finality can be known within history.

■ **Is it exclusive?** Does the finality of Jesus exclude all other claims to truth? Can Christians not learn from dialogue with people of other faiths or none? Must their attitude to other religious traditions and non-Christian cultures be wholly negative?

The finality of Jesus means that in him God has given us the *decisive* truth about himself and his purposes for us. Of course, there is truth to be found elsewhere: Christians have never denied that. If we live by the truth of Jesus, we must be open to truth wherever it is to be found and thank God for it. What God may have made available of truth and value through the many traditions of human culture we cannot know in advance.

But wherever we find truth we can relate it to the decisive truth of Jesus. He is ultimately the criterion—must be if he is truly 'God in a human life'. Whatever is worthless in human life he will expose, what is good he will bring to fulfilment. In relation to him its full signficance will come to light. And conversely, in relation to it some aspect of his significance may become clearer to us. After all Jesus is a person, and the significance of persons is found in how they relate to the rest of reality. Jesus' finality will be tested as he is seen in relationship to all truth, all value, all people. Christian faith is that he will prove to be decisive for all reality.

Index

This index has been designed to be useful to the reader rather than to be completely exhaustive. A number of themes appear very frequently in this book, and these have been indexed only where they are the chief point at issue or where representative treatment is given. Page numbers in **bold** show where an entry forms the theme of an article; page numbers in *italics* refer to charts or captions.

JESUS 2000
Acknowledgments

Lion Publishing would like to thank the following agencies and photographers for their permission to reproduce the photographs in this book:

Alinari, pages 97, 189 (top); Ancient Art and Architecture Collection, page 29; Andes Press Agency, page 163 (top); Associated Press, page 147; R.G. Bailey Ltd, page 178; Baptist Times, page 110 (top); Howard Barlow, page 185; Beneddittine di Priscilla, pages 86 (top right), 168/169; Paul Benison, pages 80, 228; Biblioteque Nationale, page 74 (bottom); Bridgeman Art Library, pages 62 (bottom right), 101, 140, 145, 150 (all), 151, 152 (top right and bottom), 202, 205, 216; Trustees of the British Museum, pages 17, 18, 34 (both), 54, 74 (top), 75 (top); British Tourist Association, page 127; Brucke Museum, Berlin, page 153 (top); Susanna Burton, pages 123, 128; Cambridge University Library, pages 45 (both), 47 (both); Camera Press, pages 36 (left), 37; Cephas Picture Library, pages 134, 141 (bottom); Christian Aid, page 119; Church Missionary Society, pages 102, 138/Chris Fairclough, page 136 (left); Nobby Clarke, pages 204, 207; Coventry Evening Telegraph, page 116 (bottom); DAS Photographs/David Simson, page 98 (bottom); Mary Evans Picture Library, pages 76 (left), 100; Format Photographers, page 118; Fritz Fankhauser, pages 55, 96, 136 (right), 137 (top), 215; Christina Gascoigne, page 191; Billy Graham Archive, page 106 (top); Sonia Halliday and Laura Lushington Photographs, pages 10, 28 (right), 31 (both), 38, 42, 62 (top right), 62/63, 65, 73, 85 (bottom), 91 (bottom), 95 (top), 131, 132 (bottom), 157, 206/F.H.C. Birch, page 189 (centre)/Barry Searle, pages 35, 67, 70, 113, 158/Jane Taylor, pages 60 (both), 77, 167, 171, 189 (bottom)/Bill White, page 160; Robert Harding Picture Library, page 212; Hulton Picture Company, pages 90, 114/15, 146, 162, 184 (both); Lion Publishing/David Alexander, pages 76 (right), 84, 85 (top and centre), 94 (lower centre), 174, 188/Claire Schwob, page 191/David Townsend, pages 19, 26, 62 (left), 83, 93, 94 (upper centre); London Features International Ltd, page 36 (right); Mansell Collection, pages 156, 175; Middle East Archive/Alisdair Duncan, pages 16, 26/27, 56, 71, 94 (top), 95 (bottom), 159; National Film Archive, pages 40 (all), 40/41; National Gallery, page 11; Werner Neumeister, page 14 (right); Picture Point, page 124; Popperfoto, pages 91 (top), 116 (top), 135, 163 (centre and bottom), 172; Jean Luc Ray, pages 98 (top), 99, 144; John Rylands Library, page 20; Jyoti Sahi, page 82; SCM Press, page 14 (left); Clifford Shirley, pages 190, 229, 230; Frank Spooner Photographs, page 86 (bottom left, bottom centre, bottom right); Staatliche Museum, page 72; Stedelijk Van Abbemuseum, page 153 (bottom); Times Newspapers, page 79; John Topham Picture Library, pages 110 (centre and bottom), 169 (right), 225; David Townsend Photography, pages 81, 94 (bottom), 133 (top), 137 (bottom),141 (top), 143, 232; Peter Trainer/London City Mission, page 105; Trinity College Library, Dublin, page 49; John Twinning, page 231; Underground Evangelism, page 92; Santosh Verma, page 141 (centre); Scripture Union, page 122; Victoria & Albert Museum, page 33; World Council of Churches, pages 121, 223, 224; World Vision, pages 109 (top), 117, 133 (bottom), 227; Xaverian Fathers, page 222; Zefa (UK) Ltd, pages 3, 9, 24, 32, 51, 58, 61, 64, 89, 106 (bottom), 107, 109 (bottom), 125, 132 (top), 155, 169 (top left), 193 (both), 197, 199, 221/Richard Nowitz, pages 22, 23, 28 (left).